The Epistles of St. Cyprian

The Epistles of St. Cyprian

St. Cyprian

The Epistles of St. Cyprian

© Lighthouse Publishing 2023

Written by: St. Cyprian (AD 200 - 258)
Translated by: Rev. Ernest Wallis, Ph.D.(1820 – 1910)
Updated into Modern U.S English: A.M. Overett (b.1960)

All rights reserved. Without limiting the rights under copyright reserved above, no part of this publication may be reproduced, stored in a retrieval system, or transmitted, in any form or by any means (electronic, mechanical, photocopying, recording or otherwise), without the prior written permission of the copyright owner of this book.

Published by
Lighthouse Publishing
SAN 257-4330
228 Freedom Parkway
Hoschton, GA 30548
United States of America

www.lighthousechristianpublishing.com

Introductory Notice to Cyprian.

[a.d. 200–258.]

If Hippolytus reflects the spirit of Irenæus in all his writings, it is not remarkable. He was the spiritual son of the great Bishop of Lyons, and deeply imbued with the family character imparted to his disciples by the blessed presbyter of Patmos and Ephesus. But while Cyprian is the spiritual son and pupil of Tertullian, we must seek his characteristics and the key to his whole ministry in the far-off See and city where the disciples were first called Christians. Cyprian is the Ignatius of the West. We see in his works how truly historical are the writings of Ignatius, and how diffused was his simple and elementary system of organic unity. It embodies no hierarchical assumption, no "lordship over God's heritage," but is conceived in the spirit of St. Peter when he disclaimed all this, and said, "The presbyters who are among you I exhort, who am also a presbyter." Cyprian was indeed a strenuous asserter of the responsibilities of his office; but he built upon that system universally recognized by the Great Councils, which the popes and their adherents have ever labored to destroy. Nothing can be more delusive than the idea that the medieval system derives any support from Cyprian's theory of the episcopate or of Church organization. His was the system of the universal parity and community of bishops. In his scheme the apostolate was perpetuated in the episcopate, and the presbyterate was an apostolic institution, by which others were associated with bishops in all their functions as co-presbyters, but not in those reserved to the presidency of the churches. Feudal ideas imposed a very different system upon the simple framework of original Catholicity. But a careful study of that primitive framework, and of the history of papal development, makes evident the following propositions:—

1. That Cyprian's maxim, Ecclesia in Episcopo, whatever else he may have meant by it, is an aphoristic statement of the Nicene Constitutions. These were embedded in the Ignatian theory of an episcopate without a trace of a papacy; and Cyprian's maxims had to be practically destroyed in the West before it was possible to raise the portentous figure of a supreme pontiff, and to subject the Latin churches to the entirely novel principle of Ecclesia in Papa. To this novelty Cyprian's system is essentially antagonistic.

2. It will be seen that Cyprian, far from being the patron of ecclesiastical despotism, is the expounder of early canons and constitutions, in the spirit of order and discipline, indeed, but with the largest exemplification of that "liberty" which is manifested wherever "the Spirit of the Lord" is operative. Cyprian is the patron and defender of the presbytery and of lay co-operation, as well as of the regimen of the episcopate. His letters illustrate the Catholic system as it was known to the Nicene Fathers; but, of all the Christian Fathers, he is the most clear and comprehensive in his conception of the body of Christ as an organic whole, in which every member has an honorable function. Popular government and representative government, the legitimate power and place of the laity, the organization of the Christian plebs into their faculty as the ἀντιλήψεις of St. Paul, the development of synods, omni plebe adstante,—all this is embodied in the Catholic system as Cyprian understood it.

3. The Orientals in large degree, even under their yoke of bondage and the superstitions engendered by their decay, have ever adhered to this Ignatian theory, of which Cyprian was the great expounder in the West; while the terrible schism of the ninth century, which removed the West from the Nicene basis, and placed the Latin churches upon the foundation of the forged Decretals, was effected by ignoring the Cyprianic maxims, and then by a practical pulverizing of their fundamental principle of unity. This change involved a subversion of the primitive episcopate, an annihilation of the rights of the presbytery, and a total abasement of the laity; in a word, the destruction of synodical constitutions and of constitutional freedom.

4. The constitutional primacy, of which Cyprian was an early promoter, had to be entirely destroyed by decretalism before the papacy could exist. Gregory the Great stood upon the Cyprianic base when he pronounced the author of a scheme for a "universal bishopric" to be a forerunner of Antichrist. It was the spirit of the Decretals to substitute the fictitious idea of a divine supremacy in one bishop and one See, for the canonical presidency of a bishop who was only primus inter pares.

5. Hence the Cyprianic system has ever been the great resource of the "Gallicans against the Ultramontanes" in the cruel but most interesting history of the West. From the Council of Frankfort to our own times Cyprian's spirit is reflected in Hincmar, in Gerbert, in the Gallican canonists, in De Marca, in Bossuet, in Launoy, in Dupin, in Pascal, in the Jansenists (Augustinians), and by the Old Catholics in their late uprising against the dogmatic triumph of Ultramontanism. Nobody can understand the history of Latin Christianity without

mastering the system of Cyprian and comprehending the entirely hostile and uncatholic system of the Decretals.

6. I am not anxious to conceal the fact that I profoundly sympathize with the free spirit, the true benignity, and the moral purity which are everywhere reflected in the writings of Cyprian. If ever American Romanism becomes sufficiently enlightened and purified to comprehend this great Carthaginian Father, and to speak in his tones to the Bishop of Rome, a glorious reformation of this alien religion will be the result; and then we may comprehend the mysterious Providence which has transferred to these shores so many subjects of the despotism of the Vatican. Meanwhile the student of the Ante-Nicene Fathers will not be slow to perceive that he has, in the eight volumes of this series, all that is needful to disarm Romanism, to refute its pretensions, and to direct honest and truth-loving spirits in the Roman Obedience to the door of escape opened by Döllinger and his associates in the "Old Catholic" effort for the restoration of the Latin churches. Let us "speak the truth in love," and pray the Lord to bless this and every endeavor to promote and to sanctify the spirit of enlightened research after the "pattern in the mount." For "thus saith the Lord, Stand ye in the ways, and see and ask for the old paths:" τὰ ἀρχαῖα ἔθη. The following Introduction, from the Edinburgh editor, supplies further answers to inquiry, and suffices to elucidate the subjoined narrative of Pontius.

Little is known of the early history of Thascius Cyprian (born probably about 200 a.d.) until the period of his intimacy with the Carthaginian presbyter Cæcilius, which led to his conversion a.d. 246. That he was born of respectable parentage, and highly educated for the profession of rhetorician, is all that can be said with any degree of certainty. At his baptism he assumed the name of his friend Cæcilius, and devoted himself, with all the energies of an ardent and vigorous mind, to the study and practice of Christianity.

His ordination and his elevation to the episcopate rapidly followed his conversion. With some resistance on his own part, and not without great objections on the part of older presbyters, who saw themselves superseded by his promotion, the popular urgency constrained him to accept the office of Bishop of Carthage (a.d. 248), which he held until his martyrdom (a.d. 258).

The writings of Cyprian, apart from their intrinsic worth, have a very considerable historical interest and value, as illustrating the social and religious feelings and usages that then prevailed among the members of the Christian community. Nothing can enable us more vividly to realize the intense convictions—the high-strained enthusiasm—which formed the common level of the Christian experience, than does the indignation with which the prelate denounces the evasions of those who dared not confess, or the lapses of those who shrank from martyrdom. Living in the atmosphere of persecution, and often in the immediate presence of a lingering death, the professors of Christianity were nerved up to a wonderful contempt of suffering and of worldly enjoyment, and saw every event that occurred around them in the glow of their excited imagination; so that many circumstances were sincerely believed and honestly recorded, which will not be for a moment received as true by the calm and critical reader. The account given by Cyprian in his treatise on the Lapsed may serve as an illustration. Of this Dean Milman observes: "In what a high-wrought state of enthusiasm must men have been, who could relate and believe such statements as miraculous!"

Before being advanced to the episcopate, Cyprian had written his Epistle to Donatus shortly after his baptism (a.d. 246); his treatise, or fragment of a treatise, on the Vanity of Idols; and his three books of Testimonies against the Jews. In the following translation the order of Migne has been adopted, which places the letter to Donatus, as seems most natural, first among the Epistles, instead of with the Treatises.

The breaking out of the Decian persecution (a.d. 250) induced Cyprian to retire into concealment for a time; and his retreat gave occasion to a sharp attack upon his conduct, in a letter from the Roman to the Carthaginian clergy. During this year he wrote many letters from his place of concealment to the clergy and others at Rome and at Carthage, controlling, warning, directing, and exhorting, and in every way maintaining his episcopal superintendence in his absence, in all matters connected with the well-being of the Church.

The first 39 of the epistles, excepting the one to Donatus, were probably written during the period of Cyprian's retirement. He appears to have returned to his public duties early in June, 251. Then follow many letters between himself and Cornelius bishop of Rome, and others, on subjects connected with the schisms of Novatian, Novatus, and Felicissimus, and with the condition of those who had been perverted by them. The question proposed in Epistle 52 was settled in the Council that was held in May, 252; and the reference to that anticipated decision limits the date of the letter to about April in the same year. In the 53d Epistle, Cyprian is alluding to the impending persecution of Gallus, under which Cornelius was banished in July, 252. The 56th Epistle was a letter of congratulation to Cornelius on his banishment; and therefore, it must have been written before September 14th in that year, the date of the death of Cornelius. Lucius, his successor, was also banished, and was congratulated on his return by Cyprian in Epistle 57, which therefore must have been written about the end of November, 252. The 59th Epistle is referred by Bishop Pearson to the beginning of the year 253.

There seems nothing to suggest the date of Epistles 60 and 61, except the probability that they were written during a time of peace; and for this reason, they are referred to the beginning of Cyprian's episcopate, before the outbreak of the Decian persecution, a.d. 249. It is usual to assign Epistle 64 to the same year, or at least to a very early period of Cyprian's official life; but it seems scarcely likely that his episcopal counsel should have been sought by a brother bishop in a matter of practice, until he had had some experience; and as it was probably written at a time of peace, when discipline had become relaxed, the date 253 seems preferable. The 68th Epistle is easily dated by the reference, on page 246, to an episcopate of six years' duration; and it must therefore have been written in a.d. 254. On the 14th September, Cyprian was banished to Curubis by the Emperor Valerian. From his place of exile, he wrote Epistle 76, which was replied to in Epistles 77, 78, and 79. Doubts are entertained as to the date of Epistle 80, whether it should be referred to a.d. 250 or 257. Pamelius prefers the latter date, on the ground that the Rogatianus to whom it is inscribed was one who survived the Decian persecution, and a younger man than the one who, as he supposes, was declared to have suffered martyrdom at the date of this Epistle. This, however, seems very unsatisfactory; and the weight of authority is in favor of the earlier date. The remaining Epistles are easily limited by their contents to the period immediately preceding Cyprian's martyrdom.

For the sake of uniformity, it has been thought well to adhere to the arrangement of Migne, in the order of the Epistles as well as in their divisions. For the convenience of reference, however, the number of each Epistle in the Oxford edition is appended in a note. For a similar reason, the general form of Migne's text has been used in the following translation; but the use of other texts and of preceding translations has not been rejected in the endeavor to approximate to the sense of the author. Moreover, such various readings as might suggest different shades of meaning in doubtful passages have been given.

The Translator has only to add, that, as a rule, an exact rendering has been sought after, sometimes in preference to a version in fluent English. But, except in cases where the corruption or obscurity of the text seems insurmountable, the meaning of the writer is believed to be given fairly and intelligibly. The style of Cyprian, like that of his master Tertullian, is marked much more by vehemence than perspicuity, and it is often no easy matter to give exact expression in another language to the idea contained in the original text. Cyprian's Life, as written by his own deacon Pontius, is subjoined.

Note by the American Editor. It is easy to speak with ridicule of such instances as Dean Milman here treats so philosophically. But, lest believers should be charged with exceptional credulity, let us recall what the father of English Deism relates of his own experiences, in the conclusion of his Autobiography: "I had no sooner spoken these words (of prayer to the Deist's deity) but a loud though yet a gentle noise came from the heavens, for it was like nothing on earth, which did so comfort and cheer me, that I took my petition as granted, and that I had the sign I demanded.... This, how strange soever it may seem, I protest, before the eternal God, is true," etc. Life of Herbert, p. 52, Popular Authors(no date). London. From Horace Walpole's edition.

The Epistles of Cyprian.

Epistle I.

To Donatus. Argument.—Cyprian Had Promised Donatus that He Would Have a Discourse with Him Concerning Things Divine, and Now Being Reminded of His Promise, He Fulfils It. Commending at Length the Grace of God Conferred in Baptism, He Declares How He Had Been Changed Thereby; And, Finally, Pointing Out the Errors of the World, He Exhorts to Contempt of It and to Reading and Prayer. 1. Cæcilius Cyprian to Donatus sends, greeting. You rightly remind me, dearest Donatus for I not only remember my promise, but I confess that this is the appropriate time for its fulfilment, when the vintage festival invites the mind to unbend in repose, and to enjoy the annual and appointed respite of the declining year. Moreover, the place is in accord with the season, and the pleasant aspect of the gardens harmonizes with the gentle breezes of a mild autumn in soothing and cheering the senses. In such a place as this it is delightful to pass the day in discourse, and, by the (study of the sacred) parables, to train the conscience of the breast to the apprehension of the divine precepts. And that no profane intruder may interrupt our converse, nor any unrestrained clatter of a noisy household disturb it, let us seek this bower. The neighboring thickets ensure us solitude, and the vagrant trailings of the vine branches creeping in pendent mazes among the reeds that support them have made for us a porch of vines and a leafy shelter. Pleasantly here we clothe our thoughts in words; and while we gratify our eyes with the agreeable outlook upon trees and vines, the mind is at once instructed by what we hear, and nourished by what we see, although at the present time your only pleasure and your only interest is in our discourse. Despising the pleasures of sight, your eye is now fixed on me. With your mind as well as your ears you are altogether a listener; and a listener, too, with an eagerness proportioned to your affection.

2. And yet, of what kind or of what amount is anything that my mind is likely to communicate to yours? The poor mediocrity of my shallow understanding produces a very limited harvest and enriches the soil with no fruitful deposits. Nevertheless, with such powers as I have, I will set about the matter; for the subject itself on which I am about to speak will assist me. In courts of justice, in the public assembly, in political debate, a copious eloquence may be the glory of a voluble ambition; but in speaking of the Lord God, a chaste simplicity of expression strives for the conviction of faith rather with the substance, than with the powers, of

eloquence. Therefore accept from me things, not clever but weighty, words, not decked up to charm a popular audience with cultivated rhetoric, but simple and fitted by their unvarnished truthfulness for the proclamation of the divine mercy. Accept what is felt before it is spoken, what has not been accumulated with tardy painstaking during the lapse of years, but has been inhaled in one breath of ripening grace.

3. While I was still lying in darkness and gloomy night, wavering hither and thither, tossed about on the foam of this boastful age, and uncertain of my wandering steps, knowing nothing of my real life, and remote from truth and light, I used to regard it as a difficult matter, and especially as difficult in respect of my character at that time, that a man should be capable of being born again—a truth which the divine mercy had announced for my salvation,—and that a man quickened to a new life in the laver of saving water should be able to put off what he had previously been; and, although retaining all his bodily structure, should be himself changed in heart and soul. "How," said I, "is such a conversion possible, that there should be a sudden and rapid divestment of all which, either innate in us has hardened in the corruption of our material nature, or acquired by us has become inveterate by long accustomed use? These things have become deeply and radically engrained within us. When does he learn thrift who has been used to liberal banquets and sumptuous feasts? And he who has been glittering in gold and purple, and has been celebrated for his costly attire, when does he reduce himself to ordinary and simple clothing? One who has felt the charm of the fasces and of civic honors shrinks from becoming a mere private and inglorious citizen. The man who is attended by crowds of

clients, and dignified by the numerous association of an officious train, regards it as a punishment when he is alone. It is inevitable, as it ever has been, that the love of wine should entice, pride inflate, anger inflame, covetousness disquiet, cruelty stimulate, ambition delight, lust hasten to ruin, with allurements that will not let go their hold."

4. These were my frequent thoughts. For as I myself was held in bonds by the innumerable errors of my previous life, from which I did not believe that I could by possibility be delivered, so I was disposed to acquiesce in my clinging vices; and because I despaired of better things, I used to indulge my sins as if they were actually parts of me, and indigenous to me. But after that, by the help of the water of new birth, the stain of former years had been washed away, and a light from above, serene and pure, had been infused into my reconciled heart,— after that, by the agency of the Spirit breathed from heaven, a second birth had restored me to a new man;— then, in a wondrous manner, doubtful things at once began to assure themselves to me, hidden things to be revealed, dark things to be enlightened, what before had seemed difficult began to suggest a means of accomplishment, what had been thought impossible, to be capable of being achieved; so that I was enabled to acknowledge that what previously, being born of the flesh, had been living in the practice of sins, was of the earth earthly, but had now begun to be of God, and was animated by the Spirit of holiness. You yourself assuredly know and recollect as well as I do what was taken away from us, and what was given to us by that death of evil, and that life of virtue. You yourself know this without my information. Anything like boasting in one's own praise

is hateful, although we cannot in reality boast but only be grateful for whatever we do not ascribe to man's virtue but declare to be the gift of God; so that now we sin not is the beginning of the work of faith, whereas that we sinned before was the result of human error. All our power is of God; I say, of God. From Him we have life, from Him we have strength, by power derived and conceived from Him we do, while yet in this world, foreknow the indications of things to come. Only let fear be the keeper of innocence, that the Lord, who of His mercy has flowed into our hearts in the access of celestial grace, may be kept by righteous submissiveness in the hostelry of a grateful mind, that the assurance we have gained may not beget carelessness, and so the old enemy creep upon us again.

5. But if you keep the way of innocence, the way of righteousness, if you walk with a firm and steady step, if, depending on God with your whole strength and with your whole heart, you only be what you have begun to be, liberty and power to do is given you in proportion to the increase of your spiritual grace. For there is not, as is the case with earthly benefits, any measure or stint in the dispensing of the heavenly gift. The Spirit freely flowing forth is restrained by no limits, is checked by no closed barriers within certain bounded spaces; it flows perpetually, it is exuberant in its affluence. Let our heart only be athirst, and be ready to receive: in the degree in which we bring to it a capacious faith, in that measure we draw from it an overflowing grace. Thence is given power, with modest chastity, with a sound mind, with a simple voice, with unblemished virtue, that is able to quench the virus of poisons for the healing of the sick, to purge out the stains of foolish souls by restored health, to

bid peace to those that are at enmity, repose to the violent, gentleness to the unruly,—by startling threats to force to avow themselves the impure and vagrant spirits that have betaken themselves into the bodies of men whom they purpose to destroy, to drive them with heavy blows to come out of them, to stretch them out struggling, howling, groaning with increase of constantly renewing pain, to beat them with scourges, to roast them with fire: the matter is carried on there, but is not seen; the strokes inflicted are hidden, but the penalty is manifest. Thus, in respect of what we have already begun to be, the Spirit that we have received possesses its own liberty of action; while in that we have not yet changed our body and members, the carnal view is still darkened by the clouds of this world. How great is this empire of the mind, and what a power it has, not alone that itself is withdrawn from the mischievous associations of the world, as one who is purged and pure can suffer no stain of a hostile irruption, but that it becomes still greater and stronger in its might, so that it can rule over all the imperious host of the attacking adversary with its sway!

6. But in order that the characteristics of the divine may shine more brightly by the development of the truth, I will give you light to apprehend it, the obscurity caused by sin being wiped away. I will draw away the veil from the darkness of this hidden world. For a brief space conceive yourself to be transported to one of the loftiest peaks of some inaccessible mountain, thence gaze on the appearances of things lying below you, and with eyes turned in various directions look upon the eddies of the billowy world, while you yourself are removed from earthly contacts,—you will at once begin to feel compassion for the world, and with self-recollection and

increasing gratitude to God, you will rejoice with all the greater joy that you have escaped it. Consider the roads blocked up by robbers, the seas beset with pirates, wars scattered all over the earth with the bloody horror of camps. The whole world is wet with mutual blood; and murder, which in the case of an individual is admitted to be a crime, is called a virtue when it is committed wholesale. Impunity is claimed for the wicked deeds, not on the plea that they are guiltless, but because the cruelty is perpetrated on a grand scale.

7. And now, if you turn your eyes and your regards to the cities themselves, you will behold a concourse more fraught with sadness than any solitude. The gladiatorial games are prepared, that blood may gladden the lust of cruel eyes. The body is fed up with stronger food, and the vigorous mass of limbs is enriched with brawn and muscle, that the wretch fattened for punishment may die a harder death. Man is slaughtered that man may be gratified, and the skill that is best able to kill is an exercise and an art. Crime is not only com mitted, but it is taught. What can be said more inhuman,—what more repulsive? Training is undergone to acquire the power to murder, and the achievement of murder is its glory. What state of things, I pray you, can that be, and what can it be like, in which men, whom none have condemned, offer themselves to the wild beasts— men of ripe age, of sufficiently beautiful person, clad in costly garments? Living men, they are adorned for a voluntary death; wretched men, they boast of their own miseries. They fight with beasts, not for their crime, but for their madness. Fathers look on their own sons; a brother is in the arena, and his sister is hard by; and although a grander display of pomp increases the price of

the exhibition, yet, oh shame! even the mother will pay the increase in order that she may be present at her own miseries. And in looking upon scenes so frightful and so impious and so deadly, they do not seem to be aware that they are parricides with their eyes.

8. Hence turn your looks to the abominations, not less to be deplored, of another kind of spectacle. In the theatres also you will behold what may well cause you grief and shame. It is the tragic buskin which relates in verse the crimes of ancient days. The old horrors of parricide and incest are unfolded in action calculated to express the image of the truth, so that, as the ages pass by, any crime that was formerly committed may not be forgotten. Each generation is reminded by what it hears, that whatever has once been done may be done again. Crimes never die out by the lapse of ages; wickedness is never abolished by process of time; impiety is never buried in oblivion. Things which have now ceased to be actual deeds of vice become examples. In the mimes, moreover, by the teaching of infamies, the spectator is attracted either to reconsider what he may have done in secret, or to hear what he may do. Adultery is learnt while it is seen; and while the mischief having public authority panders to vices, the matron, who perchance had gone to the spectacle a modest woman, returns from it immodest. Still further, what a degradation of morals it is, what a stimulus to abominable deeds, what food for vice, to be polluted by histrionic gestures, against the covenant and law of one's birth, to gaze in detail upon the endurance of incestuous abominations! Men are emasculated, and all the pride and vigor of their sex is effeminated in the disgrace of their enervated body; and he is most pleasing there who has most completely broken down the man into

the woman. He grows into praise by virtue of his crime; and the more he is degraded, the more skillful he is considered to be. Such a one is looked upon—oh shame! and looked upon with pleasure. And what cannot such a creature suggest? He inflames the senses, he flatters the affections, he drives out the more vigorous conscience of a virtuous breast; nor is there wanting authority for the enticing abomination, that the mischief may creep upon people with a less perceptible approach. They picture Venus immodest, Mars adulterous; and that Jupiter of theirs not more supreme in dominion than in vice, inflamed with earthly love in the midst of his own thunders, now growing white in the feathers of a swan, now pouring down in a golden shower, now breaking forth by the help of birds to violate the purity of boys. And now put the question, Can he who looks upon such things be healthy-minded or modest? Men imitate the gods whom they adore, and to such miserable beings their crimes become their religion.

9. Oh, if placed on that lofty watch-tower you could gaze into the secret places—if you could open the closed doors of sleeping chambers, and recall their dark recesses to the perception of sight,—you would behold things done by immodest persons which no chaste eye could look upon; you would see what even to see is a crime; you would see what people imbruted with the madness of vice deny that they have done, and yet hasten to do,—men with frenzied lusts rushing upon men, doing things which afford no gratification even to those who do them. I am deceived if the man who is guilty of such things as these does not accuse others of them. The depraved maligns the depraved, and thinks that he himself, though conscious of the guilt, has escaped, as if

consciousness were not a sufficient condemnation. The same people who are accusers in public are criminals in private, condemning themselves at the same time as they condemn the culprits; they denounce abroad what they commit at home, willingly doing what, when they have done, they accuse,—a daring which assuredly is fitly mated with vice, and an impudence quite in accordance with shameless people. And I beg you not to wonder at the things that people of this kind speak: the offence of their mouths in words is the least of which they are guilty.

10. But after considering the public roads full of pitfalls, after battles of many kinds scattered abroad over the whole world, after exhibitions either bloody or infamous, after the abominations of lust, whether exposed for sale in brothels or hidden within the domestic walls— abominations, the audacity of which is greater in proportion to the secrecy of the crime,—possibly you may think that the Forum at least is free from such things, that it is neither exposed to exasperating wrongs, nor polluted by the association of criminals. Then turn your gaze in that direction: there you will discover things more odious than ever, so that thence you will be more desirous of turning away your eyes, although the laws are carved on twelve tables, and the statutes are publicly prescribed on brazen tablets. Yet wrong is done in the midst of the laws themselves; wickedness is committed in the very face of the statutes; innocence is not preserved even in the place where it is defended. By turns the rancor of disputants rages; and when peace is broken among the togas, the Forum echoes with the madness of strife. There close at hand is the spear and the sword, and the executioner also; there is the claw that tears, the rack that stretches, the fire that burns up,—more tortures for one poor human body

than it has limbs. And in such cases who is there to help? One's patron? He makes a feint and deceives. The judge? But he sells his sentence. He who sits to avenge crimes commits them, and the judge becomes the culprit, in order that the accused may perish innocently. Crimes are everywhere common; and everywhere in the multiform character of sin, the pernicious poison acts by means of degraded minds. One man forges a will, another by a capital fraud makes a false deposition; on the one hand, children are cheated of their inheritances, on the other, strangers are endowed with their estates. The opponent makes his charge, the false accuser attacks, the witness defames, on all sides the venal impudence of hired voices sets about the falsification of charges, while in the meantime the guilty do not even perish with the innocent. There is no fear about the laws; no concern for either inquisitor or judge; when the sentence can be bought off for money, it is not cared for. It is a crime now among the guilty to be innocent; whoever does not imitate the wicked is an offence to them. The laws have come to terms with crimes, and whatever is public has begun to be allowed. What can be the modesty, what can be the integrity, that prevails there, when there are none to condemn the wicked, and one only meets with those who ought themselves to be condemned?

11. But that we may not perchance appear as if we were picking out extreme cases, and with the view of disparagement were seeking to attract your attention to those things whereof the sad and revolting view may offend the gaze of a better conscience, I will now direct you to such things as the world in its ignorance accounts good. Among these also you will behold things that will shock you. In respect of what you regard as honors, of

what you consider the fasces, what you count affluence in riches, what you think power in the camp, the glory of the purple in the magisterial office, the power of license in the chief command,—there is hidden the virus of ensnaring mischief, and an appearance of smiling wickedness, joyous indeed, but the treacherous deception of hidden calamity. Just as some poison, in which the flavor having been medicated with sweetness, craftily mingled in its deadly juices, seems, when taken, to be an ordinary draught, but when it is drunk up, the destruction that you have swallowed assails you. You see, forsooth, that man distinguished by his brilliant dress, glittering, as he thinks, in his purple. Yet with what baseness has he purchased this glitter! What contempt of the proud has he had first to submit to! what haughty thresholds has he, as an early courtier, besieged! How many scornful footsteps of arrogant great men has he had to precede, thronged in the crowd of clients, that by and by a similar procession might attend and precede him with salutations,—a train waiting not upon his person, but upon his power! for he has no claim to be regarded for his character, but for his fasces. Of these, finally, you may see the degrading end, when the time-serving sycophant has departed, and the hanger-on, deserting them, has defiled the exposed side of the man who has retired into a private condition. It is then that the mischiefs done to the squandered family-estate smite upon the conscience, then the losses that have exhausted the fortune are known,—expenses by which the favor of the populace was bought, and the people's breath asked for with fickle and empty entreaties. Assuredly, it was a vain and foolish boastfulness to have desired to set forth in the gratification of a disappointing spectacle, what the people would not receive, and what would ruin the magistrates.

12. But those, moreover, whom you consider rich, who add forests to forests, and who, excluding the poor from their neighborhood, stretch out their fields far and wide into space without any limits, who possess immense heaps of silver and gold and mighty sums of money, either in built-up heaps or in buried stores,—even in the midst of their riches those are torn to pieces by the anxiety of vague thought, lest the robber should spoil, lest the murderer should attack, lest the envy of some wealthier neighbor should become hostile, and harass them with malicious lawsuits. Such a one enjoys no security either in his food or in his sleep. In the midst of the banquet he sighs, although he drinks from a jeweled goblet; and when his luxurious bed has enfolded his body, languid with feasting, in its yielding bosom, he lies wakeful in the midst of the down; nor does he perceive, poor wretch, that these things are merely gilded torments, that he is held in bondage by his gold, and that he is the slave of his luxury and wealth rather than their master. And oh, the odious blindness of perception, and the deep darkness of senseless greed! although he might disburden himself and get rid of the load, he rather continues to brood over his vexing wealth,—he goes on obstinately clinging to his tormenting hoards. From him there is no liberality to dependents, no communication to the poor. And yet such people call that their own money, which they guard with jealous labor, shut up at home as if it were another's, and from which they derive no benefit either for their friends, for their children, or, in fine, for themselves. Their possession amounts to this only, that they can keep others from possessing it; and oh, what a marvelous perversion of names! they call those things

goods, which they absolutely put to none but bad uses.

13. Or think you that even those are secure,—that those at least are safe with some stable permanence among the chaplets of honor and vast wealth, whom, in the glitter of royal palaces, the safeguard of watchful arms surrounds? They have greater fear than others. A man is constrained to dread no less than he is dreaded. Exaltation exacts its penalties equally from the more powerful, although he may be hedged in with bands of satellites and may guard his person with the enclosure and protection of a numerous retinue. Even as he does not allow his inferiors to feel security, it is inevitable that he himself should want the sense of security. The power of those whom power makes terrible to others, is, first of all, terrible to themselves. It smiles to rage, it cajoles to deceive, it entices to slay, it lifts up to cast down. With a certain usury of mischief, the greater the height of dignity and honors attained, the greater is the interest of penalty required.

14. Hence, then, the one peaceful and trustworthy tranquility, the one solid and firm and constant security, is this, for a man to withdraw from these eddies of a distracting world, and, anchored on the ground of the harbor of salvation, to lift his eyes from earth to heaven; and having been admitted to the gift of God, and being already very near to his God in mind, he may boast, that whatever in human affairs others esteem lofty and grand, lies altogether beneath his consciousness. He who is actually greater than the world can crave nothing, can desire nothing, from the world. How stable, how free from all shocks is that safeguard; how heavenly the protection in its perennial blessings,—to be loosed from the snares of this entangling world, and to be purged from

earthly dregs, and fitted for the light of eternal immortality! He will see what crafty mischief of the foe that previously attacked us has been in progress against us. We are constrained to have more love for what we shall be, by being allowed to know and to condemn what we were. Neither for this purpose is it necessary to pay a price either in the way of bribery or of labor; so that man's elevation or dignity or power should be begotten in him with elaborate effort; but it is a gratuitous gift from God, and it is accessible to all. As the sun shines spontaneously, as the day gives light, as the fountain flows, as the shower yields moisture, so does the heavenly Spirit infuses itself into us. When the soul, in its gaze into heaven, has recognized its Author, it rises higher than the sun, and far transcends all this earthly power, and begins to be that which it believes itself to be.

15. Do you, however, whom the celestial warfare has enlisted in the spiritual camp, only observe a discipline uncorrupted and chastened in the virtues of religion. Be constant as well in prayer as in reading; now speak with God, now let God speak with you, let Him instruct you in His precepts, let Him direct you. Whom He has made rich, none shall make poor; for, in fact, there can be no poverty to him whose breast has once been supplied with heavenly food. Ceilings enriched with gold, and houses adorned with mosaics of costly marble, will seem mean to you, now when you know that it is you yourself who are rather to be perfected, you who are rather to be adorned, and that that dwelling in which God has dwelt as in a temple, in which the Holy Spirit has begun to make His abode, is of more importance than all others. Let us embellish this house with the colors of innocence, let us enlighten it with the light of justice: this

will never fall into decay with the wear of age, nor shall it be defiled by the tarnishing of the colors of its walls, nor of its gold. Whatever is artificially beautified is perishing; and such things as contain not the reality of possession afford no abiding assurance to their possessors. But this remains in a beauty perpetually vivid, in perfect honor, in permanent splendor. It can neither decay nor be destroyed; it can only be fashioned into greater perfection when the body returns to it.

16. These things, dearest Donatus, briefly for the present. For although what you profitably hear delights your patience, indulgent in its goodness, your well-balanced mind, and your assured faith—and nothing is so pleasant to your ears as what is pleasant to you in God,—yet, as we are associated as neighbors, and are likely to talk together frequently, we ought to have some moderation in our conversation; and since this is a holiday rest, and a time of leisure, whatever remains of the day, now that the sun is sloping towards the evening, let us spend it in gladness, nor let even the hour of repast be without heavenly grace. Let the temperate meal resound with psalms; and as your memory is tenacious and your voice musical, undertake this office, as is your wont. You will provide better entertainment for your dearest friends, if, while we have something spiritual to listen to, the sweetness of religious music charms our ears.

Epistle II.

From the Roman Clergy to the Carthaginian Clergy, About the Retirement of the Blessed Cyprian.

Argument.—The Roman Clergy Had Learnt from Crementius the Sub-Deacon, that in the Time of Persecution Cyprian Had Withdrawn Himself. Therefore, with Their Accustomed Zeal for the Faith, They Remind the Carthaginian Clergy of Their Duty, and Instruct Them What to Do in the Case of the Lapsed, During the Interval of the Bishop's Absence.

1. We have been informed by Crementius the sub-deacon, who came to us from you, that the blessed father Cyprian has for a certain reason withdrawn; "in doing which he acted quite rightly, because he is a person of eminence, and because a conflict is impending," which God has allowed in the world, for the sake of cooperating with His servants in their struggle against the adversary, and was, moreover, willing that this conflict should show to angels and to men that the victor shall be crowned, while the vanquished shall in himself receive the doom which has been made manifest to us. Since, moreover, it devolves upon us who appear to be placed on high, in the place of a shepherd, to keep watch over the flock; if we be found neglectful, it will be said to us, as it was said to our predecessors also, who in such wise negligent had been placed in charge, that "we have not sought for that which was lost, and have not corrected the wanderer, and have not bound up that which was broken, but have eaten their milk, and been clothed with their wool;" and then also the Lord Himself, fulfilling what had been written in the law and the prophets, teaches, saying, "I am the good

shepherd, who lay down my life for the sheep. But the hireling, whose own the sheep are not, sees the wolf coming, and leaves the sheep, and flees, and the wolf scatters them." To Simon, too, He speaks thus: "Loves thou me? He answered, I do love Thee. He saith to him, Feed my sheep." We know that this saying arose out of the very circumstance of his withdrawal, and the rest of the disciples did likewise.

2. We are unwilling, therefore, beloved brethren, that you should be found hirelings, but we desire you to be good shepherds, since you are aware that no slight danger threatens you if you do not exhort our brethren to stand steadfast in the faith, so that the brotherhood be not absolutely rooted out, as being of those who rush headlong into idolatry. Neither is it in words only that we exhort you to this; but you will be able to ascertain from very many who come to you from us, that, God blessing us, we both have done and still do all these things ourselves with all anxiety and worldly risk, having before our eyes rather the fear of God and eternal sufferings than the fear of men and a short-lived discomfort, not forsaking the brethren, but exhorting them to stand firm in the faith, and to be ready to go with the Lord. And we have even recalled those who were ascending to do that to which they were constrained. The Church stands in faith, notwithstanding that some have been driven to fall by very terror, whether that they were persons of eminence, or that they were afraid, when seized, with the fear of man: these, however, we did not abandon, although they were separated from us, but exhorted them, and do exhort them, to repent, if in any way they may receive pardon from Him who is able to grant it; lest, haply, if they should be deserted by us, they should become worse.

3. You see, then, brethren, that you also ought to do the like, so that even those who have fallen may amend their minds by your exhortation; and if they should be seized once more, may confess, and may so make amends for their previous sin. And there are other matters which are incumbent on you, which also we have here added, as that if any who may have fallen into this temptation begin to be taken with sickness, and repent of what they have done, and desire communion, it should in any wise be granted them. Or if you have widows or bedridden people who are unable to maintain themselves, or those who are in prisons or are excluded from their own dwellings, these ought in all cases to have some to minister to them. Moreover, catechumens when seized with sickness ought not to be deceived, but help is to be afforded them. And, as matter of the greatest importance, if the bodies of the martyrs and others be not buried, a considerable risk is incurred by those whose duty it is to do this office. By whomsoever of you, then, and on whatever occasion this duty may have been performed, we are sure that he is regarded as a good servant,—as one who has been faithful in the least and will be appointed ruler over ten cities. May God, however, who gives all things to them that hope in Him, grant to us that we may all be found in these works. The brethren who are in bonds greet you, as do the elders, and the whole Church, which itself also with the deepest anxiety keeps watch over all who call on the name of the Lord. And we likewise beg you in your turn to have us in remembrance. Know, moreover, that Bassianus has come to us; and we request of you who have a zeal for God, to send a copy of this letter to whomsoever you are able, as occasions may serve, or make your own opportunities, or send a message, that

they may stand firm and steadfast in the faith. We bid you, beloved brethren, ever heartily farewell.

Epistle III.

To the Presbyters and Deacons Abiding at Rome. a.d. 250.

Argument.—This is a Familiar and Friendly Epistle; So that It Requires No Formal Argument, Especially as It Can Be Sufficiently Gathered from the Title Itself. The Letter of the Roman Clergy, to Which Cyprian is Replying, is Missing.

1. Cyprian to the elders and deacons, brethren abiding at Rome, sends, greeting. When the report of the departure of the excellent man, my colleague, was still uncertain among us, my beloved brethren, and I was wavering doubtfully in my opinion on the matter, I received a letter sent to me from you by Crementius the sub-deacon, in which I was most abundantly informed of his glorious end; and I rejoiced greatly that, in harmony with the integrity of his administration, an honorable consummation also attended him. Wherein, moreover, I greatly congratulate you, that you honor his memory with a testimony so public and so illustrious, so that by your means is made known to me, not only what is glorious to you in connection with the memory of your bishop, but what ought to afford to me also an example of faith and virtue. For in proportion as the fall of a bishop is an event which tends ruinously to the fall of his followers, so on the other hand it is a useful and helpful thing when a bishop, by the firmness of his faith, sets himself forth to his brethren as an object of imitation.

2. I have, moreover, read another epistle, in which neither the person who wrote nor the persons to whom it was written were plainly declared; and inasmuch as in the same letter both the writing and the matter, and even the paper itself, gave me the idea that something had been taken away, or had been changed from the original, I have sent you back the epistle as it actually came to hand, that you may examine whether it is the very same which you gave to Crementius the sub-deacon, to carry. For it is a very serious thing if the truth of a clerical letter is corrupted by any falsehood or deceit. In order, then, that we may know this, ascertain whether the writing and subscription are yours, and write to me again what is the truth of the matter. I bid you, dearest brethren, ever heartily farewell.

Epistle IV.

To the Presbyters and Deacons.

Argument.—Cyprian Exhorts His Clergy from His Place of Retirement, that in His Absence They Should Be United; That Nothing Should Be Wanting to Prisoners or to the Rest of the Poor; And Further, that They Should Keep the People in Quiet, Lest, If They Should Rush in Crowds to Visit the Martyrs in Prison, This Privilege Should at Length Be Forbidden Them. a.d. 250.

1. Cyprian to the presbyters and deacons, his beloved brethren, greeting. Being by the grace of God in safety, dearest brethren, I salute you, rejoicing that I am informed of the prosperity of all things in respect of your safety also; and as the condition of the place does not permit me to be with you now, I beg you, by your faith

and your religion, to discharge there both your own office and mine, that there may be nothing wanting either to discipline or diligence. In respect of means, moreover, for meeting the expenses, whether for those who, having confessed their Lord with a glorious voice, have been put in prison, or for those who are laboring in poverty and want, and still stand fast in the Lord, I entreat that nothing be wanting, since the whole of the small sum which was collected there was distributed among the clergy for cases of that kind, that many might have means whence they could assist the necessities and burthens of individuals.

2. I beg also that there may be no lack, on your parts, of wisdom and carefulness to preserve peace. For although from their affection the brethren are eager to approach and to visit those good confessors, on whom by their glorious beginnings the divine consideration has already shed a brightness, yet I think that this eagerness must be cautiously indulged, and not in crowds,—not in numbers collected together at once, lest from this very thing ill will be aroused, and the means of access be denied, and thus, while we insatiably wish for all, we lose all. Take counsel, therefore, and see that this may be more safely managed with moderation, so that the presbyters also, who there offer with the confessors, may one by one take turns with the deacons individually; because, by thus changing the persons and varying the people that come together, suspicion is diminished. For, meek and humble in all things, as befits the servants of God, we ought to accommodate ourselves to the times, and to provide for quietness, and to have regard to the people. I bid you, brethren, beloved and dearly longed-for, always heartily farewell; and have me in remembrance. Greet all the brotherhood. Victor the deacon, and those who are with

me, greet you. Farewell!

Epistle V.

To the Presbyters and Deacons.

Argument.—The Argument of This Letter is Nearly the Same as that of the Preceding One, Except that the Writer Directs the Confessors Also to Be Admonished by the Clergy of Their Duty, to Give Attention to Humility, and Obey the Presbyters and Deacons. His Own Retirement Incidentally Furnishes an Occasion for This.

1. Cyprian to the presbyters and deacons, his brethren, greeting. I had wished indeed, beloved brethren, with this my letter to greet the whole of my clergy in health and safety. But since the stormy time which has in a great measure overwhelmed my people, has, moreover, added this enhancement to my sorrows, that it has touched with its desolation even a portion of the clergy, I pray the Lord that, by the divine mercy, I may hereafter greet you at all events as safe, who, as I have learned, stand fast both in faith and virtue. And although some reasons might appear to urge me to the duty of myself hastening to come to you, firstly, for instance, because of my eagerness and desire for you, which is the chief consideration in my prayers, and then, that we might be able to consult together on those matters which are required by the general advantage, in respect of the government of the Church, and having carefully examined them with abundant counsel, might wisely arrange them;—yet it seemed to me better, still to preserve my retreat and my quiet for a while, with a view to other advantages connected with the peace and safety of us all:—which

advantages an account will be given you by our beloved brother Tertullus, who, besides his other care which he zealously bestows on divine labors, was, moreover, the author of this counsel; that I should be cautious and moderate, and not rashly trust myself into the sight of the public; and especially that I should beware of that place where I had been so often inquired for and sought after.

2. Relying, therefore, upon your love and your piety, which I have abundantly known, in this letter I both exhort and command you, that those of you whose presence there is least suspicious and least perilous, should in my stead discharge my duty, in respect of doing those things which are required for the religious administration. In the meantime let the poor be taken care of as much and as well as possible; but especially those who have stood with unshaken faith and have not forsaken Christ's flock, that, by your diligence, means be supplied to them to enable them to bear their poverty, so that what the troublous time has not effected in respect of their faith, may not be accomplished by want in respect of their afflictions. Let a more earnest care, moreover, be bestowed upon the glorious confessors. And although I know that very many of those have been maintained by the vow and by the love of the brethren, yet if there be any who are in want either of clothing or maintenance, let them be supplied, with whatever things are necessary, as I formerly wrote to you, while they were still kept in prison,—only let them know from you and be instructed, and learn what, according to the authority of Scripture, the discipline of the Church requires of them, that they ought to be humble and modest and peaceable, that they should maintain the honor of their name, so that those who have achieved glory by what they have testified, may

achieve glory also by their characters, and in all things seeking the Lord's approval, may show themselves worthy, in consummation of their praise, to attain a heavenly crown. For there remains more than what is yet seen to be accomplished, since it is written "Praise not any man before his death;" and again, "Be thou faithful unto death, and I will give thee a crown of life." And the Lord also says, "He that endures to the end, the same shall be saved." Let them imitate the Lord, who at the very time of His passion was not more proud, but more humble. For then He washed His disciples' feet, saying, "If I, your Lord and Master, have washed your feet, ye ought also to wash one another's feet. For I have given you an example, that ye should do as I have done to you." Let them also follow the example of the Apostle Paul, who, after often-repeated imprisonment, after scourging, after exposures to wild beasts, in everything continued meek and humble; and even after his rapture to the third heaven and paradise, he did not proudly arrogate anything to himself when he said, "Neither did we eat any man's bread for nought, but wrought with labor and travail night and day, that we might not be chargeable to any of you."

3. These several matters, I pray you, suggest to our brethren. And as "he who humbles himself shall be exalted," now is the time when they should rather fear the ensnaring adversary, who more eagerly attacks the man that is strongest, and becoming more virulent, for the very reason that he is conquered, strives to overcome his conqueror. The Lord grant that I may soon both see them again, and by salutary exhortation may establish their minds to preserve their glory. For I am grieved when I hear that some of them run about wickedly and proudly, and give themselves up to follies or to discords; that

members of Christ, and even members that have confessed Christ, are defiled by unlawful concubinage, and cannot be ruled either by deacons or by presbyters, but cause that, by the wicked and evil characters of a few, the honorable glories of many and good confessors are tarnished; whom they ought to fear, lest, being condemned by their testimony and judgment, they be excluded from their fellowship. That, finally, is the illustrious and true confessor, concerning whom afterwards the Church does not blush, but boasts.

4. In respect of that which our fellow-presbyters, Donatus and Fortunatus, Novatus and Gordius, wrote to me, I have not been able to reply by myself, since, from the first commencement of my episcopacy, I made up my mind to do nothing on my own private opinion, without your advice and without the consent of the people. But as soon as, by the grace of God, I shall have come to you, then we will discuss in common, as our respective dignity requires, those things which either have been or are to be done. I bid you, brethren beloved and dearly longed-for, ever heartily farewell, and be mindful of me. Greet the brotherhood that is with you earnestly from me and tell them to remember me. Farewell.

Epistle VI.

To Rogatianus the Presbyter, and the Other Confessors. a.d. 250.

Argument.—He Exhorts Rogatianus and the Other Confessors to Maintain Discipline, that None Who Had Confessed Christ in Word Should Seem to Deny Him in Deed; Casually Rebuking Some of Them, Who, Being

Exiled on Account of the Faith, Were Not Afraid to Return Unbidden into Their Country.

1. Cyprian to the presbyter Rogatianus, and to the other confessors, his brethren, greeting. I had both heretofore, dearly beloved and bravest brethren, sent you a letter, in which I congratulated your faith and virtue with exulting words, and now my voice has no other object, first of all, than with joyous mind, repeatedly and always to announce the glory of your name. For what can I wish greater or better in my prayers than to see the flock of Christ enlightened by the honor of your confession? For although all the brethren ought to rejoice in this, yet, in the common gladness, the share of the bishop is the greatest. For the glory of the Church is the glory of the bishop. In proportion as we grieve over those whom a hostile persecution has cast down, in the same proportion we rejoice over you whom the devil has not been able to overcome.

2. Yet I exhort you by our common faith, by the true and simple love of my heart towards you, that, having overcome the adversary in this first encounter, you should hold fast to your glory with a brave and persevering virtue. We are still in the world; we are still placed in the battlefield; we fight daily for our lives. Care must be taken, that after such beginnings as these there should also come an increase, and that what you have begun to be with such a blessed commencement should be consummated in you. It is a slight thing to have been able to attain anything; it is more to be able to keep what you have attained; even as faith itself and saving birth makes alive, not by being received, but by being preserved. Nor is it actually the attainment, but the perfecting, that keeps a man for God. The Lord taught this in His instruction

when He said, "Behold, thou art made whole; sin no more, lest a worse thing come unto thee." Conceive of Him as saying this also to His confessor, "Lo thou art made a confessor; sin no more, lest a worse thing come unto thee." Solomon also, and Saul, and many others, so long as they walked in the Lord's ways, were able to keep the grace given to them. When the discipline of the Lord was forsaken by them, grace also forsook them.

3. We must persevere in the straight and narrow road of praise and glory; and since peacefulness and humility and the tranquility of a good life is fitting for all Christians, according to the word of the Lord, who looks to none other man than "to him that is poor and of a contrite spirit, and that trembles at" His word, it the more behooves you confessors, who have been made an example to the rest of the brethren, to observe and fulfil this, as being those whose characters should provoke to imitation the life and conduct of all. For as the Jews were alienated from God, as those on whose account "the name of God is blasphemed among the Gentiles," so on the other hand those are dear to God through whose conformity to discipline the name of God is declared with a testimony of praise, as it is written, the Lord Himself forewarning and saying, "Let your light so shine before men that they may see your good works and glorify your Father which is in heaven." And Paul the apostle says, "Shine as lights in the world." And similarly, Peter exhorts: "As strangers," says he, "and pilgrims, abstain from fleshly lusts, which war against the soul, having your conversation honest among the Gentiles; that whereas they speak against you as evil-doers, they may by your good works, which they shall behold, glorify the Lord." This, indeed, the greatest part of you, I rejoice to

say, are careful for; and, made better by the honor of your confession itself, guard and preserve its glory by tranquil and virtuous lives.

4. But I hear that some infect your number and destroy the praise of a distinguished name by their corrupt conversation; whom you yourselves, even as being lovers and guardians of your own praise, should rebuke and check and correct. For what a disgrace is suffered by your name, when one spends his days in intoxication and debauchery, another returns to that country whence he was banished, to perish when arrested, not now as being a Christian, but as being a criminal! I hear that some are puffed up and are arrogant, although it is written, "Be not high-minded, but fear: for if God spared not the natural branches, take heed lest He also spare not thee." Our Lord "was led as a sheep to the slaughter; and as a lamb before her shearers is dumb, so He opened not His mouth." "I am not rebellious," says He, "neither do I gainsay. I gave my back to the smiters, and my cheeks to the palms of their hands. I hid not my face from the filthiness of spitting." And dares any one now, who lives by and in this very One, lift up himself and be haughty, forgetful, as well of the deeds which He did, as of the commands which He left to us either by Himself or by His apostles? But if "the servant is not greater than his Lord," let those who follow the Lord humbly and peacefully and silently tread in His steps, since the lower one is, the more exalted he may become; as says the Lord, "He that is least among you, the same shall be great."

5. What, then, is that—how execrable should it appear to you—which I have learnt with extreme anguish and grief of mind, to wit, that there are not wanting those who defile the temples of God, and the members

sanctified after confession and made glorious, with a disgraceful and infamous concubinage, associating their beds promiscuously with women's! In which, even if there be no pollution of their conscience, there is a great guilt in this very thing, that by their offence originate examples for the ruin of others. There ought also to be no contentions and emulations among you, since the Lord left to us His peace, and it is written, "Thou shalt love thy neighbor as thyself." "But if ye bite and find fault with one another, take heed that ye be not consumed one of another." From abuse and revilings also I entreat you to abstain, for "revilers do not attain the kingdom of God;" and the tongue which has confessed Christ should be preserved sound and pure with its honor. For he who, according to Christ's precept, speaks things peaceable and good and just, daily confesses Christ. We had renounced the world when we were baptized; but we have now indeed renounced the world when tried and approved by God, we leave all that we have, and have followed the Lord, and stand and live in His faith and fear.

  6. Let us confirm one another by mutual exhortations, and let us more and more go forward in the Lord; so that when of His mercy He shall have made that peace which He promises to give, we may return to the Church new and almost changed men, and may be received, whether by our brethren or by the heathen, in all things corrected and renewed for the better; and those who formerly admired our glory in our courage may now admire the discipline in our lives. I bid you, beloved brethren, ever heartily farewell; and be mindful of me.

Epistle VII.

To the Clergy, Concerning Prayer to God.

Argument.—The Argument of the Present Epistle is Nearly the Same as that of the Two Preceding, Except that He Exhorts in This to Diligent Prayer.

1. Cyprian to the presbyters and deacons, his brethren, greeting. Although I know, brethren beloved, that from the fear which we all of us owe to God, you also are instantly urgent in continual petitions and earnest prayers to Him, still I myself remind your religious anxiety, that in order to appease and entreat the Lord, we must lament not only in words, but also with fasting and with tears, and with every kind of urgency. For we must perceive and confess that the so disordered ruin arising from that affliction, which has in a great measure laid waste, and is even still laying waste, our flock, has visited us according to our sins, in that we do not keep the way of the Lord, nor observe the heavenly commandments given to us for our salvation. Our Lord did the will of His Father, and we do not do the will of our Lord; eager about our patrimony and our gain, seeking to satisfy our pride, yielding ourselves wholly to emulation and to strife, careless of simplicity and faith, renouncing the world in words only, and not in deeds, every one of us pleasing himself, and displeasing all others,—therefore we are smitten as we deserve, since it is written: "And that servant, which knows his master's will, and has not obeyed his will, shall be beaten with many stripes." But what stripes, what blows, do we not deserve, when even confessors, who ought to be an example of virtuous life to others, do not maintain discipline? Therefore, while an

inflated and immodest boastfulness about their own confession excessively elates some, tortures come upon them, and tortures without any cessation of the tormentor, without any end of condemnation, without any comfort of death,—tortures which do not easily let them pass to the crown, but wrench them on the rack until they cause them to abandon their faith, unless someone taken away by the divine compassion should depart in the very midst of the torments, gaining glory not by the cessation of his torture, but by the quickness of his death.

2. These things we suffer by our own fault and our own deserving, even as the divine judgment has forewarned us, saying, "If they forsake my law and walk not in my judgments, if they profane my statutes and keep not my commandments, then will I visit their transgressions with the rod, and their iniquities with stripes." It is for this reason that we feel the rods and the stripes, because we neither please God with good deeds nor atone for our sins. Let us of our inmost heart and of our entire mind ask for God's mercy, because He Himself also adds, saying, "Nevertheless my loving-kindness will I not scatter away from them." Let us ask, and we shall receive; and if there be delay and tardiness in our receiving, since we have grievously offended, let us knock, because "to him that knocks also it shall be opened," if only our prayers, our groanings, and our tears, knock at the door; and with these we must be urgent and persevering, even although prayer be offered with one mind.

3. For,—which the more induced and constrained me to write this letter to you,—you ought to know (since the Lord has condescended to show and to reveal it) that it was said in a vision, "Ask, and ye shall obtain." Then,

afterwards, that the attending people were bidden to pray for certain persons pointed out to them, but that in their petitions there were dissonant voices, and wills disagreeing, and that this excessively displeased Him who had said, "Ask, and ye shall obtain," because the disagreement of the people was out of harmony, and there was not a consent of the brethren one and simple, and a united concord; since it is written, "God who makes men to be of one mind in a house;" and we read in the Acts of the Apostles, "And the multitude of them that believed were of one heart and of one soul." And the Lord has bidden us with His own voice, saying, "This is my command, that ye love one another." And again, "I say unto you, that if two of you shall agree on earth as touching anything that you shall ask, it shall be done for you of my Father which is in heaven." But if two of one mind can do so much, what might be affected if the unanimity prevailed among all? But if, according to the peace which our Lord gave us, there were agreement among all brethren, we should before this have obtained from the divine mercy what we seek; nor should we be wavering so long in this peril of our salvation and our faith. Yes, truly, and these evils would not have come upon the brethren, if the brotherhood had been animated with one spirit.

    4. For there also was shown that there sate the father of a family, a young man also being seated at his right hand, who, anxious and somewhat sad with a kind of indignation, holding his chin in his right hand, occupied his place with a sorrowful look. But another standing on the left hand, bore a net, which he threatened to throw, in order to catch the people standing round. And when he who saw marveled what this could be, it was told him that

the youth who was thus sitting on the right hand was saddened and grieved because his commandments were not observed; but that he on the left was exultant because an opportunity was afforded him of receiving from the father of the family the power of destroying. This was shown long before the tempest of this devastation arose. And we have seen that which had been shown fulfilled; that while we despise the commandments of the Lord, while we do not keep the salutary ordinances of the law that He has given, the enemy was receiving a power of doing mischief, and was overwhelming, by the cast of his net, those who were imperfectly armed and too careless to resist.

5. Let us urgently pray and groan with continual petitions. For know, beloved brethren, that I was not long ago reproached with this also in a vision, that we were sleepy in our prayers, and did not pray with watchfulness; and undoubtedly God, who "rebukes whom He loves," when He rebukes, rebukes that He may amend, amends that He may preserve. Let us therefore strike off and break away from the bonds of sleep, and pray with urgency and watchfulness, as the Apostle Paul bids us, saying, "Continue in prayer, and watch in the same." For the apostles also ceased not to pray day and night; and the Lord also Himself, the teacher of our discipline, and the way of our example, frequently and watchfully prayed, as we read in the Gospel: "He went out into a mountain to pray and continued all night in prayer to God." And assuredly what He prayed for, He prayed for on our behalf, since He was not a sinner, but bore the sins of others. But He so prayed for us, that in another place we read, "And the Lord said to Peter, Behold, Satan has desired to sift you as wheat: but I have prayed for thee,

that thy faith fail not." But if for us and for our sins He both labored and watched and prayed, how much more ought we to be instant in prayers; and, first of all, to pray and to entreat the Lord Himself, and then through Him, to make satisfaction to God the Father! We have an advocate and an intercessor for our sins, Jesus Christ the Lord and our God, if only we repent of our sins past, and confess and acknowledge our sins, whereby we now offend the Lord, and for the time to come engage to walk in His ways, and to fear His commandments. The Father corrects and protects us, if we still stand fast in the faith both in afflictions and perplexities, that is to say, cling closely to His Christ; as it is written, "Who shall separate us from the love of Christ? Shall tribulation, or distress, or persecution, or famine or nakedness, or peril, or sword?" None of these things can separate believers, nothing can tear away those who are clinging to His body and blood. Persecution of that kind is an examination and searching out of the heart. God wills us to be sifted and proved, as He has always proved His people; and yet in His trials help has never at any time been wanting to believers.

6. Finally, to the very least of His servants although placed among very many sins, and unworthy of His condescension, yet He has condescended of His goodness towards us to command: "Tell him," said He, "to be safe, because peace is coming; but that, in the meantime, there is a little delay, that some who still remain may be proved." But we are admonished by these divine condescension both concerning a spare diet and a temperate use of drink; to wit, lest worldly enticement should enervate the breast now elevated with celestial vigor, or lest the mind, weighed down by too abundant feasting, should be less watchful unto prayers and

supplication.

7. It was my duty not to conceal these special matters, nor to hide them alone in my own consciousness,—matters by which each one of us may be both instructed and guided. And do not you for your part keep this letter concealed among yourselves but let the brethren have it to read. For it is the part of one who desires that his brother should not be warned and instructed, to intercept those words with which the Lord condescends to admonish and instruct us. Let them know that we are proved by our Lord and let them never fail of that faith whereby we have once believed in Him, under the conflict of this present affliction. Let each one, acknowledging his own sins, even now put off the conversation of the old man. "For no man who looks back as he puts his hand to the plough is fit for the kingdom of God." And, finally, Lot's wife, who, when she was delivered, looked back in defiance of the commandment, lost the benefit of her escape. Let us look not to things which are behind, whither the devil calls us back, but to things which are before, whither Christ calls us. Let us lift up our eyes to heaven, lest the earth with its delights and enticements deceive us. Let each one of us pray God not for himself only, but for all the brethren, even as the Lord has taught us to pray, when He bids to each one, not private prayer, but enjoined them, when they prayed, to pray for all in common prayer and concordant supplication. If the Lord shall behold us humble and peaceable; if He shall see us joined one with another; if He shall see us fearful concerning His anger; if corrected and amended by the present tribulation, He will maintain us safe from the disturbances of the enemy. Discipline hath preceded; pardon also shall follow.

8. Let us only, without ceasing to ask, and with full faith that we shall receive, in simplicity and unanimity beseech the Lord, entreating not only with groaning but with tears, as it behooves those to entreat who are situated between the ruins of those who wail, and the remnants of those who fear; between the manifold slaughter of the yielding, and the little firmness of those who still stand. Let us ask that peace may be soon restored; that we may be quickly helped in our concealments and our dangers; that those things may be fulfilled which the Lord deigns to show to his servants,— the restoration of the Church, the security of our salvation; after the rains, serenity; after the darkness, light; after the storms and whirlwinds, a peaceful calm; the affectionate aids of paternal love, the accustomed grandeurs of the divine majesty whereby both the blasphemy of persecutors may be restrained, the repentance of the lapsed renewed, and the steadfast faith of the persevering may glory. I bid you, beloved brethren, ever heartily farewell; and have me in remembrance. Salute the brotherhood in my name; and remind them to remember me. Farewell.

Epistle VIII.

To the Martyrs and Confessors.

Argument.—Cyprian, Commending the African Martyrs Marvelously for Their Constancy, Urges Them to Perseverance by the Example of Their Colleague Mappalicus.

Cyprian to the martyrs and confessors in Christ our Lord and in God the Father, everlasting salvation. I gladly rejoice and am thankful, most brave and blessed brethren, at hearing of your faith and virtue, wherein the Church, our Mother, glories. Lately, indeed, she gloried, when, in consequence of an enduring confession, that punishment was undergone which drove the confessors of Christ into exile; yet the present confession is so much the more illustrious and greater in honour as it is braver in suffering. The combat has increased, and the glory of the combatants has increased also. Nor were you kept back from the struggle by fear of tortures, but by the very tortures themselves you were more and more stimulated to the conflict; bravely and firmly you have returned with ready devotion, to contend in the extremest contest. Of you I find that some are already crowned, while some are even now within reach of the crown of victory; but all whom the danger has shut up in a glorious company are animated to carry on the struggle with an equal and common warmth of virtue, as it behooves the soldiers of Christ in the divine camp: that no allurements may deceive the incorruptible steadfastness of your faith, no threats terrify you, no sufferings or tortures overcome you, because "greater is He that is in us, than he that is in the world;" nor is the earthly punishment able to do more towards casting down, than is the divine protection towards lifting up. This truth is proved by the glorious struggle of the brethren, who, having become leaders to the rest in overcoming their tortures, afforded an example of virtue and faith, contending in the strife, until the strife yielded, being overcome. With what praises can I commend you, most courageous brethren? With what vocal proclamation can I extol the strength of your heart and the perseverance of your faith? You have borne the sharpest examination by torture, even unto the glorious consummation, and have not yielded to sufferings, but rather the sufferings have given way to you. The end of torments, which the tortures themselves did not give, the crown has given. The examination by torture waxing severer, continued for a long time to this result, not to overthrow the steadfast faith, but to send the men of God more quickly to the Lord. The multitude of those who were present saw with admiration the heavenly contest,— the contest of God, the spiritual contest, the battle of Christ,—saw that His servants stood with free voice, with unyielding mind, with divine virtue—bare, indeed, of weapons of this world, but believing and armed with the weapons of faith. The tortured stood more brave than the torturers; and the limbs, beaten and torn as they were, overcame the hooks that bent and tore them. The scourge, often repeated with all its rage, could not conquer invincible faith, even although the membrane which enclosed the entrails were broken, and it was no longer the limbs but the wounds of the servants of God that were tortured. Blood was flowing which might quench the blaze of persecution, which might subdue the flames of Gehenna with its glorious gore. Oh, what a spectacle was that to the Lord,—how sublime, how great, how acceptable to the eyes of God in the allegiance and devotion of His soldiers! As it is written in the Psalms, when the Holy Spirit at once speaks to us and warns us: "Precious in the sight of the Lord is the death of His saints." Precious is the death which has bought immortality at the cost of its blood, which has received the crown from the consummation of its virtues. How did Christ rejoice therein! How willingly did He both fight and conquer in such servants of His, as the protector of their faith, and giving to believers as much as he who taketh believes that he receives! He was present at His own contest; He lifted up, strengthened, animated the champions and assertors of His name. And He who once conquered death on our behalf, always conquers it in us. "When they," says He, "deliver you up, take no thought what ye shall speak: for it shall be given you in that hour what ye shall speak. For it is not ye that speak, but the Spirit of your Father which speaks in you." The present struggle has afforded a proof of this saying. A voice filled with the Holy Spirit broke forth from the martyr's mouth when the most blessed Mappalicus said to the proconsul in the midst of his torments, "You shall see a contest tomorrow." And that which he said with the testimony of virtue and faith, the Lord fulfilled. A heavenly contest was exhibited, and the servant of God was crowned in the struggle of the promised fight. This is the contest which the prophet Isaiah of old predicted, saying, "It shall be no light contest for you with men, since God appoints the struggle." And in order to show what this struggle would be, he added the words, "Behold, a virgin shall conceive and bear a son, and ye shall call His name Emmanuel." This is the struggle of our faith in which we engage, in which we conquer, in which we are crowned. This is the struggle which the blessed Apostle Paul has shown to us, in which it behooves us to run and to attain the crown of glory. "Do ye not know," says he, "that they which run in a race, run all indeed, but one receives the prize? So run that ye may obtain." "Now they do it that they may receive a corruptible crown, but we an incorruptible." Moreover, setting forth his own struggle, and declaring that he himself should soon be a sacrifice for the Lord's sake, he says, "I am now ready to be offered, and the time of my assumption is at hand. I have fought a good fight, I have finished my course, I have kept the faith: henceforth there is laid up for me a crown of righteousness, which the Lord, the righteous judge, shall give me at that day; and not to me only, but unto all them also that love His appearing." This fight, therefore, predicted of old by the prophets, begun by the Lord, waged by the apostles, Mappalicus promised again to the proconsul in his own name and that of his colleagues. Nor did the faithful voice deceive in his promise; he exhibited the fight to which he had pledged himself, and he received the reward which he deserved. I not only beseech but exhort the rest of you, that you all should follow that martyr now most blessed, and the other partners of that engagement,—soldiers and comrades, steadfast in faith, patient in suffering, victors in tortures,—that those who are united at once by the bond of confession, and the entertainment of a dungeon, may also be united in the consummation of their virtue and a celestial crown; that you by your joy may dry the tears of our Mother, the Church, who mourns over the wreck and death of very many; and that you may confirm, by the provocation of your example, the steadfastness of others who stand also. If the battle shall call you out, if the day of your contest shall come engage bravely, fight with constancy, as knowing that you are fighting under the eyes of a present Lord, that you are attaining by the confession of His name to His own glory; who is not such a one as that He only looks on His servants, but He Himself also wrestles in us, Himself is engaged,— Himself also in the struggles of our conflict not only crowns, but is crowned. But if before the day of your contest, of the mercy of God, peace shall supervene, let there still remain to you the sound will and the glorious conscience. Nor let any one of you be saddened as if he were inferior to those who before you have suffered tortures, have overcome the world and trodden it under foot, and so have come to the Lord by a glorious road. For the Lord is the "searcher out of the reins and the hearts." He looks through secret things and beholds that which is concealed. In order to merit the crown from Him, His own testimony alone is sufficient, who will judge us. Therefore, beloved brethren, either case is equally lofty and illustrious,—the former more secure, to wit, to hasten to the Lord with the consummation of our victory,—the latter more joyous; a leave of absence, after glory, being received to flourish in the praises of the Church. O blessed Church of ours, which the honour of the divine condescension illuminates, which in our own times the glorious blood of martyrs renders illustrious! She was white before in the works of the brethren; now she has become purple in the blood of the martyrs. Among her flowers are wanting neither roses nor lilies. Now let each one strive for the largest dignity of either honour. Let them receive crowns, either white, as of labors, or of purple, as of suffering. In the heavenly camp both peace and strife have their own flowers, with which the soldier of Christ may be crowned for glory. I bid you, most brave and beloved brethren, always heartily farewell in the Lord; and have me in remembrance. Fare ye well.

Epistle IX.

To the Clergy, Concerning Certain Presbyters Who Had Rashly Granted Peace to the Lapsed Before the Persecution Had Been Appeased, and Without the Privity of the Bishops.

Argument.—The Argument of This Epistle is Contained in the Following Words of the XIVth

Epistle:—"To the Presbyters and Deacons," He Says, "Was Not Wanting the Vigor of the Priesthood, So that Some, Too Little Mindful of Discipline, and Hasty with a Rash Precipitation, Who Had Already Begun to Communicate with the Lapsed, Were Checked."

1. Cyprian to the presbyters and deacons, his brethren, greeting. I have long been patient, beloved brethren, hoping that my forbearing silence would avail to quietness. But since the unreasonable and reckless presumption of some is seeking by its boldness to disturb both the honour of the martyrs, and the modesty of the confessors, and the tranquility of the whole people, it behooves me no longer to keep silence, lest too much reticence should issue in danger both to the people and to ourselves. For what danger ought we not to fear from the Lord's displeasure, when some of the presbyters, remembering neither the Gospel nor their own place, and, moreover, considering neither the Lord's future judgment nor the bishop now placed over them, claim to themselves entire authority,—a thing which was never in any wise done under our predecessors,—with discredit and contempt of the bishop?

2. And I wish, if it could be so without the sacrifice of our brethren's safety, that they could make good their claim to all things; I could dissemble and bear the discredit of my episcopal authority, as I always have dissembled and borne it. But it is not now the occasion for dissimulating when our brotherhood is deceived by some of you, who, while without the means of restoring salvation they desire to please, become a still greater stumbling-block to the lapsed. For that it is a very great crime which persecution has compelled to be committed, they themselves know who have committed it; since our

Lord and Judge has said, "Whosoever shall confess me before men, him will I also confess before my Father which is in heaven; but whosoever shall deny me, him will I also deny." And again, He has said, "All sins shall be forgiven unto the sons of men, and blasphemies; but he that shall blaspheme against the Holy Ghost shall not have forgiveness, but is guilty of eternal sin." Also, the blessed apostle has said, "Ye cannot drink the cup of the Lord and the cup of devils; ye cannot be partakers of the Lord's table and of the table of devils." He who withholds these words from our brethren deceives them, wretched that they are; so that they who truly repenting might satisfy God, both as the Father and as merciful, with their prayers and works, are seduced more deeply to perish; and they who might raise themselves up fall the more deeply. For although in smaller sins sinners may do penance for a set time, and according to the rules of discipline come to public confession, and by imposition of the hand of the bishop and clergy receive the right of communion: now with their time still unfulfilled, while persecution is still raging, while the peace of the Church itself is not yet restored, they are admitted to communion, and their name is presented; and while the penitence is not yet performed, confession is not yet made, the hands of the bishop and clergy are not yet laid upon them, the eucharist is given to them; although it is written, "Whosoever shall eat the bread and drink the cup of the Lord unworthily, shall be guilty of the body and blood of the Lord."

3. But now they are not guilty who so little observe the law of Scripture; but they will be guilty who are in office and do not suggest these things to brethren, so that, being instructed by those placed above them, they

may do all things with the fear of God, and with the observance given and prescribed by Him. Then, moreover, they lay the blessed martyrs open to ill-will, and involve the glorious servants of God with the priest of God; so that although they, mindful of my place, have directed letters to me, and have asked that their wishes should then be examined, and peace granted them,—when our Mother, the Church herself, should first have received peace for the Lord's mercy, and the divine protection, have brought me back to His Church,—yet these, disregarding the honour which the blessed martyrs with the confessors maintain for me, despising the Lord's law and that observance, which the same martyrs and confessors bid to be maintained, before the fear of persecution is quenched, before my return, almost even before the departure of the martyrs, communicate with the lapsed, and offer and give them the eucharist: when even if the martyrs, in the heat of their glory, were to consider less carefully the Scriptures, and to desire anything more, they should be admonished by the presbyters' and deacons' suggestions, as was always done in time past.

4. For this reason the divine rebuke does not cease to chastise us night nor day. For besides the visions of the night, by day also, the innocent age of boys is among us filled with the Holy Spirit, seeing in an ecstasy with their eyes, and hearing and speaking those things whereby the Lord condescends to warn and instruct us. And you shall hear all things when the Lord, who bade me withdraw, shall bring me back again to you. In the meanwhile, let those certain ones among you who are rash and incautious and boastful, and who do not regard man, at least fear God, knowing that, if they shall persevere still in the same course, I shall use that power of admonition

which the Lord bids me use; so that they may meanwhile be withheld from offering, and have to plead their cause both before me and before the confessors themselves and before the whole people, when, with God's permission, we begin to be gathered together once more into the bosom of the Church, our Mother. Concerning this matter, I have written to the martyrs and confessors, and to the people, letters; both of which I have bidden to be read to you. I wish you, dearly beloved brethren and earnestly longed-for, ever heartily farewell in the Lord; and have me in remembrance. Fare ye well.

Epistle X.
To the Martyrs and Confessors Who Sought that Peace Should Be Granted to the Lapsed.
Argument.—The Occasion of This Letter is Given Below in Epistle XIV. As Follows:—"When I Found that Those Who Had Polluted Their Hands and Mouths with Sacrilegious Contact, or Had No Less Infected Their Conscience with Wicked Certificates," Etc.

1. Cyprian to the martyrs and confessors, his beloved brethren, greeting. The anxiety of my situation and the fear of the Lord constrain me, my brave and beloved brethren, to admonish you in my letters, that those who so devotedly and bravely maintain the faith of the Lord should also maintain the law and discipline of the Lord. For while it behooves all Christ's soldiers to keep the precepts of their commander; to you it is more especially fitting that you should obey His precepts, inasmuch as you have been made an example to others, both of valor and of the fear of God. And I had indeed believed that the presbyters and deacons who are there present with you would admonish and instruct you more

fully concerning the law of the Gospel, as was the case always in time past under my predecessors; so that the deacons passing in and out of the prison controlled the wishes of the martyrs by their counsels, and by the Scripture precepts. But now, with great sorrow of mind, I gather that not only the divine precepts are not suggested to you by them, but that they are even rather restrained, so that those things which are done by you yourselves, both in respect of God with caution, and in respect of God's priest with honour, are relaxed by certain presbyters, who consider neither the fear of God nor the honour of the bishop. Although you sent letters to me in which you ask that your wishes should be examined, and that peace should be granted to certain of the lapsed as soon as with the end of the persecution we should have begun to meet with our clergy, and to be gathered together once more; those presbyters, contrary to the Gospel law, contrary also to your respectful petition, before penitence was fulfilled, before confession even of the gravest and most heinous sin was made, before hands were placed upon the repentant by the bishops and clergy, dare to offer on their behalf, and to give them the eucharist, that is, to profane the sacred body of the Lord, although it is written, "Whosoever shall eat the bread and drink the cup of the Lord unworthily, shall be guilty of the body and blood of the Lord."

2. And to the lapsed indeed pardon may be granted in respect of this thing. For what dead person would not hasten to be made alive? Who would not be eager to attain to his own salvation? But it is the duty of those placed over them to keep the ordinance, and to instruct those that are either hurrying or ignorant, that those who ought to be shepherds of the sheep may not become their

butchers. For to concede those things which tend to destruction is to deceive. Nor is the lapsed raised in this manner, but, by offending God, he is more urged on to ruin. Let them learn, therefore, even from you, what they ought to have taught; let them reserve your petitions and wishes for the bishops and let them wait for ripe and peaceable times to give peace at your requests. The first thing is, that the Mother should first receive peace from the Lord, and then, in accordance with your wishes, that the peace of her children should be considered.

3. And since I hear, most brave and beloved brethren, that you are pressed by the shamelessness of some, and that your modesty suffers violence; I beg you with what entreaties I may, that, as mindful of the Gospel, and considering what and what sort of things in past time your predecessors the martyrs conceded, how careful they were in all respects, you also should anxiously and cautiously weigh the wishes of those who petition you, since, as friends of the Lord, and hereafter to exercise judgment with Him, you must inspect both the conduct and the doings and the deserts of each one. You must consider also the kinds and qualities of their sins, lest, in the event of anything being abruptly and unworthily either promised by you or done by me, our Church should begin to blush, even before the very Gentiles. For we are visited and chastened frequently, and we are admonished, that the commandments of the Lord may be kept without corruption or violation, which I find does not cease to be the case there among you so as to prevent the divine judgment from instructing very many of you also in the discipline of the Church. Now this can all be done, if you will regulate those things that are asked of you with a careful consideration of religion, perceiving and

restraining those who, by accepting persons, either make favors in distributing your benefits, or seek to make a profit of an unlawful trade.

4. Concerning this I have written both to the clergy and to the people, both of which letters I have directed to be read to you. But you ought also to bring back and amend that matter according to your diligence, in such a way as to designate those by name to whom you desire that peace should be granted. For I hear that certificates are so given to some as that it is said, "Let such a one be received to communion along with his friends," which was never in any case done by the martyrs so that a vague and blind petition should by and by heap reproach upon us. For it opens a wide door to say, "Such a one with his friends;" and twenty or thirty or more, may be presented to us, who may be asserted to be neighbors and connections, and freedmen and servants, of the man who receives the certificate. And for this reason, I beg you that you will designate by name in the certificate those whom you yourselves see, whom you have known, whose penitence you see to be very near to full satisfaction, and so direct to us letters in conformity with faith and discipline. I bid you, very brave and beloved brethren, ever heartily in the Lord farewell; and have me in remembrance. Fare ye well.

Epistle XI.
To the People.
Argument.—The Substance of This Letter is Also Suggested in Epistle XIV, "Among the People Also," He Says, "I Have Done What I Could to Quiet Their Minds and Have Instructed Them to Be Retained in Ecclesiastical Discipline."

1. Cyprian to his brethren among the people who stand fast, greeting. That you bewail and grieve over the downfall of our brethren I know from myself, beloved brethren, who also bewail with you and grieve for each one, and suffer and feel what the blessed apostle said: "Who is weak," said he, "and I am not weak? who is offended, and I burn not?" And again, he has laid it down in his epistle, saying, "Whether one member suffer, all the members suffer with it; or one member rejoice, all the members rejoice with it." I sympathize with you in your suffering and grief, therefore, for our brethren, who, having lapsed and fallen prostrate under the severity of the persecution, have inflicted a like pain on us by their wounds, inasmuch as they tear away part of our bowels with them,—to these the divine mercy is able to bring healing. Yet I do not think that there must be any haste, nor that anything must be done incautiously and immaturely, lest, while peace is grasped at, the divine indignation be more seriously incurred. The blessed martyrs have written to me about certain persons, requesting that their wishes may be examined into. When, as soon as peace is given to us all by the Lord, we shall begin to return to the Church, then the wishes of each one shall be looked into in your presence, and with your judgment.

2. Yet I hear that certain of the presbyters, neither mindful of the Gospel nor considering what the martyrs have written to me, nor reserving to the bishop the honour of his priesthood and of his dignity, have already begun to communicate with the lapsed, and to offer on their behalf, and to give them the eucharist, when it was fitting that they should attain to these things in due course. For, as in smaller sins which are not committed against God,

penitence may be fulfilled in a set time, and confession may be made with investigation of the life of him who fulfils the penitence, and no one can come to communion unless the hands of the bishop and clergy be first imposed upon him; how much more ought all such matters as these to be observed with caution and moderation, according to the discipline of the Lord, in these gravest and extremest sins! This warning, indeed, our presbyters and deacons ought to have given you, that they might cherish the sheep committed to their care, and by the divine authority might instruct them in the way of obtaining salvation by prayer. I am aware of the peacefulness as well as the fear of our people, who would be watchful in the satisfaction and the deprecation of God's anger, unless some of the presbyters, by way of gratifying them, had deceived them.

3. Even you, therefore, yourselves, guide them each one, and control the minds of the lapsed by counsel and by your own moderation, according to the divine precepts. Let no one pluck the unripe fruit at a time as yet premature. Let no one commit his ship, shattered and broken with the waves, anew to the deep, before he has carefully repaired it. Let none be in haste to accept and to put on a rent tunic, unless he has seen it mended by a skillful workman and has received it arranged by the fuller. Let them bear with patience my advice, I beg. Let them look for my return, that when by God's mercy I come to you, I, with many of my co-bishops, being called together according to the Lord's discipline, and in the presence of the confessors, and with your opinion also, may be able to examine the letters and the wishes of the blessed martyrs. Concerning this matter I have written both to the clergy and to the martyrs and confessors, both of which letters I have directed to be read to you. I bid

you, brethren beloved and most longed-for, ever heartily farewell in the Lord; and have me in remembrance. Fare ye well.

Epistle XII.
To the Clergy, Concerning the Lapsed and Catechumens, that They Should Not Be Left Without Superintendence.

Argument.—The Burden of This Letter, as of the Succeeding One, is Found Below in the XIVth Epistle. "But Afterwards," He Says, "When Some of the Lapsed, Whether of Their Own Accord, or by the Suggestion of Any Other, Broke Forth with a Daring Demand, as Though They Would Endeavour, by a Violent Effort, to Extort the Peace that Had Been Promised to Them by the Martyrs and Confessors," Etc.

1. Cyprian to the presbyters and deacons, his brethren, greeting. I marvel, beloved brethren, that you have answered nothing to me in reply to my many letters which I have frequently written to you, although as well the advantage as the need of our brotherhood would certainly be best provided for if, receiving information from you, I could accurately investigate and advise upon the management of affairs. Since, however, I see that there is not yet any opportunity of coming to you, and that the summer has already begun—a season that is disturbed with continual and heavy sicknesses,—I think that our brethren must be dealt with;—that they who have received certificates from the martyrs, and may be assisted by their privilege with God, if they should be seized with any misfortune and peril of sickness, should, without waiting for my presence, before any presbyter who might be present, or if a presbyter should not be

found and death begins to be imminent, before even a deacon, be able to make confession of their sin, that, with the imposition of hands upon them for repentance, they should come to the Lord with the peace which the martyrs have desired, by their letters to us, to be granted to them.

2. Cherish also by your presence the rest of the people who are lapsed, and cheer them by your consolation, that they may not fail of the faith and of God's mercy. For those shall not be forsaken by the aid and assistance of the Lord, who meekly, humbly, and with true penitence have persevered in good works; but the divine remedy will be granted to them also. To the hearers also, if there are any overtaken by danger, and placed near to death, let your vigilance not be wanting; let not the mercy of the Lord be denied to those that are imploring the divine favor. I bid you, beloved brethren, ever heartily farewell; and remember me. Greet the whole brotherhood in my name and remind them and ask them to be mindful of me. Fare ye well.

Epistle XIII.

To the Clergy, Concerning Those Who are in Haste to Receive Peace. a.d. 250.

Argument.—Peace Must Be Attained Through Penitence, and Penitence is Realized by Keeping the Commandments. They Who are Oppressed with Sickness, If They are Relieved by the Suffrages of the Martyrs, May Be Admitted to Peace; But Others are to Be Kept Back Until the Peace of the Church is Secured.

1. Cyprian to the presbyters and deacons, his brethren, greeting. I have read your letter, beloved brethren, wherein you wrote that your wholesome counsel was not wanting to our brethren, that, laying aside all rash

haste, they should manifest a religious patience to God, so that when by His mercy we come together, we may debate upon all kinds of things, according to the discipline of the Church, especially since it is written, "Remember from whence thou hast fallen, and repent." Now he repents, who, remembering the divine precept, with meekness and patience, and obeying the priests of God, deserves well of the Lord by his obedience and his righteous works.

2. Since, however, you intimate that some are petulant, and eagerly urge their being received to communion, and have desired in this matter that some rule should be given by me to you, I think I have sufficiently written on this subject in the last letter that was sent to you, that they who have received a certificate from the martyrs, and can be assisted by their help with the Lord in respect of their sins, if they begin to be oppressed with any sickness or risk; when they have made confession, and have received the imposition of hands on them by you in acknowledgment of their penitence, should be remitted to the Lord with the peace promised to them by the martyrs. But others who, without having received any certificate from the martyrs, are envious (since this is the cause not of a few, nor of one church, nor of one province, but of the whole world), must wait, in dependence on the protection of the Lord, for the public peace of the Church itself. For this is suitable to the modesty and the discipline, and even the life of all of us, that the chief officers meeting together with the clergy in the presence also of the people who stand fast, to whom themselves, moreover, honor is to be shown for their faith and fear, we may be able to order all things with the religiousness of a common consultation. But how

irreligious is it, and mischievous, even to those themselves who are eager, that while such as are exiles, and driven from their country, and spoiled of all their property, have not yet returned to the Church, some of the lapsed should be hasty to anticipate even confessors themselves, and to enter into the Church before them! If they are so over-anxious, they have what they require in their own power, the times themselves offering them freely more than they ask. The struggle is still going forward, and the strife is daily celebrated. If they truly and with constancy repent of what they have done, and the fervor of their faith prevails, he who cannot be delayed may be crowned. I bid you, beloved brethren, ever heartily farewell; and have me in remembrance. Greet all the brotherhood in my name and tell them to be mindful of me. Fare ye well.

Epistle XIV.
To the Presbyters and Deacons Assembled at Rome.
Argument.—He Gives an Account of His Withdrawal and of the Things Which He Did Therein, Having Sent to Rome for His Justification, Copies of the Letters Which He Had Written to His People; Nay, He Makes Use of the Same Words Which He Had Employed in Them.

1. Cyprian to his brethren the presbyters and deacons assembled at Rome, greeting. Having ascertained, beloved brethren, that what I have done and am doing has been told to you in a somewhat garbled and untruthful manner, I have thought it necessary to write this letter to you, wherein I might give an account to you of my doings, my discipline, and my diligence; for, as the

Lord's commands teach, immediately the first burst of the disturbance arose, and the people with violent clamor repeatedly demanded me, I, taking into consideration not so much my own safety as the public peace of the brethren, withdrew for a while, lest, by my over-bold presence, the tumult which had begun might be still further provoked. Nevertheless, although absent in body, I was not wanting either in spirit, or in act, or in my advice, so as to fail in any benefit that I could afford my brethren by my counsel, according to the Lord's precepts, in anything that my poor abilities enabled me.

2. And what I did, these thirteen letters sent forth at various times declare to you, which I have transmitted to you; in which neither counsel to the clergy, nor exhortation to the confessors, nor rebuke, when it was necessary, to the exiles, nor my appeals and persuasions to the whole brotherhood, that they should entreat the mercy of God, were wanting to the full extent that, according to the law of faith and the fear of God, with the Lord's help, my poor abilities could endeavor. But afterward, when tortures came, my words reached both to our tortured brethren and to those who as yet were only imprisoned with a view to torture, to strengthen and console them. Moreover, when I found that those who had polluted their hands and mouths with sacrilegious contact, or had no less infected their consciences with wicked certificates, were everywhere soliciting the martyrs, and were also corrupting the confessors with importunate and excessive entreaties, so that, without any discrimination or examination of the individuals themselves, thousands of certificates were daily given, contrary to the law of the Gospel, I wrote letters in which I recalled by my advice, as much as possible, the martyrs and confessors to the

Lord's commands. To the presbyters and deacons also was not wanting the vigor of the priesthood; so that some, too little mindful of discipline, and hasty, with a rash precipitation, who had already begun to communicate with the lapsed, were restrained by my interposition. Among the people, moreover, I have done what I could to quiet their minds and have instructed them to maintain ecclesiastical discipline.

3. But afterward, when some of the lapsed, whether of their own accord, or by the suggestion of any other, broke forth with a daring demand, as though they would endeavor by a violent effort to extort the peace that had been promised to them by the martyrs and confessors; concerning this also I wrote twice to the clergy, and commanded it to be read to them; that for the mitigation of their violence in any manner for the meantime, if any who had received a certificate from the martyrs were departing from this life, having made confession, and received the imposition of hands on them for repentance, they should be remitted to the Lord with the peace promised them by the martyrs. Nor in this did I give them a law, or rashly constitute myself the author of the direction; but as it seemed fit both that honor should be paid to the martyrs, and that the vehemence of those who were anxious to disturb everything should be restrained; and when, besides, I had read your letter which you lately wrote hither to my clergy by Crementius the sub-deacon, to the effect that assistance should be given to those who might, after their lapse, be seized with sickness, and might penitently desire communion; I judged it well to stand by your judgment, lest our proceedings, which ought to be united and to agree in all things, should in any respect be different. The cases of the rest, even although they might

have received certificates from the martyrs, I ordered altogether to be put off, and to be reserved till I should be present, that so, when the Lord has given to us peace, and several bishops shall have begun to assemble into one place, we may be able to arrange and reform everything, having the advantage also of your counsel. I bid you, beloved brethren, ever heartily farewell.

Epistle XV.
To Moyses and Maximus, and the Rest of the Confessors.

Argument.—The Burden of This Letter is Given in Epistle XXXI. Below, Where the Roman Clergy Say: "On Which Subject We Owe You, and Give You Our Deepest and Abundant Thanks, that You Threw Light into the Gloom of Their Prison by Your Letters."

1. Cyprian to Moyses and Maximus, the presbyters and the other confessors, his brethren, greeting. Celerinus, a companion both of your faith and virtue, and God's soldier in glorious engagements, has come to me, beloved brethren, and represented all of you, as well as each individual, forcibly to my affection. I beheld in him, when he came, the whole of you; and when he spoke sweetly and often of your love to me, in his words I heard you. I rejoice very greatly when such things are brought to me from you by such men as he. In a certain manner I am also there with you in prison. I think that I who am thus bound to your hearts, enjoy with you the delights of the divine approval. Your individual love associates me with your honour; the Spirit does not allow our love to be separated. Confession shuts you up in prison; affection shuts me up there. And I indeed, remembering you day and night, both when in the

sacrifices I offer prayer with many, and when in retirement I pray with private petition, beseech of the Lord a full acknowledgment to your crowns and your praises. But my poor ability is too weak to recompense you; you give more when you remember me in prayer, since, already breathing only celestial things, and meditating only divine things, you ascend to loftier heights, even by the delay of your suffering; and by the long lapse of time, are not wasting, but increasing your glory. A first and single confession makes blessed; you confess as often as, when asked to retire from prison, you prefer the prison with faith and virtue; your praises are as numerous as the days; as the months roll onward, ever your merits increase. He conquers once who suffers at once; but he who continues always battling with punishments, and is not overcome with suffering, is daily crowned.

2. Now, therefore, let magistrates and consuls or proconsuls go by; let them glory in the ensigns of their yearly dignity, and in their twelve fasces. Behold, the heavenly dignity in you is sealed by the brightness of a year's honour, and already, in the continuance of its victorious glory, has passed over the rolling circle of the returning year. The rising sun and the waning moon enlightened the world; but to you, He who made the sun and moon was a greater light in your dungeon, and the brightness of Christ glowing in your hearts and minds, irradiated with that eternal and brilliant light the gloom of the place of punishment, which to others was so horrible and deadly. The winter has passed through the vicissitudes of the months; but you, shut up in prison, were undergoing, instead of the inclemency of winter, the winter of persecution. To the winter succeeded the

mildness of spring, rejoicing with roses and crowned with flowers; but to you were present roses and flowers from the delights of paradise, and celestial garlands wreathed your brows. Behold, the summer is fruitful with the fertility of the harvest, and the threshing-floor is filled with grain; but you who have sown glory, reap the fruit of glory, and, placed in the Lord's threshing-floor, behold the chaff burnt up with unquenchable fire; you yourselves as grains of wheat, winnowed and precious corn, now purged and garnered, regard the dwelling-place of a prison as your granary. Nor is there wanting to the autumn spiritual grace for discharging the duties of the season. The vintage is pressed out of doors, and the grape which shall hereafter flow into the cups is trodden in the presses. You, rich bunches out of the Lord's vineyard, and branches with fruit already ripe, trodden by the tribulation of worldly pressure, fill your winepress in the torturing prison, and shed your blood instead of wine; brave to bear suffering, you willingly drink the cup of martyrdom. Thus, the year rolls on with the Lord's servants,—thus is celebrated the vicissitude of the seasons with spiritual deserts, and with celestial rewards.

3. Abundantly blessed are they who, from your number, passing through these footprints of glory, have already departed from the world; and, having finished their journey of virtue and faith, have attained to the embrace and the kiss of the Lord, to the joy of the Lord Himself. But yet your glory is not less, who are still engaged in contest, and, about to follow the glories of your comrades, are long waging the battle, and with an unmoved and unshaken faith standing fast, are daily exhibiting in your virtues a spectacle in the sight of God. The longer is your strife, the loftier will be your crown.

The struggle is one, but it is crowded with a manifold multitude of contests; you conquer hunger, and despise thirst, and tread underfoot the squalor of the dungeon, and the horror of the very abode of punishment, by the vigor of your courage. Punishment is there subdued; torture is worn out; death is not feared but desired, being overcome by the reward of immortality, so that he who has conquered is crowned with eternity of life. What now must be the mind in you, how elevated, how large the heart, when such and so great things are resolved, when nothing but the precepts of God and the rewards of Christ are considered! The will is then only God's will; and although you are still placed in the flesh, it is the life not of the present world, but of the future, that you now live.

4. It now remains, beloved brethren, that you should be mindful of me; that, among your great and divine considerations, you should also think of me in your mind and spirit; and that I should be in your prayers and supplications, when that voice, which is illustrious by the purification of confession, and praiseworthy for the continual tenor of its honour, penetrates to God's ears, and heaven being open to it, passes from these regions of the world subdued, to the realms above, and obtains from the Lord's goodness even what it asks. For what do you ask from the Lord's mercy which you do not deserve to obtain?—you who have thus observed the Lord's commands, who have maintained the Gospel discipline with the simple vigor of your faith, who, with the glory of your virtue uncorrupted, have stood bravely by the Lord's commands, and by His apostles, and have confirmed the wavering faith of many by the truth of your martyrdom? Truly, Gospel witnesses, and truly, Christ's martyrs, resting upon His roots, founded with strong foundation

upon the Rock, you have joined discipline with virtue, you have brought others to the fear of God, you have made your martyrdoms, examples. I bid you, brethren, very brave and beloved, ever heartily farewell; and remember me.

>Epistle XVI.
>The Confessors to Cyprian.
>Argument.—A Certificate Written in the Name of the Martyrs by Lucianus. All the confessors to father Cyprian, greeting. Know that, to all, concerning whom the account of what they have done since the commission of their sin has been, in your estimation, satisfactory, we have granted peace; and we have desired that this rescript should be made known by you to the other bishops also. We bid you to have peace with the holy martyrs. Lucianus wrote this, there being present of the clergy, both an exorcist and a reader.

>Epistle XVII.
>To the Presbyters and Deacons About the Foregoing and the Following Letters.
>Argument.—No Account is to Be Made of Certificates from the Martyrs Before the Peace of the Church is Restored. Cyprian to the presbyters and deacons, his brethren, greeting. The Lord speaks and saith, "Upon whom shall I look, but upon him that is humble and quiet, and that trembles at my words?" Although we ought all to be this, yet especially those ought to be so who must labor, that, after their grave lapse, they may, by true penitence and absolute humility, deserve well of the Lord. Now I have read the letter of the whole body of confessors, which they wish to be made

known by me to all my colleagues, and in which they requested that the peace given by themselves should be assured to those concerning whom the account of what they have done since their crime has been, in our estimation, satisfactory; which matter, as it waits for the counsel and judgment of all of us, I do not dare to prejudge, and so to assume a common cause for my own decision. And therefore, in the meantime, let us abide by the letters which I lately wrote to you, of which I have now sent a copy to many of my colleagues, who wrote in reply, that they were pleased with what I had decided, and that there must be no departure therefrom, until, peace being granted to us by the Lord, we shall be able to assemble together into one place, and to examine into the cases of individuals. But that you may know both what my colleague Caldonius wrote to me, and what I replied to him, I have enclosed with my letter a copy of each letter, the whole of which I beg you to read to our brethren, that they may be more and more settled down to patience, and not add another fault to what had hitherto been their former fault, not being willing to obey either me or the Gospel, nor allowing their cases to be examined in accordance with the letters of all the confessors. I bid you, beloved brethren, ever heartily farewell; and have me in remembrance. Salute all the brotherhood. Fare ye well!

>Epistle XVIII.
>Caldonius to Cyprian.
>Argument.—When, in the Urgency of a New Persecution, Certain of the Lapsed Had Confessed Christ, and So, Before They Went Away into Exile, Sought for Peace, Caldonius Consults Cyprian as to Whether Peace Should Be Granted Them.

Caldonius to Cyprian and his fellow-presbyters abiding at Carthage, greeting. The necessity of the times induces us not hastily to grant peace. But it was well to write to you, that they who, after having sacrificed, were again tried, became exiles. And thus, they seem to me to have atoned for their former crime, in that they now let go their possessions and homes, and, repenting, follow Christ. Thus Felix, who assisted in the office of presbyter under Decimus, and was very near to me in bonds (I knew that same Felix very thoroughly), Victoria, his wife, and Lucius, being faithful, were banished, and have left their possessions, which the treasury now has in keeping. Moreover, a woman, Bona by name, who was dragged by her husband to sacrifice, and (with no conscience guilty of the crime, but because those who held her hands, sacrificed) began to cry against them, "I did not do it; you it was who did it!"—was also banished. Since, therefore, all these were asking for peace, saying, "We have recovered the faith which we had lost, we have repented, and have publicly confessed Christ"—although it seems to me that they ought to receive peace,—yet I have referred them to your judgment, that I might not appear to presume anything rashly. If, therefore, you should wish me to do anything by the common decision, write to me. Greet our brethren; our brethren greet you. I bid you, beloved brethren, ever heartily farewell.

Epistle XIX.
Cyprian Replies to Caldonius.
Argument.—Cyprian Treats of Nothing Peculiar in This Epistle, Beyond Acquiescing in the Opinion of Caldonius, to Wit, that Peace Should Not Be Refused to Such Lapsed As, by a True Repentance and Confession of

the Name of Christ, Have Deserved It, and Have Therefore Returned to Him.

Cyprian to Caldonius, his brother, greeting. We have received your letter, beloved brother, which is abundantly sensible, and full of honesty and faith. Nor do we wonder that, skilled and exercised as you are in the Scriptures of the Lord, you do everything discreetly and wisely. You have judged quite correctly about granting peace to our brethren, which they, by true penitence and by the glory of a confession of the Lord, have restored to themselves, being justified by their words, by which before they had condemned themselves. Since, then, they have washed away all their sin, and their former stain, by the help of the Lord, has been done away by a more powerful virtue, they ought not to lie any longer under the power of the devil, as it were, prostrate; when, being banished and deprived of all their property, they have lifted themselves up and have begun to stand with Christ. And I wish that the others also would repent after their fall, and be transferred into their former condition; and that you may know how we have dealt with these, in their urgent and eager rashness and importunity to extort peace, I have sent a book to you, with letters to the number of five, that I wrote to the clergy and to the people, and to the martyrs also and confessors, which letters have already been sent to many of our colleagues, and have satisfied them; and they replied that they also agree with me in the same opinion according to the Catholic faith; which very thing do you also communicate to as many of our colleagues as you can, that among all these, may be observed one mode of action and one agreement, according to the Lord's precepts. I bid you, beloved brother, ever heartily farewell.

Epistle XX.
Celerinus to Lucian.
Argument.—Celerinus, on Behalf of His Lapsed Sisters at Rome, Beseeches Peace from the Carthaginian Confessors.
1. Celerinus to Lucian, greeting. In writing this letter to you, my lord and brother, I have been rejoicing and sorrowful,—rejoicing in that I had heard that you had been tried on behalf of the name of our Lord Jesus Christ our Savior, and had confessed His name in the presence of the magistrates of the world; but sorrowful, in that from the time when I was in your company I have never been able to receive your letters. And now lately a twofold sorrow has fallen upon me; that although you knew that Montanus, our common brother, was coming to me from you out of the dungeon, you did not intimate anything to me concerning your wellbeing, nor about anything that is done in connection with you. This, however, continually happens to the servants of God, especially to those who are appointed for the confession of Christ. For I know that everyone looks not now to the things that are of the world, but that he is hoping for a heavenly crown. Moreover, I said that perhaps you had forgotten to write to me. For if from the lowest place I may be called by you yours, or brother, if I should be worthy to hear myself named Celerinus; yet, when I also was in such a purple confession, I remembered my oldest brethren, and I took notice of them in my letters, that their former love was still around me and mine. Yet I beseech, beloved of the Lord, that if, first of all, you are washed in that sacred blood, and have suffered for the name of our Lord Jesus Christ before my letters find you in this world,

or should they now reach you, that you would answer them to me. So may He crown you whose name you have confessed. For I believe, that although in this world we do not see each other, yet in the future we shall embrace one another in the presence of Christ. Entreat that I may be worthy, even I, to be crowned along with your company.

2. Know, nevertheless, that I am placed in the midst of a great tribulation; and, as if you were present with me, I remember your former love day and night, God only knows. And therefore, I ask that you grant my desire, and that you will grieve with me at the (spiritual) death of my sister, who in this time of devastation has fallen from Christ; for she has sacrificed and provoked our Lord, as seems manifest to us. And for her deeds I in this day of paschal rejoicing, weeping day and night, have spent the days in tears, in sackcloth, and ashes, and I am still spending them so to this day, until the aid of our Lord Jesus Christ, and affection manifested through you, or through those my lords who have been crowned, from whom you are about to ask it, shall come to the help of so terrible a shipwreck. For I remember your former love, that you will grieve with all the rest for our sisters whom you also knew well—that is, Numeria and Candida,—for whose sin, because they have us as brethren, we ought to keep watch. For I believe that Christ, according to their repentance and the works which they have done towards our banished colleagues who came from you—by whom themselves you will hear of their good works,—that Christ, I say, will have mercy upon them, when you, His martyrs, beseech Him.

3. For I have heard that you have received the ministry of the purpled ones. Oh, happy are you, even sleeping on the ground, to obtain your wishes which you

have always desired! You have desired to be sent into prison for His name's sake, which now has come to pass; as it is written, "The Lord grant thee according to thine own heart;" and now made a priest of God over them, and the same their minister has acknowledged it. I ask, therefore my lord, and I entreat by our Lord Jesus Christ, that you will refer the case to the rest of your colleagues, your brethren, my lords, and ask from them, that whichever of you is first crowned, should remit such a great sin to those our sisters, Numeria and Candida. For this latter I have always called Etecusa—God is my witness,—because she gave gifts for herself that she might not sacrifice; but she appears only to have ascended to the Tria Fata, and thence to have descended. I know, therefore, that she has not sacrificed. Their cause having been lately heard, the chief rulers commanded them in the meantime to remain as they are, until a bishop should be appointed. But, as far as possible, by your holy prayers and petitions, in which we trust, since you are friends as well as witnesses of Christ, (we pray) that you would be indulgent in all these matters.

4. I entreat, therefore, beloved lord Lucian, be mindful of me, and acquiesce in my petition; so may Christ grant you that sacred crown which he has given you not only in confession but also in holiness, in which you have always walked and have always been an example to the saints as well as a witness, that you will relate to all my lords, your brethren the confessors, all about this matter, that they may receive help from you. For this, my lord and brother, you ought to know, that it is not I alone who ask this on their behalf, but also Statius and Severianus, and all the confessors who have come thence hither from you; to whom these very sisters went

down to the harbor and took them up into the city, and they have ministered to sixty-five, and even to this day have tended them in all things. For all are with them. But I ought not to burden that sacred heart of yours anymore, since I know that you will labor with a ready will. Macharius, with his sisters Cornelia and Emerita, salute you, rejoicing in your sanguinary confession, as well as in that of all the brethren, and Saturninus, who himself also wrestled with the devil, who also bravely confessed the name of Christ, who moreover, under the torture of the grappling claws, bravely confessed, and who also strongly begs and entreats this. Your brethren Calphurnius and Maria, and all the holy brethren, salute you. For you ought to know this too, that I have written also to my lords your brethren letters, which I request that you deign to read to them.

>Epistle XXI.
>Lucian Replies to Celerinus.
>Argument.—Lucian Assents to the Petition of Celerinus.

1. Lucian to Celerinus, his lord, and (if I shall be worthy to be called so) colleague in Christ, greeting. I have received your letter, most dearly beloved lord and brother, in which you have so laden me with expressions of kindness, that by reason of your so burdening me I was almost overcome with such excessive joy; so that I exulted in reading, by the benefit of your so great humility, the letter, which I also earnestly desired after so long a time to read, in which you deigned to call me to remembrance, saying to me in your writing, "if I may be worthy to be called your brother," of a man such as I am who confessed the name of God with trembling before the

inferior magistrates. For you, by God's will, when you confessed, not only frightened back the great serpent himself, the pioneer of Antichrist, (but) have conquered him, by that voice and those divine words, whereby I know how you love the faith, and how zealous you are for Christ's discipline, in which I know and rejoice that you are actively occupied. Now beloved, already to be esteemed among the martyrs, you have wished to overload me with your letter, in which you told us concerning our sisters, on whose behalf I wish that we could by possibility mention them without remembering also so great a crime committed. Assuredly we should not then think of them with so many tears as we do now.

2. You ought to know what has been done concerning us. When the blessed martyr Paulus was still in the body, he called me and said to me: "Lucian, in the presence of Christ I say to you, If anyone, after my being called away, shall ask for peace from you, grant it in my name." Moreover, all of us whom the Lord has condescended in such tribulation to call away, by our letters, by mutual agreement, have given peace to all. You see, then, brother, how (I have done this) in part of what Paulus bade me, as what we in all cases decreed when we were in this tribulation, wherein by the command of the emperor we were ordered to be put to death by hunger and thirst, and were shut up in two cells, that so they might weaken us by hunger and thirst. Moreover, the fire from the effect of our torture was so intolerable that nobody could bear it. But now we have attained the brightness itself. And therefore, beloved brother, greet Numeria and Candida, who (shall have peace) according to the precept of Paulus, and the rest of the martyrs whose names I subjoin: viz., Bassus in the dungeon of the

perjured, Mappalicus at the torture, Fortunio in prison, Paulus after torture, Fortunata, Victorinus, Victor, Herennius, Julia, Martial, and Aristo, who by God's will were put to death in the prison by hunger, of whom in a few days you will hear of me as a companion. For now, there are eight days, from the day in which I was shut up again, to the day in which I wrote my letter to you. For before these eight days, for five intervening days, I received a morsel of bread and water by measure. And therefore, brother, as here, since the Lord has begun to give peace to the Church itself, according to the precept of Paulus, and our tractate, the case being set forth before the bishop, and confession being made, I ask that not only these may have peace, but also (all) those whom you know to be very near to our heart.

3. All my colleagues greet you. Do you greet the confessors of the Lord who are there with you, whose names you have intimated, among whom also are Saturninus, with his companions, but who also is my colleague, and Maris, Collecta, and Emerita, Calphurnius and Maria, Sabina, Spesina, and the sisters, Januaria, Dativa, Donata. We greet Saturus with his family, Bassianus and all the clergy, Uranius, Alexius, Quintianus, Colonica, and all whose names I have not written, because I am already weary. Therefore they must pardon me. I bid you heartily farewell, and Alexius, and Getulicus, and the moneychangers, and the sisters. My sisters Januaria and Sophia, whom I commend to you, greet you.

Epistle XXII.

To the Clergy Abiding at Rome, Concerning Many of the Confessors, and Concerning the Forwardness of Lucian and the Modesty of Celerinus the Confessor.

Argument.—In This Letter Cyprian Informs the Roman Clergy of the Seditious Demand of the Lapsed to Be Restored to Peace, and of the Forwardness of Lucian. In Order that They May Better Understand These Matters, Cyprian Takes Care that Not Only His Own Letters, But Also Those of Celerinus and Lucian, Should Be Sent to Them.

1. Cyprian to the presbyters and deacons abiding at Rome, his brethren, greeting. After the letters that I wrote to you, beloved brethren, in which what I had done was explained, and some slight account was given of my discipline and diligence, there came another matter which, any more than the others, ought not to be concealed from you. For our brother Lucian, who himself also is one of the confessors, earnest indeed in faith, and robust in virtue, but little established in the reading of the Lord's word, has attempted certain things, constituting himself for a time an authority for unskilled people, so that certificates written by his hand were given indiscriminately to many persons in the name of Paulus; whereas Mappalicus the martyr, cautious and modest, mindful of the law and discipline, wrote no letters contrary to the Gospel, but only, moved with domestic affection for his mother, who had fallen, commanded peace to be given to her. Saturninus, moreover, after his torture, still remaining in prison, sent out no letters of this kind. But Lucian, not only while Paulus was still in prison, gave everywhere in his name certificates written with his own hand, but even after his decease persisted in

doing the same things under his name, saying that this had been commanded him by Paulus, ignorant that he must obey the Lord rather than his fellow-servant. In the name also of Aurelius, a young man who had undergone the torture, many certificates were given, written by the hand of the same Lucian, because Aurelius did not know how to write himself.

2. In order, in some measure, to put a stop to this practice, I wrote letters to them, which I have sent to you under the enclosure of the former letter, in which I did not fail to ask and persuade them that consideration might be had for the law of the Lord and the Gospel. But after I sent my letters to them, that, as it were, something might be done more moderately and temperately; the same Lucian wrote a letter in the name of all the confessors, in which well nigh every bond of faith, and fear of God, and the Lord's command, and the sacredness and sincerity of the Gospel were dissolved. For he wrote in the name of all, that they had given peace to all, and that he wished that this decree should be communicated through me to the other bishops, of which letter I transmitted a copy to you. It was added indeed, "of whom the account of what they have done since their crime has been satisfactory;"— a thing this which excites a greater odium against me, because I, when I have begun to hear the cases of each one and to examine into them, seem to deny to many what they now are all boasting that they have received from the martyrs and confessors.

3. Finally, this seditious practice has already begun to appear; for in our province, through some of its cities, an attack has been made by the multitude upon their rulers, and they have compelled that peace to be given to them immediately which they all cried out had

been once given to them by the martyrs and confessors. Their rulers, being frightened and subdued, were of little avail to resist them, either by vigor of mind or by strength of faith. With us, moreover, some turbulent spirits, who in time past were with difficulty governed by me, and were delayed till my coming, were inflamed by this letter as if by a firebrand, and began to be more violent, and to extort the peace granted to them. I have sent a copy to you of the letters that I wrote to my clergy about these matters, and, moreover, what Caldonius, my colleague, of his integrity and faithfulness wrote, and what I replied to him. I have sent both to you to read. Copies also of the letter of Celerinus, the good and stout confessor, which he wrote to Lucian the same confessor—also what Lucian replied to him,—I have sent to you; that you may know both my labor in respect of everything, and my diligence, and might learn the truth itself, how moderate and cautious is Celerinus the confessor, and how reverent both in his humility and fear for our faith; while Lucian, as I have said, is less skillful concerning the understanding of the Lord's word, and by his facility, is mischievous on account of the dislike that he causes for my reverential dealing. For while the Lord has said that the nations are to be baptized in the name of the Father, and of the Son, and of the Holy Ghost, and their past sins are to be done away in baptism; this man, ignorant of the precept and of the law, commands peace to be granted and sins to be done away in the name of Paulus; and he says that this was commanded him by Paulus, as you will observe in the letter sent by the same Lucian to Celerinus, in which he very little considered that it is not martyrs that make the Gospel, but that martyrs are made by the Gospel; since Paul also, the apostle whom the Lord called a chosen vessel unto Him, laid down in his epistle: "I marvel that ye are so soon removed from Him that called you into the grace of Christ, unto another gospel: which is not another; but there be some that trouble you, and would pervert the Gospel of Christ. But though we, or an angel from heaven, preach any other gospel unto you than that which we have preached unto you, let him be accursed. As we said before, so say I now again, If any man preach any other gospel unto you than that ye have received, let him be accursed."

4. But your letter, which I received, written to my clergy, came opportunely; as also did those which the blessed confessors, Moyses and Maximus, Nicostratus, and the rest, sent to Saturninus and Aurelius, and the others, in which are contained the full vigor of the Gospel and the robust discipline of the law of the Lord. Your words much assisted me as I labored here, and withstood with the whole strength of faith the onset of ill-will, so that my work was shortened from above, and that before the letters which I last sent you reached you, you declared to me, that according to the Gospel law, your judgment also strongly and unanimously concurred with mine. I bid you, brethren, beloved and longed-for, ever heartily farewell.

Epistle XXIII.
To the Clergy, on the Letters Sent to Rome, and About the Appointment of Saturus as Reader, and Optatus as Sub-Deacon. a.d. 250.

Argument.—The Clergy are Informed by This Letter of the Ordination of Saturus and Optatus, and What Cyprian Had Written to Rome.

Cyprian to the presbyters and deacons, his

brethren, greeting. That nothing may be unknown to your consciousness, beloved brethren, of what was written to me and what I replied, I have sent you a copy of each letter, and I believe that my rejoinder will not displease you. But I ought to acquaint you in my letter concerning this, that for a very urgent reason I have sent a letter to the clergy who abide in the city. And since it behooved me to write by clergy, while I know that very many of ours are absent, and the few that are there are hardly sufficient for the ministry of the daily duty, it was necessary to appoint some new ones, who might be sent. Know, then, that I have made Saturus a reader, and Optatus, the confessor, a sub-deacon; whom already, by the general advice, we had made next to the clergy, in having entrusted to Saturus on Easter-day, once and again, the reading; and when with the teacher-presbyters we were carefully trying readers—in appointing Optatus from among the readers to be a teacher of the hearers;—examining, first of all, whether all things were found fitting in them, which ought to be found in such as were in preparation for the clerical office. Nothing new, therefore, has been done by me in your absence; but what, on the general advice of all of us had been begun, has, upon urgent necessity, been accomplished. I bid you, beloved brethren, ever heartily farewell; and remember me. Fare ye well.

Epistle XXIV.
To Moyses and Maximus and the Rest of the Confessors.
Argument.—This Letter is One of Congratulation to the Roman Confessors.
1. Cyprian to Moyses and Maximus, the presbyters, and to the other confessors, his very beloved

brethren, greeting. I had already known from rumor, most brave and blessed brethren, the glory of your faith and virtue, rejoicing greatly and abundantly congratulating you, that the highest condescension of our Lord Jesus Christ should have prepared you for the crown by confession of His name. For you, who have become chiefs and leaders in the battle of our day, have set forward the standard of the celestial warfare; you have made a beginning of the spiritual contest which God has purposed to be now waged by your valor; you, with unshaken strength and unyielding firmness, have broken the first onset of the rising war. Thence have arisen happy openings of the fight; thence have begun good auspices of victory. It happened that here martyrdoms were consummated by tortures. But he who, preceding in the struggle, has been made an example of virtue to the brethren, is on common ground with the martyrs in honour. Hence you have delivered to us garlands woven by your hand and have pledged your brethren from the cup of salvation.

2. To these glorious beginnings of confession and the omens of a victorious warfare, has been added the maintenance of discipline, which I observed from the vigor of your letter that you lately sent to your colleagues joined with you to the Lord in confession, with anxious admonition, that the sacred precepts of the Gospel and the commandments of life once delivered to us should be kept with firm and rigid observance. Behold another lofty degree of your glory; behold, with confession, a double title to deserving well of God,—to stand with a firm step, and to drive away in this struggle, by the strength of your faith, those who endeavor to make a breach in the Gospel, and bring impious hands to the work of undermining the

Lord's precepts:—to have before afforded the indications of courage, and now to afford lessons of life. The Lord, when, after His resurrection, He sent forth His apostles, charges them, saying, "All power is given unto me in heaven and in earth. Go ye therefore, and teach all nations, baptizing them in the name of the Father, and of the Son, and of the Holy Ghost: teaching them to observe all things whatsoever I have commanded you." And the Apostle John, remembering this charge, subsequently lays it down in his epistle: "Hereby," says he, "we do know that we know Him, if we keep His commandments. He that says he knows Him, and keeps not His commandments, is a liar, and the truth is not in him." You prompt the keeping of these precepts; you observe the divine and heavenly commands. This is to be a confessor of the Lord; this is to be a martyr of Christ,—to keep the firmness of one's profession inviolate among all evils, and secure. For to wish to become a martyr for the Lord, and to try to overthrow the Lord's precepts; to use against Him the condescension that He has granted you;—to become, as it were, a rebel with arms that you have received from Him;—this is to wish to confess Christ, and to deny Christ's Gospel. I rejoice, therefore, on your behalf, most brave and faithful brethren; and as much as I congratulate the martyrs there honored for the glory of their strength, so much do I also equally congratulate you for the crown of the Lord's discipline. The Lord has shed forth His condescension in manifold kinds of liberality. He has distributed the praises of good soldiers and their spiritual glories in plentiful variety. We also are sharers in your honour; we count your glory our glory, whose times have been brightened by such a felicity, that it should be the fortune of our day to see the proved servants of God and Christ's soldiers crowned. I bid you, most brave and blessed brethren, ever heartily farewell; and remember me.

Epistle XXV.
Moyses, Maximus, Nicostratus, and the Other Confessors Answer the Foregoing Letter. a.d. 250.
Argument.—They Gratefully Acknowledge the Consolation Which the Roman Confessors Had Received from Cyprian's Letter. Martyrdom is Not a Punishment, But a Happiness. The Words of the Gospel are Brands to Inflame Faith. In the Case of the Lapsed, the Judgment of Cyprian is Acquiesced in.

1. To Cæcilius Cyprian, bishop of the church of the Carthaginians, Moyses and Maximus, presbyters, and Nicostratus and Rufinus, deacons, and the other confessors persevering in the faith of the truth, in God the Father, and in His Son Jesus Christ our Lord, and in the Holy Spirit, greeting. Placed, brother, as we are among various and manifold sorrows, on account of the present desolations of many brethren throughout almost the whole world, this chief consolation has reached us, that we have been lifted up by the receipt of your letter and have gathered some alleviation for the griefs of our saddened spirit. From which we can already perceive that the grace of divine providence wished to keep us so long shut up in the prison chains, perhaps for no other reason than that, instructed and more vigorously animated by your letter, we might with a more earnest will attain to the destined crown. For your letter has shone upon us as a calm in the midst of a tempest, and as the longed-for tranquility in the midst of a troubled sea, and as repose in labors, as health in dangers and pains, as in the densest darkness, the bright

and glowing light. Thus, we drank it up with a thirsty spirit, and received it with a hungry desire; so that we rejoice to find ourselves by it sufficiently fed and strengthened for encounter with the foe. The Lord will reward you for that love of yours, and will restore you the fruit due to this so good work; for he who exhorts is not less worthy of the reward of the crown than he who suffers; not less worthy of praise is he who has taught, than he who has acted also; he is not less to be honored who has warned, than he who has fought; except that sometimes the weight of glory more redounds to him who trains, than to him who has shown himself a teachable learner; for the latter, perchance, would not have had what he has practiced, unless the former had taught him.

2. Therefore, again, we say, brother Cyprian, we have received great joy, great comfort, great refreshment, especially in that you have described, with glorious and deserved praises, the glorious, I will not say, deaths, but immortalities of martyrs. For such departures should have been proclaimed with such words, that the things which were related might be told in such manner as they were done. Thus, from your letter, we saw those glorious triumphs of the martyrs; and with our eyes in some sort have followed them as they went to heaven, and have contemplated them seated among angels, and the powers and dominions of heaven. Moreover, we have in some manner perceived with our ears the Lord giving them the promised testimony in the presence of the Father. It is this, then, which also raises our spirit day by day, and inflames us to the following of the track of such dignity.

3. For what more glorious, or what more blessed, can happen to any man from the divine condescension, than to confess the Lord God, in death itself, before his

very executioners? Than among the raging and varied and exquisite tortures of worldly power, even when the body is racked and torn and cut to pieces, to confess Christ the Son of God with a spirit still free, although departing? Than to have mounted to heaven with the world left behind? Than, having forsaken men, to stand among the angels? Than, all worldly impediments being broken through, already to stand free in the sight of God? Than to enjoy the heavenly kingdom without any delay? Than to have become an associate of Christ's passion in Christ's name? Than to have become by the divine condescension the judge of one's own judge? Than to have brought off an unstained conscience from the confession of His name? Than to have refused to obey human and sacrilegious laws against the faith? Than to have borne witness to the truth with a public testimony? Than, by dying, to have subdued death itself, which is dreaded by all? Than, by death itself, to have attained immortality? Than when torn to pieces, and tortured by all the instruments of cruelty, to have overcome the torture by the tortures themselves? Than by strength of mind to have wrestled with all the agonies of a mangled body? Than not to have shuddered at the flow of one's own blood? Than to have begun to love one's punishments, after having faith to bear them? Than to think it an injury to one's life not to have left it?

4. For to this battle our Lord, as with the trumpet of His Gospel, stimulates us when He says, "He that loveth father or mother more than me is not worthy of me: and he that loveth his own soul more than me is not worthy of me. And he that takes not his cross, and follow after me, is not worthy of me." And again, "Blessed are they which are persecuted for righteousness' sake: for

theirs is the kingdom of heaven. Blessed shall ye be, when men shall persecute you, and hate you. Rejoice, and be exceeding glad: for so did their fathers persecute the prophets which were before you." And again, "Because ye shall stand before kings and powers, and the brother shall deliver up the brother to death, and the father the son, and he that endures to the end shall be saved;" and "To him that overcomes will I give to sit on my throne, even as I also overcame and am set down on the throne of my Father." Moreover, the apostle: "Who shall separate us from the love of Christ? Shall tribulation, or distress, or persecution, or famine, or nakedness, or peril, or sword? (As it is written, For thy sake are we killed all the day long; we are accounted as sheep for the slaughter.) Nay, in all these things we are more than conquerors for Him who hath loved us."

5. When we read these things, and things of the like kind, brought together in the Gospel, and feel, as it were, torches placed under us, with the Lord's words to inflame our faith, we not only do not dread, but we even provoke the enemies of the truth; and we have already conquered the opponents of God, by the very fact of our not yielding to them, and have subdued their nefarious laws against the truth. And although we have not yet shed our blood, we are prepared to shed it. Let no one think that this delay of our departure is any clemency; for it obstructs us, it makes a hindrance to our glory, it puts off heaven, it withholds the glorious sight of God. For in a contest of this kind, and in the kind of contest when faith is struggling in the encounter, it is not true clemency to put off martyrs by delay. Entreat therefore, beloved Cyprian, that of His mercy the Lord will every day more and more arm and adorn every one of us with greater

abundance and readiness, and will confirm and strengthen us by the strength of His power; and, as a good captain, will at length bring forth His soldiers, whom He has hitherto trained and proved in the camp of our prison, to the field of the battle set before them. May He hold forth to us the divine arms, those weapons that know not how to be conquered,—the breastplate of righteousness, which is never accustomed to be broken,—the shield of faith, which cannot be pierced through,—the helmet of salvation, which cannot be shattered,—and the sword of the Spirit, which has never been wont to be injured. For to whom should we rather commit these things for him to ask for us, than to our so reverend bishop, as destined victims asking help of the priest?

6. Behold another joy of ours, that, in the duty of your episcopate, although in the meantime you have been, owing to the condition of the times, divided from your brethren, you have frequently confirmed the confessors by your letters; that you have ever afforded necessary supplies from your own just acquisitions; that in all things you have always shown yourself in some sense present; that in no part of your duty have you hung behind as a deserter. But what more strongly stimulated us to a greater joy we cannot be silent upon but must describe with all the testimony of our voice. For we observe that you have both rebuked with fitting censure, and worthily, those who, unmindful of their sins, had, with hasty and eager desire, extorted peace from the presbyters in your absence, and those who, without respect for the Gospel, had with profane facility granted the holiness of the Lord unto dogs, and pearls to swine; although a great crime, and one which has extended with incredible destructiveness almost over the whole earth, ought only,

as you yourself write, to be treated cautiously and with moderation, with the advice of all the bishops, presbyters, deacons, confessors, and even the laymen who abide fast, as in your letters you yourself also testify; so that, while wishing unseasonably to bring repairs to the ruins, we may not appear to be bringing about other and greater destruction, for where is the divine word left, if pardon be so easily granted to sinners? Certainly, their spirits are to be cheered and to be nourished up to the season of their maturity, and they are to be instructed from the Holy Scriptures how great and surpassing a sin they have committed. Nor let them be animated by the fact that they are many, but rather let them be checked by the fact that they are not few. An unblushing number has never been accustomed to have weight in extenuation of a crime; but shame, modesty, patience, discipline, humility, and subjection, waiting for the judgment of others upon itself, and bearing the sentence of others upon its own judgment,—this it is which proves penitence; this it is which skins over a deep wound; this it is which raises up the ruins of the fallen spirit and restores them, which quells and restrains the burning vapor of their raging sins. For the physician will not give to the sick the food of healthy bodies, lest the unseasonable nourishment, instead of repressing, should stimulate the power of the raging disease,—that is to say, lest what might have been sooner diminished by abstinence, should, through impatience, be prolonged by growing indigestion.

7. Hands, therefore, polluted with impious sacrifices must be purified with good works, and wretched mouths defiled with accursed food must be purged with words of true penitence, and the spirit must be renewed and consecrated in the recesses of the faithful

heart. Let the frequent groanings of the penitents be heard; let faithful tears be shed from the eyes not once only, but again and again, so that those very eyes which wickedly looked upon idols may wash away, with tears that satisfy God, the unlawful things that they had done. Nothing is necessary for diseases but patience: they who are weary and weak wrestle with their pain; and so at length hope for health, if, by tolerating it, they can overcome their suffering; for unfaithful is the scar which the physician has too quickly produced; and the healing is undone by any little casualty, if the remedies be not used faithfully from their very slowness. The flame is quickly recalled again to a conflagration, unless the material of the whole fire be extinguished even to the extremest spark; so that men of this kind should justly know that even they themselves are more advantaged by the very delay, and that more trusty remedies are applied by the necessary postponement. Besides, where shall it be said that they who confess Christ are shut up in the keeping of a squalid prison, if they who have denied Him are in no peril of their faith? Where, that they are bound in the cincture of chains in God's name, if they who have not kept the confession of God are not deprived of communion? Where, that the imprisoned martyrs lay down their glorious lives, if those who have forsaken the faith do not feel the magnitude of their dangers and their sins? But if they betray too much impatience, and demand communion with intolerable eagerness, they vainly utter with petulant and unbridled tongues those querulous and invidious reproaches which avail nothing against the truth, since they might have retained by their own right what now by a necessity, which they of their own free will have sought, they are compelled to sue for. For the faith which could confess Christ, could also have been kept by Christ in communion. We bid you, blessed and most glorious father, ever heartily farewell in the Lord; and have us in remembrance.

    Epistle XXVI.
    Cyprian to the Lapsed.
    Argument.—The Argument of This Letter is Found Below in Letter XXVII. "They Wrote to Me," Says He, "Not Asking that Peace Should Be Granted Them, But Claiming It for Themselves as Already Granted, Because They Say that Paulus Has Given Peace to All; As You Will Read in Their Letter of Which I Have Sent You a Copy, Together with What I Briefly Replied to Them." But the Letter of the Lapsed to Which He Replies is Wanting.

    1. Our Lord, whose precepts and admonitions we ought to observe, describing the honour of a bishop and the order of His Church, speaks in the Gospel, and says to Peter: "I say unto thee, That thou art Peter, and upon this rock will I build my Church; and the gates of hell shall not prevail against it. And I will give unto thee the keys of the kingdom of heaven: and whatsoever thou shalt bind on earth shall be bound in heaven: and whatsoever thou shalt loose on earth shall be loosed in heaven." Thence, through the changes of times and successions, the ordering of bishops and the plan of the Church flow onwards; so that the Church is founded upon the bishops, and every act of the Church is controlled by these same rulers. Since this, then, is founded on the divine law, I marvel that some, with daring temerity, have chosen to write to me as if they wrote in the name of the Church; when the Church is established in the bishop and the

clergy, and all who stand fast in the faith. For far be it from the mercy of God and His uncontrolled might to suffer the number of the lapsed to be called the Church; since it is written, "God is not the God of the dead, but of the living." For we indeed desire that all may be made alive; and we pray that, by our supplications and groans, they may be restored to their original state. But if certain lapsed ones claim to be the Church, and if the Church be among them and in them, what is left but for us to ask of these very persons that they would deign to admit us into the Church? Therefore, it behooves them to be submissive and quiet and modest, as those who ought to appease God, in remembrance of their sin, and not to write letters in the name of the Church, when they should rather be aware that they are writing to the Church.

 2. But some who are of the lapsed have lately written to me, and are humble and meek and trembling and fearing God, and who have always labored in the Church gloriously and liberally, and who have never made a boast of their labor to the Lord, knowing that He has said, "When ye shall have done all these things, say, We are unprofitable servants: we have done that which was our duty to do." Thinking of which things, and although they had received certificates from the martyrs, nevertheless, that their satisfaction might be admitted by the Lord, these persons beseeching have written to me that they acknowledge their sin, and are truly repentant, and do not hurry rashly or importunately to secure peace; but that they are waiting for my presence, saying that even peace itself, if they should receive it when I was present, would be sweeter to them. How greatly I congratulate these, the Lord is my witness, who hath condescended to tell what such, and such sort of servants

deserve of His kindness. Which letters, as I lately received, and now read that you have written very differently, I beg that you will discriminate between your wishes; and whoever you are who have sent this letter, add your names to the certificate, and transmit the certificate to me with your several names. For I must first know to whom I have to reply; then I will respond to each of the matters that you have written, having regard to the mediocrity of my place and conduct. I bid you, beloved brethren, ever heartily farewell, and live quietly and tranquilly according to the Lord's discipline. Fare ye well.

Epistle XXVII.
To the Presbyters and Deacons. Argument.—The Argument of This Letter is Sufficiently in Agreement with the Preceding, and It Appears that It is the One of Which He Speaks in the Following Letter; For He Praises His Clergy for Having Rejected from Communion Gaius of Didda, a Presbyter, and His Deacon, Who Rashly Communicated with the Lapsed; And Exhorts Them to Do the Same with Certain Others.

1. Cyprian to the presbyters and deacons, his brethren, greeting. You have done uprightly and with discipline, beloved brethren, that, by the advice of my colleagues who were present, you have decided not to communicate with Gaius the presbyter of Didda, and his deacon; who, by communicating with the lapsed, and offering their oblations, have been frequently taken in their wicked errors; and who once and again, as you wrote to me, when warned by my colleagues not to do this, have persisted obstinately, in their presumption and audacity, deceiving certain brethren also from among our people, whose benefit we desire with all humility to consult, and

whose salvation we take care for, not with affected adulation, but with sincere faith, that they may supplicate the Lord with true penitence and groaning and sorrow, since it is written, "Remember from whence thou art fallen, and repent." And again, the divine Scripture says, "Thus saith the Lord, When thou shalt be converted and lament, then thou shalt be saved, and shalt know where thou hast been."

2. Yet how can those mourn and repent, whose groanings and tears some of the presbyters obstruct when they rashly think that they may be communicated with, not knowing that it is written, "They who call you happy cause you to err, and destroy the path of your feet?" Naturally, our wholesome and true counsels have no success, whilst the salutary truth is hindered by mischievous blandishments and flatteries, and the wounded and unhealthy mind of the lapsed suffers what those also who are bodily diseased and sick often suffer; that while they refuse wholesome food and beneficial drink as bitter and distasteful, and crave those things which seem to please them and to be sweet for the present, they are inviting to themselves mischief and death by their recklessness and intemperance. Nor does the true remedy of the skillful physician avail to their safety, whilst the sweet enticement is deceiving with its charms.

3. Do you, therefore, according to my letters, take counsel about this faithfully and wholesomely, and do not recede from better counsels; and be careful to read these same letters to my colleagues also, if there are any present, or if any should come to you; that, with unanimity and concord, we may maintain a healthful plan for soothing and healing the wounds of the lapsed,

intending to deal very fully with all when, by the Lord's mercy, we shall begin to assemble together. In the meantime, if any unrestrained and impetuous person, whether of our presbyters or deacons or of strangers, should dare, before our decree, to communicate with the lapsed, let him be expelled from our communion, and plead the cause of his rashness before all of us when, by the Lord's permission, we shall assemble together again. Moreover, you wished me to reply what I thought concerning Philumenus and Fortunatus, sub-deacons, and Favorinus, an acolyte, who retired in the midst of the time of trial and have now returned. Of which thing I cannot make myself sole judge, since many of the clergy are still absent, and have not considered, even thus late, that they should return to their place; and this case of each one must be considered separately and fully investigated, not only with my colleagues, but also with the whole of the people themselves. For a matter which hereafter may constitute an example as regards the ministers of the Church must be weighed and adjudged with careful deliberation. In the meanwhile, let them only abstain from the monthly division, not so as to seem to be deprived of the ministry of the Church, but that all matters being in a sound state, they may be reserved till my coming. I bid you, beloved brethren, ever heartily farewell. Greet all the brotherhood, and fare ye well.

Epistle XXVIII.
To the Presbyters and Deacons Abiding at Rome.
Argument.—The Roman Clergy are Informed of the Temerity of the Lapsed Who Were Demanding Peace.
Cyprian to the presbyters and deacons abiding at Rome, his brethren, greeting. Both our common love and

the reason of the thing demand, beloved brethren, that I should keep back from your knowledge nothing of those matters which are transacted among us, that so we may have a common plan for the advantage of the administration of the Church. For after I wrote to you the letter which I sent by Saturus the reader, and Optatus the sub-deacon, the combined temerity of certain of the lapsed, who refuse to repent and to make satisfaction to God, wrote to me, not asking that peace might be given to them, but claiming it as already given; because they say that Paulus has given peace to all, as you will read in their letter of which I have sent you a copy, as well as what I briefly replied to them in the meantime. But that you may also know what sort of a letter I afterwards wrote to the clergy, I have, moreover, sent you a copy of this. But if, after all, their temerity should not be repressed either by my letters or by yours, and should not yield to wholesome counsels, I shall take such proceedings as the Lord, according to His Gospel, has enjoined to be taken. I bid you, beloved brethren, ever heartily farewell.

Epistle XXIX.
The Presbyters and Deacons Abiding at Rome, to Cyprian.
Argument.—The Roman Church Declares Its Judgment Concerning the Lapsed to Be in Agreement with the Carthaginian Decrees. Any Indulgence Shown to the Lapsed is Required to Be in Accordance with the Law of the Gospel. That the Peace Granted by the Confessors Depends Only Upon Grace and Good-Will, is Manifest from the Fact that the Lapsed are Referred to the Bishops. The Seditious Demand for Peace Made by Felicissimus is to Be Attributed to Faction.

1. The presbyters and deacons abiding at Rome, to Father Cyprian, greeting. When, beloved brother, we carefully read your letter which you had sent by Fortunatus the sub☐deacon, we were smitten with a double sorrow, and disordered with a twofold grief, that there was not any rest given to you in such necessities of the persecution, and that the unreasonable petulance of the lapsed brethren was declared to be carried even to a dangerous boldness of expression. But although those things which we have spoken of severely afflicted us and our spirit, yet your rigour and the severity that you have used, according to the proper discipline, moderates the so heavy load of our grief, in that you rightly restrain the wickedness of some, and, by your exhortation to repentance, show the legitimate way of salvation. That they should have wished to hurry to such an extreme as this, we are indeed considerably surprised; as that with such urgency, and at so unseasonable and bitter a time, being in so great and excessive a sin, they should not so much ask for, as claim, peace for themselves; nay, should say that they already have it in heaven. If they have it, why do they ask for what they possess? But if, by the very fact that they are asking for it, it is proved that they have it not, wherefore do they not accept the judgment of those from whom they have thought fit to ask for the peace, which they certainly have not got? But if they think that they have from any other source the prerogative of communion, let them try to compare it with the Gospel, that so at length it may abundantly avail them, if it is not out of harmony with the Gospel law. But on what principle can that give Gospel communion which seems to be established contrary to Gospel truth? For since every prerogative contemplates the privilege of association,

precisely on the assumption of its not being out of harmony with the will of Him with whom it seeks to be associated; then, because this is alien from His will with whom it seeks to be associated, it must of necessity lose the indulgence and privilege of the association.

2. Let them, then, see what it is they are trying to do in this matter. For if they say that the Gospel has established one decree, but the martyrs have established another; then they, setting the martyrs at variance with the Gospel, will be in danger on both sides. For, on the one hand, the majesty of the Gospel will already appear shattered and cast down, if it can be overcome by the novelty of another decree; and, on the other, the glorious crown of confession will be taken from the heads of the martyrs, if they be not found to have attained it by the observation of that Gospel whence they become martyrs; so that, reasonably, no one should be more careful to determine nothing contrary to the Gospel, than he who strives to receive the name of martyr from the Gospel. We should like, besides, to be informed of this: if martyrs become martyrs for no other reason than that by not sacrificing they may keep the peace of the Church even to the shedding of their own blood, lest, overcome by the suffering of the torture, by losing peace, they might lose salvation; on what principle do they think that the salvation, which if they had sacrificed they thought that they should not have, was to be given to those who are said to have sacrificed; although they ought to maintain that law in others, which they themselves appear to have held before their own 308 eyes? In which thing we observe that they have put forward against their own cause the very thing which they thought made for them. For if the martyrs thought that peace was to be granted to

them, why did not they themselves grant it? Why did they think that, as they themselves say, they were to be referred to the bishops? For he who orders a thing to be done, can assuredly do that which he orders to be done. But, as we understand, nay, as the case itself speaks and proclaims, the most holy martyrs thought that a proper measure of modesty and of truth must be observed on both sides. For as they were urged by many, in remitting them to the bishop they conceived that they would consult their own modesty so as to be no further disquieted; and in themselves not holding communion with them, they judged that the purity of the Gospel law ought to be maintained unimpaired.

3. But of your charity, brother, never desist from soothing the spirits of the lapsed and affording to the erring the medicine of truth, although the temper of the sick is wont to reject the kind offices of those who would heal them. This wound of the lapsed is as yet fresh, and the sore is still rising into a tumor; and therefore we are certain, that when, in the course of more protracted time, that urgency of theirs shall have worn out, they will love that very delay which refers them to a faithful medicine; if only there be not those who arm them for their own danger, and, instructing them perversely, demand on their behalf, instead of the salutary remedies of delay, the fatal poisons of a premature communion. For we do not believe that without the instigation of certain people they would all have dared so petulantly to claim peace for themselves. We know the faith of the Carthaginian church, we know her training, we know her humility; whence also we have marveled that we should observe certain things somewhat rudely suggested against you by letter, although we have often become aware of your mutual love and charity, in

many illustrations of reciprocal affection of one another. It is time, therefore, that they should repent of their fault, that they should prove their grief for their lapse, that they should show modesty, that they should manifest humility, that they should exhibit some shame, that, by their submission, they should appeal to God's clemency for themselves, and by due honour for God's priest should draw forth upon themselves the divine mercy. How vastly better would have been the letters of these men themselves, if the prayers of those who stood fast had been aided by their own humility! since that which is asked for is more easily obtained, when he for whom it is asked is worthy, that what is asked should be obtained.

4. In respect, however, of Privatus of Lambesa, you have acted as you usually do, in desiring to inform us of the matter, as being an object of anxiety; for it becomes us all to watch for the body of the whole Church, whose members are scattered through every various province. But the deceitfulness of that crafty man could not be hid from us even before we had your letters; for previously, when from the company of that very wickedness a certain Futurus came, a standard-bearer of Privatus, and was desirous of fraudulently obtaining letters from us, we were neither ignorant who he was, nor did he get the letters which he wanted. We bid you heartily farewell in the Lord.

    Epistle XXX.
    The Roman Clergy to Cyprian.
    Argument.—The Roman Clergy Enter into the Matters Which They Had Spoken of in the Foregoing Letter, More Fully and Substantially in the Present One; Replying, Moreover, to Another Letter of Cyprian, Which

is Thought Not to Be Extant, and from Which They Quote a Few Words. They Thank Cyprian for His Letters Sent to the Roman Confessors and Martyrs.

1. To Father Cyprian, the presbyters and deacons abiding at Rome, greeting. Although a mind conscious to itself of uprightness, and relying on the vigor of evangelical discipline, and made a true witness to itself in the heavenly decrees, is accustomed to be satisfied with God for its only judge, and neither to seek the praises nor to dread the charges of any other, yet those are worthy of double praise, who, knowing that they owe their conscience to God alone as the judge, yet desire that their doings should be approved also by their brethren themselves. It is no wonder, brother Cyprian, that you should do this, who, with your usual modesty and inborn industry, have wished that we should be found not so much judges of, as sharers in, your counsels, so that we might find praise with you in your doings while we approve them; and might be able to be fellow-heirs with you in your good counsels, because we entirely accord with them. In the same way we are all thought to have labored in that in which we are all regarded as allied in the same agreement of censure and discipline.

2. For what is there either in peace so suitable, or in a war of persecution so necessary, as to maintain the due severity of the divine rigour? Which he who resists, will of necessity wander in the unsteady course of affairs, and will be tossed hither and thither by the various and uncertain storms of things; and the helm of counsel being, as it were, wrenched from his hands he will drive the ship of the Church's safety among the rocks; so that it would appear that the Church's safety can be no otherwise secured, than by repelling any who set themselves against

it as adverse waves, and by maintaining the ever-guarded rule of discipline itself as if it were the rudder of safety in the tempest. Nor is it now but lately that this counsel has been considered by us, nor have these sudden appliances against the wicked but recently occurred to us; but this is read of among us as the ancient severity, the ancient faith, the ancient discipline, since the apostle would not have published such praise concerning us, when he said "that your faith is spoken of throughout the whole world" unless already from thence that vigor had borrowed the roots of faith from those times; from which praise and glory it is a very great crime to have become degenerate. For it is less disgrace never to have attained to the heraldry of praise, than to have fallen from the height of praise; it is a smaller crime not to have been honored with a good testimony, than to have lost the honour of good testimonies; it is less discredit to have lain without the announcement of virtues, ignoble without praise, than, disinherited of the faith, to have lost our proper praises. For those things which are proclaimed to the glory of anyone, unless they are maintained by anxious and careful pains, swell up into the odium of the greatest crime.

3. That we are not saying this dishonestly, our former letters have proved, wherein we have declared our opinion to you with a very plain statement, both against those who had betrayed themselves as unfaithful by the unlawful presentation of wicked certificates, as if they thought that they would escape those ensnaring nets of the devil; whereas, not less than if they had approached to the wicked altars, they were held fast by the very fact that they had testified to him; and against those who had used those certificates when made, although they had not been present when they were made, since they had certainly

asserted their presence by ordering that they should be so written. For he is not guiltless of wickedness who has bidden it to be done; nor is he unconcerned in the crime with whose consent it is publicly spoken of, although it was not committed by him. And since the whole mystery of faith is understood to be contained in the confession of the name of Christ, he who seeks for deceitful tricks to excuse himself, has denied Christ; and he who wants to appear to have satisfied either edicts or laws put forth against the Gospel, has obeyed those edicts by the very fact by which he wished to appear to have obeyed them. Moreover, also, we have declared our faith and consent against those, too, who had polluted their hands and their mouths with unlawful sacrifices, whose own minds were before polluted; whence also their very hands and mouths were polluted also. Far be it from the Roman Church to slacken her vigor with so profane a facility, and to loosen the nerves of her severity by overthrowing the majesty of faith; so that, when the wrecks of your ruined brethren are still not only lying, but are falling around, remedies of a too hasty kind, and certainly not likely to avail, should be afforded for communion; and by a false mercy, new wounds should be impressed on the old wounds of their transgression; so that even repentance should be snatched from these wretched beings, to their greater overthrow. For where can the medicine of indulgence profit, if even the physician himself, by intercepting repentance, makes easy way for new dangers, if he only hides the wound, and does not suffer the necessary remedy of time to close the scar? This is not to cure, but, if we wish to speak the truth, to slay.

4. Nevertheless, you have letters agreeing with our letters from the confessors, whom the dignity of their

confession has still shut up here in prison, and whom, for the Gospel contest, their faith has once already crowned in a glorious confession; letters wherein they have maintained the severity of the Gospel discipline, and have revoked the unlawful petitions, so that they might not be a disgrace to the Church. Unless they had done this, the ruins of Gospel discipline would not easily be restored, especially since it was to none so fitting to maintain the tenor of evangelical vigor unimpaired, and its dignity, as to those who had given themselves up to be tortured and cut to pieces by raging men on behalf of the Gospel, that they might not deservedly forfeit the honour of martyrdom, if, on the occasion of martyrdom, they had wished to be betrayers of the Gospel. For he who does not guard what he has, in that condition whereon he possesses it, by violating the condition whereon he possesses it, loses what he possessed.

5. In which matter we ought to give you also, and we do give you, abundant thanks, that you have brightened the darkness of their prison by your letters; that you came to them in whatever way you could enter; that you refreshed their minds, robust in their own faith and confession, by your addresses and letters; that, following up their felicities with worthy praises, you have inflamed them to a much more ardent desire of heavenly glory; that you urged them forward; that you animated, by the power of your discourse, those who, as we believe and hope, will be victors by and by; so that although all may seem to come from the faith of those who confess, and from the divine mercy, yet they seem in their martyrdom to have become in some sort debtors to you. But once more, to return to the point whence our discourse appears to have digressed, you shall find subjoined the sort of

letters that we also sent to Sicily; although upon us is incumbent a greater necessity of delaying this affair; having, since the departure of Fabian of most noble memory, had no bishop appointed as yet, on account of the difficulties of affairs and times, who can arrange all things of this kind, and who can take account of those who are lapsed, with authority and wisdom. However, what you also have yourself declared in so important a matter, is satisfactory to us, that the peace of the Church must first be maintained; then, that an assembly for counsel being gathered together, with bishops, presbyters, deacons, and confessors, as well as with the laity who stand fast, we should deal with the case of the lapsed. For it seems extremely invidious and burdensome to examine into what seems to have been committed by many, except by the advice of many; or that one should give a sentence when so great a crime is known to have gone forth, and to be diffused among so many; since that cannot be a firm decree which shall not appear to have had the consent of very many. Look upon almost the whole world devastated and observe that the remains and the ruins of the fallen are lying about on every side and consider that therefore an extent of counsel is asked for, large in proportion as the crime appears to be widely propagated. Let not the medicine be less than the wound, let not the remedies be fewer than the deaths, that in the same manner as those who fell, fell for this reason that they were too incautious with a blind rashness, so those who strive to set in order this mischief should use every moderation in counsels, lest anything done as it ought not to be, should, as it were, be judged by all of no effect.

6. Thus, with one and the same counsel, with the same prayers and tears, let us, who up to the present time

seem to have escaped the destruction of these times of ours, as well as those who appear to have fallen into those calamities of the time, entreat the divine majesty, and ask peace for the Church's name. With mutual prayers, let us by turns cherish, guard, arm one another; let us pray for the lapsed, that they may be raised up; let us pray for those who stand, that they may not be tempted to such a degree as to be destroyed; let us pray that those who are said to have fallen may acknowledge the greatness of their sin, and may perceive that it needs no momentary nor over-hasty cure; let us pray that penitence may follow also the effects of the pardon of the lapsed; that so, when they have understood their own crime, they may be willing to have patience with us for a while, and no longer disturb the fluctuating condition of the Church, lest they may seem themselves to have inflamed an internal persecution for us, and the fact of their unquietness be added to the heap of their sins. For modesty is very greatly fitting for them in whose sins it is an immodest mind that is condemned. Let them indeed knock at the doors, but assuredly let them not break them down; let them present themselves at the threshold of the church, but certainly let them not leap over it; let them watch at the gates of the heavenly camp, but let them be armed with modesty, by which they perceive that they have been deserters; let them resume the trumpet of their prayers, but let them not therewith sound a point of war; let them arm themselves indeed with the weapons of modesty, and let them resume the shield of faith, which they had put off by their denial through the fear of death, but let those that are even now armed believe that they are armed against their foe, the devil, not against the Church, which grieves over their fall. A modest petition will much avail them; a bashful entreaty, a necessary humility, a patience which is not careless. Let them send tears as their ambassadors for their sufferings; let groanings, brought forth from their deepest heart, discharge the office of advocate, and prove their grief and shame for the crime they have committed.

7. Nay, if they shudder at the magnitude of the guilt incurred; if with a truly medicinal hand they deal with the deadly wound of their heart and conscience and the deep recesses of the subtle mischief, let them blush even to ask; except, again, that it is a matter of greater risk and shame not to have besought the aid of peace. But let all this be in the sacrament; in the law of their very entreaty let consideration be had for the time; let it be with downcast entreaty, with subdued petition, since he also who is besought ought to be bent, not provoked; and as the divine clemency ought to be looked to, so also ought the divine censure; and as it is written, "I forgave thee all that debt, because thou desired me," so it is written, "Whosoever shall deny me before men, him will I also deny before my Father and before His angels." For God, as He is merciful, so He exacts obedience to His precepts, and indeed carefully exacts it; and as He invites to the banquet, so the man that hath not a wedding garment He binds hands and feet, and casts him out beyond the assembly of the saints. He has prepared heaven, but He has also prepared hell. He has prepared places of refreshment, but He has also prepared eternal punishment. He has prepared the light that none can approach unto, but He has also prepared the vast and eternal gloom of perpetual night.

8. Desiring to maintain the moderation of this middle course in these matters, we for a long time, and indeed many of us, and, moreover, with some of the

bishops who are near to us and within reach, and some whom, placed afar off, the heat of the persecution had driven out from other provinces, have thought that nothing new was to be done before the appointment of a bishop; but we believe that the care of the lapsed must be moderately dealt with, so that, in the meantime, whilst the grant of a bishop is withheld from us by God, the cause of such as are able to bear the delays of postponement should be kept in suspense; but of such as impending death does not suffer to bear the delay, having repented and professed a detestation of their deeds with frequency; if with tears, if with groans, if with weeping they have betrayed the signs of a grieving and truly penitent spirit, when there remains, as far as man can tell, no hope of living; to them, finally, such cautious and careful help should be ministered, God Himself knowing what He will do with such, and in what way He will examine the balance of His judgment; while we, however, take anxious care that neither ungodly men should praise our smooth facility, nor truly penitent men accuse our severity as cruel. We bid you, most blessed and glorious father, ever heartily farewell in the Lord; and have us in memory.

Epistle XXXI.
To the Carthaginian Clergy, About the Letters Sent to Rome, and Received Thence.
Argument.—The Carthaginian Clergy are Requested to Take Care that the Letters of the Roman Clergy and Cyprian's Answer are Communicated. Cyprian to the presbyters and deacons, his brethren, greeting. That you, my beloved brethren, might know what letters I have sent to the clergy acting at Rome, and what they have replied to me, and, moreover, what

Moyses and Maximus, the presbyters, and Rufinus and Nicostratus, the deacons, and the rest of the confessors that with them are kept in prison, replied likewise to my letters, I have sent you copies to read. Do you take care, with as much diligence as you can, that what I have written, and what they have replied, be made known to our brethren. And, moreover, if any bishops from foreign places, my colleagues, or presbyters, or deacons, should be present, or should arrive among you, let them hear all these matters from you; and if they wish to transcribe copies of the letters and to take them to their own people, let them have the opportunity of transcribing them; although I have, moreover, bidden Saturus the reader, our brother, to give liberty of copying them to any individuals who wish it; so that, in ordering, for the present, the condition of the Church in any manner, an agreement, one and faithful, may be observed by all. But about the other matters which were to be dealt with, as I have also written to several of my colleagues, we will more fully consider them in a common council, when, by the Lord's permission, we shall begin to assemble into one place. I bid you, brethren, beloved and longed-for, ever heartily farewell. Salute the brotherhood. Fare ye well.

    Epistle XXXII.
    To the Clergy and People, About the Ordination of Aurelius as a Reader.
    Argument.—Cyprian Tells the Clergy and People that Aurelius the Confessor Has Been Ordained a Reader by Him, and Commends, by the Way, the Constancy of His Virtue and His Mind, Whereby He Was Even Deserving of a Higher Degree in the Church.
    1. Cyprian to the elders and deacons, and to the

whole people, greeting. In ordinations of the clergy, beloved brethren, we usually consult you beforehand, and weigh the character and deserts of individuals, with the general advice. But human testimonies must not be waited for when the divine approval precedes. Aurelius, our brother, an illustrious youth, already approved by the Lord, and dear to God, in years still very young, but, in the praise of virtue and of faith, advanced; inferior in the natural abilities of his age, but superior in the honour he has merited,—has contended here in a double conflict, having twice confessed and twice been glorious in the victory of his confession, both when he conquered in the course and was banished, and when at length he fought in a severer conflict, he was triumphant and victorious in the battle of suffering. As often as the adversary wished to call forth the servants of God, so often this prompt and brave soldier both fought and conquered. It had been a slight matter, previously to have engaged under the eyes of a few when he was banished; he deserved also in the forum to engage with a more illustrious virtue so that, after overcoming the magistrates, he might also triumph over the proconsul, and, after exile, might vanquish tortures also. Nor can I discover what I ought to speak most of in him,—the glory of his wounds or the modesty of his character; that he is distinguished by the honour of his virtue, or praiseworthy for the admirableness of his modesty. He is both so excellent in dignity and so lowly in humility, that it seems that he is divinely reserved as one who should be an example to the rest for ecclesiastical discipline, of the way in which the servants of God should in confession conquer by their courage, and, after confession, be conspicuous for their character.

2. Such a one, to be estimated not by his years but

by his deserts, merited higher degrees of clerical ordination and larger increase. But, in the meantime, I judged it well, that he should begin with the office of reading; because nothing is more suitable for the voice which has confessed the Lord in a glorious utterance, than to sound Him forth in the solemn repetition of the divine lessons; than, after the sublime words which spoke out the witness of Christ, to read the Gospel of Christ whence martyrs are made; to come to the desk after the scaffold; there to have been conspicuous to the multitude of the Gentiles, here to be beheld by the brethren; there to have been heard with the wonder of the surrounding people, here to be heard with the joy of the brotherhood. Know, then, most beloved brethren, that this man has been ordained by me and by my colleagues who were then present. I know that you will both gladly welcome these tidings, and that you desire that as many such as possible may be ordained in our church. And since joy is always hasty, and gladness can bear no delay, he reads on the Lord's day, in the meantime, for me; that is, he has made a beginning of peace, by solemnly entering on his office of a reader. Do you frequently be urgent in supplications, and assist my prayers by yours, that the Lord's mercy favoring us may soon restore both the priest safe to his people, and the martyr for a reader with the priest. I bid you, beloved brethren in God the Father, and in Jesus Christ, ever heartily farewell.

Epistle XXXIII.
To the Clergy and People, About the Ordination of Celerinus as Reader.
Argument.—This Letter is About the Same in

Purport with the Preceding, Except that He Largely Commends the Constancy of Celerinus in His Confession of the Faith. Moreover, that Both of These Letters Were Written During His Retreat, is Sufficiently Indicated by the Circumstances of the Context.

1. Cyprian to the presbyters and deacons, and to the whole people, his brethren in the Lord, greeting. The divine benefits, beloved brethren, should be acknowledged and embraced, wherewith the Lord has condescended to embellish and illustrate His Church in our times by granting a respite to His good confessors and His glorious martyrs, that they who had grandly confessed Christ should afterwards adorn Christ's clergy in ecclesiastical ministries. Exult, therefore, and rejoice with me on receiving my letter, wherein I and my colleagues who were then present mention to you Celerinus, our brother, glorious alike for his courage and his character, as added to our clergy, not by human recommendation, but by divine condescension; who, when he hesitated to yield to the Church, was constrained by her own admonition and exhortation, in a vision by night, not to refuse our persuasions; and she had more power, and constrained him, because it was not right, nor was it becoming, that he should be without ecclesiastical honour, whom the Lord honored with the dignity of heavenly glory.

2. This man was the first in the struggle of our days; he was the leader among Christ's soldiers; he, in the midst of the burning beginnings of the persecution, engaged with the very chief and author of the disturbance, in conquering with invincible firmness the adversary of his own conflict. He made a way for others to conquer; a victor with no small number of wounds, but triumphant

by a miracle, with the long-abiding and permanent penalties of a tedious conflict. For nineteen days, shut up in the close guard of a dungeon, he was racked and in irons; but although his body was laid in chains, his spirit remained free and at liberty. His flesh wasted away by the long endurance of hunger and thirst; but God fed his soul, that lived in faith and virtue, with spiritual nourishments. He lay in punishments, the stronger for his punishments; imprisoned, greater than those that imprisoned him; lying prostrate, but loftier than those who stood; as bound, and firmer than the links which bound him; judged, and more sublime than those who judged him; and although his feet were bound on the rack, yet the serpent was trodden on and ground down and vanquished. In his glorious body shines the bright evidence of his wounds; their manifest traces show forth, and appear on the man's sinews and limbs, worn out with tedious wasting away. Great things are they—marvelous things are they—which the brotherhood may hear of his virtues and of his praises. And should anyone appear like Thomas, who has little faith in what he hears, the faith of the eyes is not wanting, so that what one hears he may also see. In the servant of God, the glory of the wounds made the victory; the memory of the scars preserves that glory.

3. Nor is that kind of title to glories in the case of Celerinus, our beloved, an unfamiliar and novel thing. He is advancing in the footsteps of his kindred; he rivals his parents and relations in equal honors of divine condescension. His grandmother, Celerina, was some time since crowned with martyrdom. Moreover, his paternal and maternal uncles, Laurentius and Egnatius, who themselves also were once warring in the camps of the world, but were true and spiritual soldiers of God,

casting down the devil by the confession of Christ, merited palms and crowns from the Lord by their illustrious passion. We always offer sacrifices for them, as you remember, as often as we celebrate the passions and days of the martyrs in the annual commemoration. Nor could he, therefore, be degenerate and inferior whom this family dignity and a generous nobility provoked, by domestic examples of virtue and faith. But if in a worldly family it is a matter of heraldry and of praise to be a patrician, of how much greater praise and honour is it to become of noble rank in the celestial heraldry! I cannot tell whom I should call more blessed,—whether those ancestors, for a posterity so illustrious, or him, for an origin so glorious. So equally between them does the divine condescension flow, and pass to and fro, that, just as the dignity of their offspring brightens their crown, so the sublimity of his ancestry illuminates his glory.

4. When this man, beloved brethren, came to us with such condescension of the Lord, illustrious by the testimony and wonder of the very man who had persecuted him, what else behooved to be done except that he should be placed on the pulpit, that is, on the tribunal of the Church; that, resting on the loftiness of a higher station, and conspicuous to the whole people for the brightness of his honour, he should read the precepts and Gospel of the Lord, which he so bravely and faithfully follows? Let the voice that has confessed the Lord daily be heard in those things which the Lord spoke. Let it be seen whether there is any further degree to which he can be advanced in the Church. There is nothing in which a confessor can do more good to the brethren than that, while the reading of the Gospel is heard from his lips, everyone who hears should imitate the faith of the

reader. He should have been associated with Aurelius in reading; with whom, moreover, he was associated in the alliance of divine honour; with whom, in all the insignia of virtue and praise, he had been united. Equal both, and each like to the other, in proportion as they were sublime in glory, in that proportion they were humble in modesty. As they were lifted up by divine condescension, so they were lowly in their own peacefulness and tranquility, and equally affording examples to every one of virtues and character, and fitted both for conflict and for peace; praiseworthy in the former for strength, in the latter for modesty.

5. In such servants the Lord rejoices; in confessors of this kind He glories,—whose way and conversation is so advantageous to the announcement of their glory, that it affords to others a teaching of discipline. For this purpose Christ has willed them to remain long here in the Church; for this purpose He has kept them safe, snatched from the midst of death,—a kind of resurrection, so to speak, being wrought on their behalf; so that, while nothing is seen by the brethren loftier in honour, nothing more lowly in humility, the way of life of the brotherhood may accompany these same persons. Know, then, that these for the present are appointed readers, because it was fitting that the candle should be placed in a candlestick, whence it may give light to all, and that their glorious countenance should be established in a higher place, where, beheld by all the surrounding brotherhood, they may give an incitement of glory to the beholders. But know that I have already purposed the honour of the presbytery for them, that so they may be honored with the same presents as the presbyters, and may share the monthly divisions in equaled quantities, to sit with us

hereafter in their advanced and strengthened years; although in nothing can he seem to be inferior in the qualities of age who has consummated his age by the dignity of his glory. I bid you, brethren, beloved and earnestly longed-for, ever heartily farewell.

    Epistle XXXIV.
    To the Same, About the Ordination of Numidicus as Presbyter.
    Argument.—Cyprian Tells the Clergy and People that Numidicus Has Been Ordained by Him Presbyter; And Briefly Commends His Worth.
    Cyprian to the presbyters and deacons, and to the whole people, his brethren, very dear and longed-for, greeting. That which belongs, dearest brethren, both to the common joy and to the greatest glory of our Church ought to be told to you; for you must know that I have been admonished and instructed by divine condescension, that Numidicus the presbyter should be appointed in the number of Carthaginian presbyters, and should sit with us among the clergy,—a man illustrious by the brightest light of confession, exalted in the honour both of virtue and of faith; who by his exhortation sent before himself an abundant number of martyrs, slain by stones and by the flames, and who beheld with joy his wife abiding by his side, burned (I should rather say, preserved) together with the rest. He himself, half consumed, overwhelmed with stones, and left for dead,—when afterwards his daughter, with the anxious consideration of affection, sought for the corpse of her father,—was found half dead, was drawn out and revived, and remained unwillingly from among the companions whom he himself had sent before. But the reason of his remaining behind, as we see, was this: that

the Lord might add him to our clergy and might adorn with glorious priests the number of our presbyters that had been desolated by the lapse of some. And when God permits, he shall be advanced to a larger office in his region, when, by the Lord's protection, we have come into your presence once more. In the meantime, let what is revealed be done, that we receive this gift of God with thanksgiving, hoping from the Lord's mercy more ornaments of the same kind, that so the strength of His Church being renewed, He may make men so meek and lowly to flourish in the honour of our assembly. I bid you, brethren, very dear and longed-for, ever heartily farewell.

Epistle XXXV.

To the Clergy, Concerning the Care of the Poor and Strangers.

Argument.—He Cautions Them Against Neglecting the Widows, the Sick, or the Poor, or Strangers. Cyprian to the presbyters and deacons, his beloved brethren, greeting. In safety, by God's grace, I greet you, beloved brethren, desiring soon to come to you, and to satisfy the wish as well of myself and you, as of all the brethren. It behooves me also, however, to have regard to the common peace, and, in the meantime, although with weariness of spirit, to be absent from you, lest my presence should provoke the jealousy and violence of the heathens, and I should be the cause of breaking the peace, who ought rather to be careful for the quiet of all. When, therefore, you write that matters are arranged, and that I ought to come, or if the Lord should condescend to intimate it to me before, then I will come to you. For where could I be better or more joyful than there where the Lord willed me both to believe and to grow up?

I request that you will diligently take care of the widows, and of the sick, and of all the poor. Moreover, you may supply the expenses for strangers, if any should be indigent, from my own portion, which I have left with Rogatianus, our fellow-presbyter; which portion, lest it should be all appropriated, I have supplemented by sending to the same by Naricus the acolyte another share, so that the sufferers may be more largely and promptly dealt with. I bid you, beloved brethren, ever heartily farewell; and have me in remembrance. Greet your brotherhood in my name and tell them to be mindful of me.

 Epistle XXXVI.
To the Clergy, Bidding Them Show Every Kindness to the Confessors in Prison.
 Argument.—He Exhorts His Clergy that Every Kindness and Care Should Be Exercised Towards the Confessors, as Well Towards Those Who Were Alive, as Those Who Died, in Prison; That the Days of Their Death Should Be Carefully Noted, for the Purpose of Celebrating Their Memory Annually; And, Finally, that They Should Not Forget the Poor Also.
 1. Cyprian to the presbyters and deacons, his brethren, greeting. Although I know, dearest brethren, that you have frequently been admonished in my letters to manifest all care for those who with a glorious voice have confessed the Lord, and are confined in prison; yet, again and again, I urge it upon you, that no consideration be wanting to them to whose glory there is nothing wanting. And I wish that the circumstances of the place and of my station would permit me to present myself at this time with them; promptly and gladly would I fulfil all the

duties of love towards our most courageous brethren in my appointed ministry. But I beseech you, let your diligence be the representative of my duty, and do all those things which behoove to be done in respect of those whom the divine condescension has rendered illustrious in such merits of their faith and virtue. Let there be also a more zealous watchfulness and care bestowed upon the bodies of all those who, although they were not tortured in prison, yet depart thence by the glorious exit of death. For neither is their virtue nor their honour too little for them also to be allied with the blessed martyrs. As far as they could, they bore whatever they were prepared and equipped to bear. He who under the eyes of God has offered himself to tortures and to death, has suffered whatever he was willing to suffer; for it was not he that was wanting to the tortures, but the tortures that were wanting to him. "Whosoever shall confess me before men, him will I also confess before my Father which is in heaven," saith the Lord. They have confessed Him. "He that endures to the end, the same shall be saved," saith the Lord. They have endured and have carried the uncorrupted and unstained merits of their virtues through, even unto the end. And, again, it is written, "Be thou faithful unto death, and I will give thee a crown of life." They have persevered in their faithfulness, and steadfastness, and invincibleness, even unto death. When to the willingness and the confession of the name in prison and in chains is added also the conclusion of dying, the glory of the martyr is consummated.

2. Finally, also, take note of their days on which they depart, that we may celebrate their commemoration among the memorials of the martyrs, although Tertullus, our most faithful and devoted brother, who, in addition to

the other solicitude and care which he shows to the brethren in all service of labor, is not wanting besides in that respect in any care of their bodies, has written, and does write and intimate to me the days, in which our blessed brethren in prison pass by the gate of a glorious death to their immortality; and there are celebrated here by us oblations and sacrifices for their commemorations, which things, with the Lord's protection, we shall soon celebrate with you. Let your care also (as I have already often written) and your diligence not be wanting to the poor,—to such, I mean, as stand fast in the faith and bravely fight with us, and have not left the camp of Christ; to whom, indeed, we should now show a greater love and care, in that they are neither constrained by poverty nor prostrated by the tempest of persecution, but faithfully serve with the Lord, and have given an example of faith to the other poor. I bid you, brethren beloved, and greatly longed-for, ever heartily farewell; and remember me. Greet the brotherhood in my name. Fare ye well.

Epistle XXXVII.
To Caldonius, Herculanus, and Others, About the Excommunication of Felicissimus.
Argument.—Felicissimus, Together with His Companions in Sedition, is to Be Restrained from the Communion of All.
1. Cyprian to Caldonius and Herculanus, his colleagues, also to Rogatianus and Numidicus, his fellow-presbyters, greeting. I have been greatly grieved, dearest brethren, at the receipt of your letter, that although I have always proposed to myself and wished to keep all our brotherhood safe, and to preserve the flock unharmed, as charity requires, you tell me now that Felicissimus has

been attempting many things with wickedness and craft; so that, besides his old frauds and plundering, of which I had formerly known a good deal, he has now, moreover, tried to divide with the bishop a portion of the people; that is, to separate the sheep from the shepherd, and sons from their parents, and to scatter the members of Christ. And although I sent you as my substitutes to discharge the necessities of our brethren, with funds, and if any, moreover, wished to exercise their crafts, to assist their wishes with such an addition as might be sufficient, and at the same time also to take note of their ages and conditions and deserts,—that I also, upon whom falls the charge of knowing all of them thoroughly, might promote any that were worthy and humble and meek to the offices of the ecclesiastical administration;—he has interfered, and directed that no one should be relieved, and that those things which I had desired should not be ascertained by careful examination; he has also threatened our brethren, who had first approached to be relieved, with a wicked exercise of power, and with a violent dread that those who desired to obey me should not communicate with him in death.

2. And since, after all these things, neither moved by the honour of my station, nor shaken by your authority and presence, but of his own impulse, disturbing the peace of the brethren he hath rushed forth with many more, and asserted himself as a leader of a faction and chief of a sedition with a hasty madness—in which respect, indeed, I congratulate several of the brethren that they have withdrawn from this boldness, and have rather chosen to consent with you, so that they may remain with the Church, their mother, and receive their stipends from the bishop who dispenses them, which, indeed, I know for

certain, that others also will peaceably do, and will quickly withdraw from their rash error,—in the meantime, since Felicissimus has threatened that they should not communicate with him in death who had obeyed us, that is, who communicated with us, let him receive the sentence which he first of all declared, that he may know that he is excommunicated by us; inasmuch as he adds to his frauds and rapines, which we have known by the clearest truth, the crime also of adultery, which our brethren, grave men, have declared that they have discovered, and have asseverated that they will prove; all which things we shall then judicially examine, when, with the Lord's permission, we shall assemble in one place with many of our colleagues. But Augendus also, who, considering neither his bishop nor his Church, has equally associated himself with him in this conspiracy and faction, if he should further persevere with him, let him bear the sentence which that factious and impetuous man has provoked on himself. Moreover, whoever shall ally himself with his conspiracy and faction, let him know that he shall not communicate in the Church with us, since of his own accord he has preferred to be separated from the Church. Read this letter of mine to our brethren, and also transmit it to Carthage to the clergy, the names being added of those who have joined themselves with Felicissimus. I bid you, beloved brethren, ever heartily farewell; and remember me. Fare ye well.

Epistle XXXVIII.
The Letter of Caldonius, Herculanus, and Others, on the Excommunication of Felicissimus with His People.
Argument.—Caldonius, Herculanus, and Others

Carry into Effect What the Preceding Letter Had Bidden Them.

Caldonius, with Herculanus and Victor, his colleagues, also with Rogatianus and Numidicus, presbyters. We have rejected Felicissimus and Augendus from communion; also Repostus from among the exiles, and Irene of the Blood-stained ones; and Paula the sempstress; which you ought to know from my subscription; also we have rejected Sophronius and Soliassus (budinarius),—himself also one of the exiles.

Epistle XXXIX.

To the People, Concerning Five Schismatic Presbyters of the Faction of Felicissimus.

Argument.—In Like Manner, as in the Epistle But One Before This, Cyprian Told the Clergy, So Now He Tells the People, that Felicissimus is to Be Avoided, Together with Five Presbyters of His Faction, Who Not Only Granted Peace to the Lapsed Without Any Discrimination, But Stirred Up Sedition and Schism Against Himself.

1. Cyprian to the whole people, greeting. Although, dearest brethren, Virtius, a most faithful and upright presbyter, and also Rogatianus and Numidicus, presbyters, confessors, and illustrious by the glory of the divine condescension, and also the deacons, good men and devoted to the ecclesiastical administration in all its duties, with the other ministers, afford you the full attention of their presence, and do not cease to confirm individuals by their assiduous exhortations, and, moreover, to govern and reform the minds of the lapsed by their wholesome counsels, yet, as much as I can, I admonish, and as I can, I visit you with my letters. By my

letters I say, dearest brethren; for the malignity and treachery of certain of the presbyters has accomplished this, that I should not be allowed to come to you before Easter-day; since mindful of their conspiracy, and retaining that ancient venom against my episcopate, that is, against your suffrage and God's judgment, they renew their old attack upon me, and once more begin their sacrilegious machinations with their accustomed craft. And, indeed, of God's providence, neither by our wish nor desire, nay, although we were forgiving and silent, they have suffered the punishment which they had deserved; so that, not cast out by us, they of their own accord have cast themselves out. They themselves, before their own conscience, have passed sentence on themselves in accordance with your suffrage and the divine. These conspirators and evil men of their own accord have driven themselves from the Church.

2. Now it has appeared whence came the faction of Felicissimus; on what root and by what strength it stood. These men supplied in former times encouragements and exhortations to certain confessors, not to agree with their bishop, not to maintain the ecclesiastical discipline with faith and quietness according to the Lord's precepts, not to keep the glory of their confession with an uncorrupt and unspotted conversation. And lest it should be too little to have corrupted the minds of certain confessors, and to have wished to arm a portion of our broken fraternity against God's priesthood, they have now turned their attention with their envenomed deceitfulness to the ruin of the lapsed, to turn away from the healing of their wound the sick and the wounded, and those who, by the misfortune of their fall, are less fit and less sturdy to take stronger counsel; and invite them, by

the falsehood of a fallacious peace, to a fatal rashness, leaving off prayers and supplications, whereby, with long and continual satisfaction, the Lord is to be appeased.

3. But I pray you, brethren, watch against the snares of the devil, and, taking care for your own salvation, be diligently on your guard against this death-bearing fallacy. This is another persecution and another temptation. Those five presbyters are none other than the five leaders who were lately associated with the magistrates in an edict, that they might overthrow our faith, that they might turn away the feeble hearts of the brethren to their deadly nets by the prevarication of the truth. Now the same scheme, the same overturning, is again brought about by the five presbyters, linked with Felicissimus, to the destruction of salvation, that God should not be besought, and that he who has denied Christ should not appeal for mercy to the same Christ whom he had denied; that after the fault of the crime, repentance also should be taken away; and that the Lord should not be appeased through bishops and priests, but that the Lord's priests being forsaken, a new tradition of a sacrilegious appointment should arise, contrary to the evangelical discipline. And although it was once arranged as well by us as by the confessors and the city clergy, and moreover by all the bishops appointed either in our province or beyond the sea, that no novelty should be introduced in respect of the case of the lapsed unless we all assembled into one place, and our counsels being compared, should decide upon a moderate sentence, tempered alike with discipline and with mercy;—against this our counsel they have rebelled, and all priestly authority and power is destroyed by factious conspiracies.

4. What sufferings do I now endure, dearest

brethren, that I myself am not able to come to you at the present juncture, that I myself cannot approach you each one, that I myself cannot exhort you according to the teaching of the Lord and of His Gospel! An exile of, now, two years was not sufficient, and a mournful separation from you, from your countenance, and from your sight,— continual grief and lamentation, which, in my loneliness without you, breaks me to pieces with my constant mourning, nor my tears flowing day and night, that there is not even an opportunity for the priest, whom you made with so much love and eagerness, to greet you, nor to be enfolded in your embraces. This greater grief is added to my worn spirit, that in the midst of so much solicitude and necessity I am not able myself to hasten to you, since, by the threats and by the snares of perfidious men, we are anxious that on our coming a greater tumult may not arise there; and so, although the bishop ought to be careful for peace and tranquility in all things, he himself should seem to have afforded material for sedition, and to have embittered persecution anew. Hence, however, beloved brethren, I not only admonish but counsel you, not rashly to trust to mischievous words, nor to yield an easy consent to deceitful sayings, nor to take darkness for light, night for day, hunger for food, thirst for drink, poison for medicine, death for safety. Let not the age nor the authority deceive you of those who, answering to the ancient wickedness of the two elders; as they attempted to corrupt and violate the chaste Susannah, are thus also attempting, with their adulterous doctrines, to corrupt the chastity of the Church and violate the truth of the Gospel.

5. The Lord cries aloud, saying, "Hearken not unto the words of the false prophets, for the visions of their own hearts deceive them. They speak, but not out of the

mouth of the Lord. They say to them that despise the word of the Lord, Ye shall have peace." They are now offering peace who have not peace themselves. They are promising to bring back and recall the lapsed into the Church, who themselves have departed from the Church. There is one God, and Christ is one, and there is one Church, and one chair founded upon the rock by the word of the Lord. Another altar cannot be constituted, nor a new priesthood be made, except the one altar and the one priesthood. Whosoever gathered elsewhere, scattered. Whatsoever is appointed by human madness, so that the divine disposition is violated, is adulterous, is impious, is sacrilegious. Depart far from the contagion of men of this kind, and flee from their words, avoiding them as a cancer and a plague, as the Lord warns you and says, "They are blind leaders of the blind. But if the blind lead the blind, they shall both fall into the ditch." They intercept your prayers, which you pour forth with us to God day and night, to appease Him with a righteous satisfaction. They intercept your tears with which you wash away the guilt of the sin you have committed; they intercept the peace which you truly and faithfully ask from the mercy of the Lord; and they do not know that it is written, "And that prophet, or that dreamer of dreams, that hath spoken to turn you away from the Lord your God, shall be put to death." Let no one, beloved brethren, make you to err from the ways of the Lord; let no one snatch you, Christians, from the Gospel of Christ; let no one take sons of the Church away from the Church; let them perish alone for themselves who have wished to perish; let them remain outside the Church alone who have departed from the Church; let them alone be without bishops who have rebelled against bishops; let them alone undergo the penalties of their conspiracies who formerly, according to your votes, and now according to God's judgment, have deserved to undergo the sentence of their own conspiracy and malignity.

6. The Lord warns us in His Gospel, saying, "Ye reject the commandment of God, that ye may establish your own tradition." Let them who reject the commandment of God and endeavor to keep their own tradition be bravely and firmly rejected by you; let one downfall be sufficient for the lapsed; let no one by his fraud hurl down those who wish to rise; let no one cast down more deeply and depress those who are down, on whose behalf we pray that they may be raised up by God's hand and arm; let no one turn away from all hope of safety those who are half alive and entreating that they may receive their former health; let no one extinguish every light of the way of salvation to those that are wavering in the darkness of their lapse. The apostle instructs us, saying, "If any man teach otherwise, and consent not to the wholesome words of our Lord Jesus Christ and His doctrine, he is lifted up with foolishness: from such withdraw thyself." And again, he says, "Let no man deceive you with vain words; for because of these things cometh the wrath of God upon the children of disobedience. Be not ye therefore partakers with them." There is no reason that you should be deceived with vain words and begin to be partakers of their depravity. Depart from such, I entreat you, and acquiesce in our counsels, who daily pour out for you continual prayers to the Lord, who desire that you should be recalled to the Church by the clemency of the Lord, who pray for the fullest peace from God, first for the mother, and then for her children. Join also your petitions and prayers with our prayers and

petitions; mingle your tears with our wailings. Avoid the wolves who separate the sheep from the shepherd; avoid the envenomed tongue of the devil, who from the beginning of the world, always deceitful and lying, lies that he may deceive, cajoles that he may injure, promises good that he may give evil, promises life that he may put to death. Now also his words are evident, and his poisons are plain. He promises peace, in order that peace may not possibly be attained; he promises salvation, that he who has sinned may not come to salvation; he promises a Church, when he so contrives that he who believes him may utterly perish apart from the Church.

7. It is now the occasion, dearly beloved brethren, both for you who stand fast to persevere bravely, and to maintain your glorious stability, which you kept in persecution with a continual firmness; and if any of you by the circumvention of the adversary have fallen, that in this second temptation you should faithfully take counsel for your hope and your peace; and in order that the Lord may pardon you, that you should not depart from the priests of the Lord, since it is written, "And the man that will do presumptuously, and will not hearken unto the priest or unto the judge that shall be in those days, even that man shall die." Of this persecution this is the latest and final temptation, which itself also, by the Lord's protection, shall quickly pass away; so that I shall be again presented to you after Easter-day with my colleagues, who, being present, we shall be able as well to arrange as to complete the matters which require to be done according to your judgment and to the general advice of all of us as it has been decided before. But if anybody, refusing to repent and to make satisfaction to God, shall yield to the party of Felicissimus and his

satellites, and shall join himself to the heretical faction, let him know that he cannot afterwards return to the Church and communicate with the bishops and the people of Christ. I bid you, dearest brethren, ever heartily farewell, and that you plead with me in continual prayer that the mercy of God may be entreated.

>Epistle XL.
>To Cornelius, on His Refusal to Receive Novatian's Ordination.

Argument.—The Messengers Sent by Novatian to Intimate His Ordination to the Church of Carthage are Rejected by Cyprian.

1. Cyprian to Cornelius, his brother, greeting. There have come to us, beloved brother, sent by Novatian, Maximus the presbyter, and Augendus the deacon, and a certain Machæus and Longinus. But, as we discovered, as well from the letters which they brought with them, as from their discourse and declaration, that Novatian had been made bishop; disturbed by the wickedness of an unlawful ordination made in opposition to the Catholic Church, we considered at once that they must be restrained from communion with us; and having, in the meanwhile, refuted and repelled the things which they pertinaciously and obstinately endeavored to assert, I and several of my colleagues, who had come together to me, were awaiting the arrival of our colleagues Caldonius and Fortunatus, whom we had lately sent to you as ambassadors, and to our fellow-bishops, who were present at your ordination, in order that, when they came and reported the truth of the matter, the wickedness of the adverse party might be quelled through them, by greater authority and manifest proof. But there came, in addition,

Pompeius and Stephanus, our colleagues, who themselves also, by way of instructing us thereon, put forward manifest proofs and testimonies in conformity with their gravity and faithfulness, so that it was not even necessary that those who had come, as sent by Novatian, should be heard any further. And when in our solemn assembly they burst in with invidious abuse and turbulent clamor, demanding that the accusations, which they said that they brought and would prove, should be publicly investigated by us and by the people, we said that it was not consistent with our gravity to suffer the honour of our colleague, who had already been chosen and ordained and approved by the laudable sentence of many, to be called into question any further by the abusive voice of rivals. And because it would be a long business to collect into a letter the matters in which they have been refuted and repressed, and in which they have been manifested as having caused heresy by their unlawful attempts, you shall hear everything most fully from Primitivus our co-presbyter, when he shall come to you.

2. And lest their raging boldness should ever cease, they are striving here also to distract the members of Christ into schismatical parties, and to cut and tear the one body of the Catholic Church, so that, running about from door to door, through the houses of many, or from city to city, through certain districts, they seek for companions in their obstinacy and error to join to themselves in their schism. To whom we have once given this reply, nor shall we cease to command them to lay aside their pernicious dissensions and disputes, and to be aware that it is an impiety to forsake their Mother; and to acknowledge and understand that when a bishop is once made and approved by the testimony and judgment of his

colleagues and the people, another can by no means be appointed. Thus, if they consult their own interest peaceably and faithfully, if they confess themselves to be maintainers of the Gospel of Christ, they must return to the Church. I bid you, dearest brother, ever heartily farewell.

Epistle XLI.
To Cornelius, About Cyprian's Approval of His Ordination, and Concerning Felicissimus.
Argument.—Cyprian Excuses Himself for Not Having Without Hesitation Believed in the Ordination of Cornelius, Until He Received the Letters of His Colleagues Caldonius And Fortunatus, Which Fully Testified to Its Legitimacy; And Incidentally Repeats, in Respect of the Contrary Faction of the Novatian Party, that He Did Not in the Very First Instance Give His Adhesion to That, But Rather to Cornelius, Even to the Extent of Refusing to Receive Accusations Against Him.

1. Cyprian to Cornelius his brother, greeting. As was fitting for God's servants, and especially for upright and peaceable priests, dearest brother, we recently sent our colleagues Caldonius and Fortunatus, that they might, not only by the persuasion of our letters, but by their presence and the advice of all of you, strive and labor with all their power to bring the members of the divided body into the unity of the Catholic Church, and associate them into the bond of Christian charity. But since the obstinate and inflexible pertinacity of the adverse party has not only rejected the bosom and the embrace of its root and Mother, but even, with a discord spreading and reviving itself worse and worse, has appointed a bishop for itself, and, contrary to the sacrament once delivered of

the divine appointment and of Catholic Unity, has made an adulterous and opposed head outside the Church; having received your letters as well as those of our colleagues, at the coming also of our colleagues Pompeius and Stephanus, good men and very dear to us, by whom all these things were undoubtedly alleged and proved to us with general gladness, in conformity with the requirements alike of the sanctity and the truth of the divine tradition and ecclesiastical institution, we have directed our letters to you. Moreover, bringing these same things under the notice of our several colleagues throughout the province, we have bidden also that our brethren, with letters from them, be directed to you.

2. This has been done, although our mind and intention had been already plainly declared to the brethren, and to the whole of the people in this place, when, having received letters lately from both parties, we read your letters, and intimated your ordination to the episcopate, in the ears of everyone. Moreover, remembering the common honour, and having respect for the sacerdotal gravity and sanctity, we repudiated those things which from the other party had been heaped together with bitter virulence into a document transmitted to us; alike considering and weighing, that in so great and so religious an assembly of brethren, in which God's priests were sitting together, and His altar was set, they ought neither to be read nor to be heard. For those things should not easily be put forward, nor carelessly and rudely published, which may move a scandal by means of a quarrelsome pen in the minds of the hearers, and confuse brethren, who are placed far apart and dwelling across the sea, with uncertain opinions. Let those beware, who, obeying either their own rage or lust, and unmindful

of the divine law and holiness, rejoice to throw abroad in the meantime things which they cannot prove; and although they may not be successful in destroying and ruining innocence, are satisfied with scattering stains upon it with lying reports and false rumors. Assuredly, we should exert ourselves, as it is fitting for prelates and priests to do, that such things, when they are written by any, should be repudiated as far as we are concerned. For otherwise, what will become of that which we learn and which we declare to be laid down in Scripture: "Keep thy tongue from evil, and thy lips from speaking guile?" And elsewhere: "Thy mouth abounded in malice, and thy tongue embraced deceit. Thou sates and speaks against thy brother, and slanders thine own mother's son." Also, what the apostle says: "Let no corrupt communication proceed from thy mouth, but that which is good to the edifying of faith, that it may minister grace unto the hearers." Further, we show what the right course of conduct to pursue is, if, when such things are written by the calumnious temerity of some, we do not allow them to be read among us: and therefore, dearest brother, when such letters came to me against you, even though they were the letters of your co-presbyter sitting with you, as they breathed a tone of religious simplicity, and did not echo with any barking of curses and reviling, I ordered them to be read to the clergy and the people.

3. But in desiring letters from our colleagues, who were present at your ordination at that place, we did not forget the ancient usage, nor did we seek for any novelty. For it was sufficient for you to announce yourself by letters to have been made bishop, unless there had been a dissenting faction on the other side, who by their slanderous and calumnious fabrications disturbed the

minds and perplexed the hearts of our colleagues, as well as of several of the brethren. To set this matter at rest, we judged it necessary to obtain thence the strong and decided authority of our colleagues who wrote to us; and they, declaring the testimony of their letters to be fully deserved by your character, and life, and teaching, have deprived even your rivals, and those who delight either in novelty or evil, of every scruple of doubt or of difference; and, according to our advice weighed in wholesome reason, the minds of the brethren tossing about in this sea have sincerely and decidedly approved your priesthood. For this, my brother, we especially both labor after, and ought to labor after, to be careful to maintain as much as we can the unity delivered by the Lord, and through His apostles to us their successors, and, as far as in us lies, to gather into the Church the dispersed and wandering sheep which the willful faction and heretical temptation of some is separating from their Mother; those only being left outside, who by their obstinacy and madness have persisted, and have been unwilling to return to us; who themselves will have to give an account to the Lord of the dissension and separation made by them, and of the Church that they have forsaken.

4. But, so far as pertains to the cause of certain presbyters here, and of Felicissimus, that you may know what has been done here, our colleagues have sent you letters subscribed by their own hand, that you may learn, when you have heard the parties, from their letters what they have thought and what they have pronounced. But you will do better, brother, if you will also bid copies of the letters which I had sent lately by our colleagues Caldonius and Fortunatus to you, to be read for the common satisfaction, which I had written concerning the

same Felicissimus and his presbytery to the clergy there, and also to the people, to be read to the brethren there; declaring your ordination, and the course of the whole transaction, that so as well there as here the brotherhood may be informed of all things by us. Moreover, I have here transmitted also copies of the same by Mettius the sub-deacon, sent by me, and by Nicephorus the acolyte. I bid you, dearest brother, ever heartily farewell.

Epistle XLII.
To the Same, on His Having Sent Letters to the Confessors Whom Novatian Had Seduced.
Argument.—The Argument of This Letter Sufficiently Appears from the Title. It is Manifest that This Letter and the Following Were Sent by One Messenger. Cyprian to Cornelius his brother, greeting. I have thought it both obligatory on me, and necessary for you, dearest brother, to write a short letter to the confessors who are there with you, and, seduced by the obstinacy and depravity of Novatian and Novatus, have departed from the Church; in which letter I might induce them, for the sake of our mutual affection, to return to their Mother, that is, to the Catholic Church. This letter I have first of all entrusted to you by Mettius the sub-deacon, for your perusal, lest anyone should pretend that I had written otherwise than according to the contents of my letter. I have, moreover, charged the same Mettius sent by me to you, that he should be guided by your decision; and if you should think that this letter should be given to the confessors, then that he should deliver it. I bid you, dearest brother, ever heartily farewell.

Epistle XLIII.
To the Roman Confessors, that They Should Return to Unity.

Argument.—He Exhorts the Roman Confessors Who Had Been Seduced by the Faction of Novatian and Novatus, to Return to Unity. Cyprian to Maximus and Nicostratus, and the other confessors, greeting. As you have frequently gathered from my letters, beloved, what honour I have ever observed in my mode of speaking for your confession, and what love for the associated brotherhood; believe, I entreat you, and acquiesce in these my letters, wherein I both write and with simplicity and fidelity consult for you, and for your doings, and for your praise. For it weighs me down and saddens me, and the intolerable grief of a smitten, almost prostrate, spirit seizes me, when I find that you there, contrary to ecclesiastical order, contrary to evangelical law, contrary to the unity of the Catholic institution, had consented that another bishop should be made. That is what is neither right nor allowable to be done; that another church should be set up; that Christ's members should be torn asunder; that the one mind and body of the Lord's flock should be lacerated by a divided emulation. I entreat that in you, at all events, that unlawful rending of our brotherhood may not continue; but remembering both your confession and the divine tradition, you may return to the Mother whence you have gone forth; whence you came to the glory of confession with the rejoicing of the same Mother. And think not that you are thus maintaining the Gospel of Christ when you separate yourselves from the flock of Christ, and from His peace and concord; since it is more fitting for glorious and good soldiers to sit down within their own camp, and so placed within to manage and provide for those things which are to be dealt with in common. For as our unanimity and concord ought by no means to be divided, and because we cannot forsake the Church and go outside her to come to you, we beg and entreat you with what exhortations we can, rather to return to the Church your Mother, and to our brotherhood. I bid you, dearest brethren, ever heartily farewell.

Epistle XLIV.
To Cornelius, Concerning Polycarp the Adrumetine.
Argument.—He Excuses Himself in This Letter for What Had Occurred, in That, During the Time that He Was at Adrumetum, Letters Had Been Sent Thence by the Clergy of Polycarp, Not to Cornelius, But to the Roman Clergy, Notwithstanding that Previously Polycarp Himself Had Written Rather to Cornelius. It Appears Tolerably Plain from the Context Itself that This Was Written After the Preceding Ones.

1. Cyprian to Cornelius his brother, greeting. I have read your letters, dearest brother, which you sent by Primitivus our co-presbyter, in which I perceived that you were annoyed that, whereas letters from the Adrumetine colony in the name of Polycarp were directed to you, yet after Liberalis and I came to that place, letters began to be directed thence to the presbyters and to the deacons.

2. In respect of which I wish you to know, and certainly to believe, that it was done from no levity or contempt. But when several of our colleagues who had assembled into one place had determined that, while our co-bishops Caldonius and Fortunatus were sent as ambassadors to you, all things should be in the meantime suspended as they were, until the same colleagues of ours,

having reduced matters there to peace, or, having discovered their truth, should return to us; the presbyters and deacons abiding in the Adrumetine colony; in the absence of our co-bishop Polycarp, were ignorant of what had been decided in common by us. But when we came before them, and our purpose was understood, they themselves also began to observe what the others did, so that the agreement of the churches abiding there was in no respect broken.

3. Some people, however, sometimes disturb men's minds and spirits by their words, in that they relate things otherwise than is the truth. For we, who furnish every person who sails hence with a plan that they may sail without any offence, know that we have exhorted them to acknowledge and hold the root and matrix of the Catholic Church. But since our province is wide-spread, and has Numidia and Mauritania attached to it; lest a schism made in the city should confuse the minds of the absent with uncertain opinions, we decided—having obtained by means of the bishops the truth of the matter, and having got a greater authority for the proof of your ordination, and so at length every scruple being got rid of from the breast of every one—that letters should be sent you by all who were placed anywhere in the province; as in fact is done, that so the whole of our colleagues might decidedly approve of and maintain both you and your communion, that is as well to the unit of the Catholic Church as to its charity. That all which has by God's direction come to pass, and that our design has under Providence been forwarded, we rejoice.

4. For thus as well the truth as the dignity of your episcopate has been established in the most open light, and with the most manifest and substantial approval; so

that from the replies of our colleagues, who have thence written to us, and from the account and from the testimonies of our co-bishops Pompeius, and Stephanus, and Caldonius, and Fortunatus, both the needful cause and the right order, and moreover the glorious innocence, of your ordination might be known by all. That we, with the rest of our colleagues, may steadily and firmly administer this office, and keep it in the concordant unanimity of the Catholic Church, the divine condescension will accomplish; so that the Lord who condescends to elect and appoint for Himself priests in His Church, may protect them also when elected and appointed by His good-will and help, inspiring them to govern, and supplying both vigor for restraining the contumacy of the wicked, and gentleness for cherishing the penitence of the lapsed. I bid you, dearest brother, ever heartily farewell.

Epistle XLV.
Cornelius to Cyprian, on the Return of the Confessors to Unity.
Argument.—Cornelius Informs Cyprian of the Solemn Return of the Confessors to the Church, and Describes It.
1. Cornelius to Cyprian his brother, greeting. In proportion to the solicitude and anxiety that we sustained in respect of those confessors who had been circumvented and almost deceived and alienated from the Church by the craft and malice of that wily and subtle man, was the joy with which we were affected, and the thanks which we gave to Almighty God and to our Lord Christ, when they, acknowledging their error, and perceiving the poisoned cunning of the malignant man, as if of a serpent, came back, as they with one heart profess, with singleness of

will to the Church from which they had gone forth. And first, indeed, our brethren of approved faith, loving peace and desiring unity, announced that the swelling pride of these men was already soothed; yet there was no fitting assurance to induce us easily to believe that they were thoroughly changed. But afterwards, Urbanus and Sidonius the confessors came to our presbyters, affirming that Maximus the confessor and presbyter, equally with themselves, desired to return into the Church; but since many things had preceded this which they had contrived, of which you also have been made aware from our co-bishops and from my letters, so that faith could not hastily be reposed in them, we determined to hear from their own mouth and confession those things which they had sent by the messengers. And when they came, and were required by the presbyters to give an account of what they had done, and were charged with having very lately repeatedly sent letters full of calumnies and reproaches, in their name, through all the churches, and had disturbed nearly all the churches; they affirmed that they had been deceived, and that they had not known what was in those letters; that only through being misled they had also committed schismatical acts, and been the authors of heresy, so that they suffered hands to be imposed on him as if upon a bishop. And when these and other matters had been charged upon them, they entreated that they might be done away and altogether discharged from memory.

2. The whole of this transaction therefore being brought before me, I decided that the presbytery should be brought together; (for there were present five bishops, who were also present to-day;) so that by well-grounded counsel it might be determined with the consent of all what ought to be observed in respect of their persons. And

that you may know the feeling of all, and the advice of each one, I decided also to bring to your knowledge our various opinions, which you will read subjoined. When these things were done, Maximus, Urbanus, Sidonius, and several brethren who had joined themselves to them, came to the presbytery, desiring with earnest prayers that what had been done before might fall into oblivion, and no mention might be made of it; and promising that henceforth, as though nothing had been either done or said, all things on both sides being forgiven, they would now exhibit to God a heart clean and pure, following the evangelical word which says, "Blessed are the pure in heart, for they shall see God." What remained was, that the people should be informed of all this proceeding, that they might see those very men established in the Church whom they had long seen and mourned as wanderers and scattered. Their will being known, a great concourse of the brotherhood was assembled. There was one voice from all, giving thanks to God; all were expressing the joy of their heart by tears, embracing them as if they had this day been set free from the penalty of the dungeon. And to quote their very own words,—"We," they say, "know that Cornelius is bishop of the most holy Catholic Church elected by Almighty God, and by Christ our Lord. We confess our error; we have suffered imposture; we were deceived by captious perfidy and loquacity. For although we seemed, as it were, to have held a kind of communion with a man who was a schismatic and a heretic, yet our mind was always sincere in the Church. For we are not ignorant that there is one God; that there is one Christ the Lord whom we have confessed, and one Holy Spirit; and that in the Catholic Church there ought to be one bishop." Were we not rightly induced by that confession of theirs, to allow that what they had confessed before the power of the world they might approve of when established in the Church? Wherefore we bade Maximus the presbyter to take his own place; the rest we received with great approbation of the people. But we remitted all things to Almighty God, in whose power all things are reserved.

3. These things therefore, brother, written to you in the same hour, at the same moment, we have transmitted; and I have sent away at once Nicephorus the acolyte, hastening to descend to embarkation, that so, no delay being made, you might, as if you had been present among that clergy and in that assembly of people, give thanks to Almighty God and to Christ our Lord. But we believe—nay, we confide in it for certain—that the others also who have been ranged in this error will shortly return into the Church when they see their leaders acting with us. I think. brother, that you ought to send these letters also to the other churches, that all may know that the craft and prevarication of this schismatic and heretic are from day to day being reduced to nothing. Farewell, dearest brother.

Epistle XLVI.

Cyprian's Answer to Cornelius, Congratulating Him on the Return of the Confessors from Schism.

Argument.—He Congratulates Him on the Return of the Confessors to the Church and Reminds Him How Much that Return Benefits the Catholic Church.

1. Cyprian to Cornelius his brother, greeting. I profess that I both have rendered and do render the greatest thanks without ceasing, dearest brother, to God the Father Almighty, and to His Christ the Lord and our God and Savior, that the Church is thus divinely

protected, and its unity and holiness is not constantly nor altogether corrupted by the obstinacy of perfidy and heretical wickedness. For we have read your letter, and have exultingly received the greatest joy from the fulfilment of our common desire; to wit, that Maximus the presbyter, and Urbanus, the confessors, with Sidonius and Macarius, have re-entered into the Catholic Church, that is, that they have laid aside their error, and given up their schismatical, nay, their heretical madness, and have sought again in the soundness of faith the home of unity and truth; that whence they had gone forth to glory, thither they might gloriously return; and that they who had confessed Christ should not afterwards desert the camp of Christ, and that they might not tempt the faith of their charity and unity, who had not been overcome in strength and courage. Behold the safe and unspotted integrity of their praise; behold the uncorrupted and substantial dignity of these confessors, that they have departed from the deserters and fugitives, that they have left the betrayers of the faith, and the impugners of the Catholic Church. With reason did both the people and the brotherhood receive them when they returned, as you write, with the greatest joy; since in the glory of confessors who had maintained their glory, and returned to unity, there is none who does not reckon himself a partner and a sharer.

2. We can estimate the joy of that day from our own feelings. For if, in this place, the whole number of the brethren rejoiced at your letter which you sent concerning their confession, and received this tidings of common rejoicing with the greatest alacrity, what must have been the joy there when the matter itself, and the general gladness, was carried on under the eyes of all?

For since the Lord in His Gospel says that there is the highest "joy in heaven over one sinner that repented," how much greater is the joy in earth, no less than in heaven, over confessors who return with their glory and with praise to the Church of God, and make a way of returning for others by the faith and approval of their example? For this error had led away certain of our brethren, so that they thought they were following the communion of confessors. When this error was removed, light was infused into the breasts of all, and the Catholic Church has been shown to be one, and to be able neither to be cut nor divided. Nor can anyone now be easily deceived by the talkative words of a raging schismatic, since it has been proved that good and glorious soldiers of Christ could not long be detained without the Church by the deceitfulness and perfidy of others. I bid you, dearest brother, ever heartily farewell.

    Epistle XLVII.
    Cornelius to Cyprian, Concerning the Faction of Novatian with His Party.
    Argument.—Cornelius Gives Cyprian an Account of the Faction of Novatian.
    Cornelius to Cyprian his brother, greeting. That nothing might be wanting to the future punishment of this wretched man, when cast down by the powers of God, (on the expulsion by you of Maximus, and Longinus, and Machæus;) he has risen again; and, as I intimated in my former letter which I sent to you by Augendus the confessor, I think that Nicostratus, and Novatus, and Evaristus, and Primus, and Dionysius, have already come thither. Therefore let care be taken that it be made known to all our co-bishops and brethren, that Nicostratus is

accused of many crimes, and that not only has he committed frauds and plunders on his secular patroness, whose affairs he managed; but, moreover (which is reserved to him for a perpetual punishment), he has abstracted no small deposits of the Church; that Evaristus has been the author of a schism; and that Zetus has been appointed bishop in his room, and his successor to the people over whom he had previously presided. But he contrived greater and worse things by his malice and insatiable wickedness than those which he was then always practicing among his own people; so that you may know what kind of leaders and protectors that schismatic and heretic constantly had joined to his side. I bid you, dearest brother, ever heartily fare well.

Epistle XLVIII.
Cyprian's Answer to Cornelius, Concerning the Crimes of Novatus.
Argument.—He Praises Cornelius, that He Had Given Him Timely Warning, Seeing that the Day After the Guilty Faction Had Come to Him He Had Received Cornelius' Letter. Then He Describes at Length Novatus' Crimes, and the Schism that Had Before Been Stirred Up by Him in Africa.

1. Cyprian to Cornelius his brother, greeting. You have acted, dearest brother, both with diligence and love, in sending us in haste Nicephorus the acolyte, who both told us the glorious gladness concerning the return of the confessors, and most fully instructed us against the new and mischievous devices of Novatian and Novatus for attacking the Church of Christ. For whereas on the day before, that mischievous faction of heretical wickedness had arrived here, itself already lost and ready to ruin

others who should join it, on the day after, Nicephorus arrived with your letter. From which we both learnt ourselves, and have begun to teach and to instruct others, that Evaristus from being a bishop has now not remained even a layman; but, banished from the see and from the people, and an exile from the Church of Christ, he roves about far and wide through other provinces, and, himself having made shipwreck of truth and faith, is preparing for some who are like him, as fearful shipwrecks. Moreover, that Nicostratus, having lost the diaconate of sacred administrations, because he had abstracted the Church's money by a sacrilegious fraud, and disowned the deposits of the widows and orphans, did not wish so much to come into Africa as to escape thither from the city, from the consciousness of his rapines and his frightful crimes. And now a deserter and a fugitive from the Church, as if to have changed the clime were to change the man, he goes on to boast and announce himself a confessor, although he can no longer either be or be called a confessor of Christ who has denied Christ's Church. For when the Apostle Paul says, "For this cause shall a man leave his father and mother and shall cleave unto his wife; and they two shall be one flesh. This is a great mystery; but I speak concerning Christ and the Church;"—when, I say, the blessed apostle says this, and with his sacred voice testifies to the unity of Christ with the Church, cleaving to one another with indivisible links, how can he be with Christ who is not with the spouse of Christ, and in His Church? Or how does he assume to himself the charge of ruling or governing the Church, who has spoiled and wronged the Church of Christ?

2. For about Novatus there need have been nothing told by you to us, since Novatus ought rather to

have been shown by us to you, as always greedy of novelty, raging with the rapacity of an insatiable avarice, inflated with the arrogance and stupidity of swelling pride; always known with bad repute to the bishops there; always condemned by the voice of all the priests as a heretic and a perfidious man; always inquisitive, that he may betray: he flatters for the purpose of deceiving, never faithful that he may love; a torch and fire to blow up the flames of sedition; a whirlwind and tempest to make shipwrecks of the faith; the foe of quiet, the adversary of tranquility, the enemy of peace. Finally, when Novatus withdrew thence from among you, that is, when the storm and the whirlwind departed, calm arose there in part, and the glorious and good confessors who by his instigation had departed from the Church, after he retired from the city, returned to the Church. This is the same Novatus who first sowed among us the flames of discord and schism; who separated some of the brethren here from the bishop; who, in the persecution itself, was to our people, as it were, another persecution, to overthrow the minds of the brethren. He it is who, without my leave or knowledge, of his own factiousness and ambition appointed his attendant Felicissimus a deacon, and with his own tempest sailing also to Rome to overthrow the Church, endeavored to do similar and equal things there, forcibly separating a part of the people from the clergy, and dividing the concord of the fraternity that was firmly knit together and mutually loving one another. Since Rome from her greatness plainly ought to take precedence of Carthage, he there committed still greater and graver crimes. He who in the one place had made a deacon contrary to the Church, in the other made a bishop. Nor let anyone be surprised at this in such men. The wicked are always madly carried away by their own furious passions; and after they have committed crimes, they are agitated by the very consciousness of a depraved mind. Neither can those remain in God's Church, who have not maintained its divine and ecclesiastical discipline, either in the conversation of their life or the peace of their character. Orphans despoiled by him, widows defrauded, money moreover of the Church withheld, exact from him those penalties which we behold inflicted in his madness. His father also died of hunger in the street, and afterwards even in death was not buried by him. The womb of his wife was smitten by a blow to his heel; and in the miscarriage that soon followed, the offspring was brought forth, the fruit of a father's murder. And now does he dare to condemn the hands of those who sacrifice, when he himself is more guilty in his feet, by which the son, who was about to be born, was slain?

3. He long ago feared this consciousness of crime. On account of this he regarded it as certain that he would not only be turned out of the presbytery, but restrained from communion; and by the urgency of the brethren, the day of investigation was coming on, on which his cause was to be dealt with before us, if the persecution had not prevented. He, welcoming this, with a sort of desire of escaping and evading condemnation, committed all these crimes, and wrought all this stir; so that he who was to be ejected and excluded from the Church, anticipated the judgment of the priests by a voluntary departure, as if to have anticipated the sentence were to have escaped the punishment.

4. But in respect to the other brethren, over whom we grieve that they were circumvented by him, we labor that they may avoid the mischievous neighborhood of the

crafty impostor, that they may escape the deadly nets of his solicitations, that they may once more seek the Church from which he deserved by divine authority to be expelled. Such indeed, with the Lord's help, we trust may return by His mercy, for one cannot perish unless it is plain that he must perish, since the Lord in His Gospel says, "Every planting which my heavenly Father hath not planted shall be rooted up." He alone who has not been planted in the precepts and warnings of God the Father, can depart from the Church: he alone can forsake the bishops and abide in his madness with schismatics and heretics. But the mercy of God the Father, and the indulgence of Christ our Lord, and our own patience, will unite the rest with us. I bid you, dearest brother, ever heartily farewell.

Epistle XLIX.
Maximus and the Other Confessors to Cyprian, About Their Return from Schism.
Argument.—They Inform Cyprian that They Had Returned to the Church. Maximus, Urbanus, Sidonius, and Macharius, to Cyprian their brother, greeting. We are certain, dearest brother, that you also rejoice together with us with equal earnestness, that we having taken advice, and especially, considering the interests and the peace of the Church, having passed by all other matters, and reserved them to God's judgment, have made peace with Cornelius our bishop, as well as with the whole clergy. You ought most certainly to know from these our letters that this was done with the joy of the whole Church, and even with the forward affection of the brethren. We pray, dearest brother, that for many years you may fare well.

Epistle L.
From Cyprian to the Confessors, Congratulating Them on Their Return from Schism.
Argument.—Cyprian Congratulates the Roman Confessors on Their Return into the Church and Replies to Their Letters.
1. Cyprian to Maximus the presbyter, also to Urbanus, and Sidonius, and Macharius, his brethren, greeting. When I read your letters, dearest brethren, that you wrote to me about your return, and about the peace of the Church, and the brotherly restoration, I confess that I was as greatly overjoyed as I had before been overjoyed when I learnt the glory of your confession, and thankfully received tidings of the heavenly and spiritual renown of your warfare. For this, moreover, is another confession of your faith and praise; to confess that the Church is one, and not to become a sharer in other men's error, or rather wickedness; to seek anew the same camp whence you went forth, whence with the most vigorous strength you leapt forth to wage the battle and to subdue the adversary. For the trophies from the battlefield ought to be brought back thither whence the arms for the field had been received, lest the Church of Christ should not retain those same glorious warriors whom Christ had furnished for glory. Now, however, you have kept in the peace of the Lord the fitting tenor of your faith and the law of undivided charity and concord, and have given by your walk an example of love and peace to others; so that the truth of the Church, and the unity of the Gospel mystery which is held by us, are also linked together by your consent and bond; and confessors of Christ do not become the leaders of error, after having stood forth as praiseworthy originators of virtue and honour.

2. Let others consider how much they may congratulate you, or how much each one may glory for himself: I confess that I congratulate you more, and I more boast of you to others, in respect of this your peaceful return and charity. For you ought in simplicity to hear what was in my heart. I grieved vehemently, and I was greatly afflicted, that I could not hold communion with those whom once I had begun to love. After the schismatical and heretical error laid hold of you, on your going forth from prison, it seemed as if your glory had been left in the dungeon. For there the dignity of your name seemed to have stayed behind when the soldiers of Christ did not return from the prison to the Church, although they had gone into the prison with the praise and congratulations of the Church.

3. For although there seem to be tares in the Church, yet neither our faith nor our charity ought to be hindered, so that because we see that there are tares in the Church we ourselves should withdraw from the Church: we ought only to labor that we may be wheat, that when the wheat shall begin to be gathered into the Lord's barns, we may receive fruit for our labor and work. The apostle in his epistle says, "In a great house there are not only vessels of gold and silver, but also of wood and of earth, and some to honour and some to dishonor." Let us strive, dearest brethren, and labor as much as we possibly can, that we may be vessels of gold or silver. But to the Lord alone it is granted to break the vessels of earth, to whom also is given the rod of iron. The servant cannot be greater than his lord, nor may any one claim to himself what the Father has given to the Son alone, so as to think that he can take the fan for winnowing and purging the threshing-floor or can separate by human judgment all the tares

from the wheat. That is a proud obstinacy and a sacrilegious presumption which a depraved madness assumes to itself. And while some are always assuming to themselves more dominion than meek justice demands, they perish from the Church; and while they insolently extol themselves, blinded by their own swelling, they lose the light of truth. For which reason we also, keeping moderation, and considering the Lord's balances, and thinking of the love and mercy of God the Father, have long and carefully pondered with ourselves, and have weighed what was to be done with due moderation.

4. All which matters you can look into thoroughly, if you will read the tracts which I have lately read here, and have, for the sake of our mutual love, transmitted to you also for you to read; wherein there is neither wanting for the lapsed, censure which may rebuke, nor medicine which may heal. Moreover, my feeble ability has expressed as well as it could the unity of the Catholic Church.2449 Which treatise I now more and more trust will be pleasing to you, since you now read it in such a way as both to approve and love it; inasmuch as what we have written in words you fulfil in deeds, when you return to the Church in the unity of charity and peace. I bid you, dearest brethren, and greatly longed-for, ever heartily farewell.

Epistle LI.
To Antonianus About Cornelius and Novatian.
Argument.—When Antonianus, Having Received Letters from Novatian, Had Begun to Be Disposed in His Mind Towards His Party, Cyprian Confirms Him in His

Former Opinion, Namely, that of Continuing to Hold Communion with His Bishop and So with the Catholic Church. He Excuses Himself for His Own Change of Opinion in Respect of the Lapsed, and at the End He Explains Wherein Consists the Novatian Heresy.

1. Cyprian to Antonianus his brother, greeting. I received your first letters, dearest brother, firmly maintaining the concord of the priestly college, and adhering to the Catholic Church, in which you intimated that you did not hold communion with Novatian, but followed my advice, and held one common agreement with Cornelius our co-bishop. You wrote, moreover, for me to transmit a copy of those same letters to Cornelius our colleague, so that he might lay aside all anxiety, and know at once that you held communion with him, that is, with the Catholic Church.

2. But subsequently there arrived other letters of yours sent by Quintus our co-presbyter, in which I observed that your mind, influenced by the letters of Novatian, had begun to waver. For although previously you had settled your opinion and consent firmly, you desired in these letters that I should write to you once more what heresy Novatian had introduced, or on what grounds Cornelius holds communion with Trophimus and the sacrificers. In which matters, indeed, if you are anxiously careful, from solicitude for the faith, and are diligently seeking out the truth of a doubtful matter, the hesitating anxiety of a mind undecided in the fear of God, is not to be blamed.

3. Yet, as I see that after the first opinion expressed in your letter, you have been disturbed subsequently by letters of Novatian, I assert this first of all, dearest brother, that grave men, and men who are

once established upon the strong rock with solid firmness, are not moved, I say not with a light air, but even with a wind or a tempest, lest their mind, changeable and uncertain, be frequently agitated hither and thither by various opinions, as by gusts of wind rushing on them, and so be turned from its purpose with some reproach of levity. That the letters of Novatian may not do this with you, nor with any one, I will set before you, as you have desired, my brother, an account of the matter in few words. And first of all indeed, as you also seem troubled about what I too have done, I must clear my own person and cause in your eyes, lest any should think that I have lightly withdrawn from my purpose, and while at first and at the commencement I maintained evangelical vigor, yet subsequently I seem to have turned my mind from discipline and from its former severity of judgment, so as to think that those who have stained their conscience with certificates, or have offered abominable sacrifices, are to have peace made easy to them. Both of which things have been done by me, not without long balanced and pondered reasons.

4. For when the battle was still going on, and the struggle of a glorious contest was raging in the persecution, the courage of the soldiers had to be excited with every exhortation, and with full urgency, and especially the minds of the lapsed had to be roused with the trumpet call, as it were, of my voice, that they might pursue the way of repentance, not only with prayers and lamentations; but, since an opportunity was given of repeating the struggle and of regaining salvation, that they might be reproved by my voice, and stimulated rather to the ardor of confession and the glory of martyrdom. Finally, when the presbyters and deacons had written to

me about some persons, that they were without moderation and were eagerly pressing forward to receive communion; replying to them in my letter which is still in existence, then I added also this: "If these are so excessively eager, they have what they require in their own power, the time itself providing for them more than they ask: the battle is still being carried on, and the struggle is daily celebrated: if they truly and substantially repent of what they have done, and the ardor of their faith prevails, he who cannot be delayed may be crowned." But I put off deciding what was to be arranged about the case of the lapsed, so that when quiet and tranquility should be granted, and the divine indulgence should allow the bishops to assemble into one place, then the advice gathered from the comparison of all opinions being communicated and weighed, we might determine what was necessary to be done. But if anyone, before our council, and before the opinion decided upon by the advice of all, should rashly wish to communicate with the lapsed, he himself should be withheld from communion.

5. And this also I wrote very fully to Rome, to the clergy who were then still acting without a bishop, and to the confessors, Maximus the presbyter, and the rest who were then shut up in prison, but are now in the Church, joined with Cornelius. You may know that I wrote this from their reply, for in their letter they wrote thus: "However, what you have yourself also declared in so important a matter is satisfactory to us, that the peace of the Church must first be maintained; then, that an assembly for counsel being gathered together, with bishop, presbyters, deacons, and confessors, as well as with the laity who stand fast, we should deal with the case of the lapsed." It was added also—Novatian then writing

and reciting with his own voice what he had written, and the presbyter Moyses, then still a confessor, but now a martyr, subscribing—that peace ought to be granted to the lapsed who were sick and at the point of departure. Which letter was sent throughout the whole world and was brought to the knowledge of all the churches and all the brethren.

6. According, however, to what had been before decided, when the persecution was quieted, and opportunity of meeting was afforded; a large number of bishops, whom their faith and the divine protection had preserved in soundness and safety, we met together; and the divine Scriptures being brought forward on both sides, we balanced the decision with wholesome moderation, so that neither should hope of communion and peace be wholly denied to the lapsed, lest they should fail still more through desperation, and, because the Church was closed to them, should, like the world, live as heathens; nor yet, on the other hand, should the censure of the Gospel be relaxed, so that they might rashly rush to communion, but that repentance should be long protracted, and the paternal clemency be sorrowfully besought, and the cases, and the wishes, and the necessities of individuals be examined into, according to what is contained in a little book, which I trust has come to you, in which the several heads of our decisions are collected. And lest perchance the number of bishops in Africa should seem unsatisfactory, we also wrote to Rome, to Cornelius our colleague, concerning this thing, who himself also holding a council with very many bishops, concurred in the same opinion as we had held, with equal gravity and wholesome moderation.

7. Concerning which it has now become necessary

to write to you, that you may know that I have done nothing lightly, but, according to what I had before comprised in my letters, had put off everything to the common determination of our council, and indeed communicated with no one of the lapsed as yet, so long as there still was an opening by which the lapsed might receive not only pardon, but also a crown. Yet afterwards, as the agreement of our college, and the advantage of gathering the fraternity together and of healing their wound required, I submitted to the necessity of the times, and thought that the safety of the many must be provided for; and I do not now recede from these things which have once been determined in our council by common agreement, although many things are ventilated by the voices of many, and lies against God's priests uttered from the devil's mouth, and tossed about everywhere, to the rupture of the concord of Catholic unity. But it behooves you, as a good brother and a fellow-priest likeminded, not easily to receive what malignants and apostates may say, but carefully to weigh what your colleagues, modest and grave men, may do, from an investigation of our life and teaching.

8. I come now, dearest brother, to the character of Cornelius our colleague, that with us you may more justly know Cornelius, not from the lies of malignants and detractors, but from the judgment of the Lord God, who made him a bishop, and from the testimony of his fellow-bishops, the whole number of whom has agreed with an absolute unanimity throughout the whole world. For,—a thing which with laudable announcement commends our dearest Cornelius to God and Christ, and to His Church, and also to all his fellow priests,—he was not one who on a sudden attained to the episcopate; but, promoted

through all the ecclesiastical offices, and having often deserved well of the Lord in divine administrations, he ascended by all the grades of religious service to the lofty summit of the Priesthood. Then, moreover, he did not either ask for the episcopate itself, nor did he wish it; nor, as others do when the swelling of their arrogance and pride inflates them, did he seize upon it; but quiet otherwise, and meek and such as those are accustomed to be who are chosen of God to this office, having regard to the modesty of his virgin continency, and the humility of his inborn and guarded veneration, he did not, as some do, use force to be made a bishop, but he himself suffered compulsion, so as to be forced to receive the episcopal office. And he was made bishop by very many of our colleagues who were then present in the city of Rome, who sent to us letters concerning his ordination, honorable and laudatory, and remarkable for their testimony in announcement of him. Moreover, Cornelius was made bishop by the judgment of God and of His Christ, by the testimony of almost all the clergy, by the suffrage of the people who were then present, and by the assembly of ancient priests and good men, when no one had been made so before him, when the place of Fabian, that is, when the place of Peter and the degree of the sacerdotal throne was vacant; which being occupied by the will of God, and established by the consent of all of us, whosoever now wishes to become a bishop, must needs be made from without; and he cannot have the ordination of the Church who does not hold the unity of the Church. Whoever he may be, although greatly boasting about himself, and claiming very much for himself, he is profane, he is an alien, he is without. And as after the first there cannot be a second, whosoever is made after one who ought to be alone, is not second to him, but is in fact none at all.

9. Then afterwards, when he had undertaken the episcopate, not obtained by solicitation nor by extortion, but by the will of God who makes priests; what a virtue there was in the very undertaking of his episcopate, what strength of mind, what firmness of faith,—a thing that we ought with simple heart both thoroughly to look into and to praise,—that he intrepidly sate at Rome in the sacerdotal chair at that time when a tyrant, odious to God's priests, was threatening things that can, and cannot be spoken, inasmuch as he would much more patiently and tolerantly hear that a rival prince was raised up against himself than that a priest of God was established at Rome. Is not this man, dearest brother, to be commended with the highest testimony of virtue and faith? Is not he to be esteemed among the glorious confessors and martyrs, who for so long a time sate awaiting the manglers of his body and the avengers of a ferocious tyrant, who, when Cornelius resisted their deadly edicts, and trampled on their threats and sufferings and tortures by the vigor of his faith, would either rush upon him with the sword, or crucify him, or scorch him with fire, or rend his bowels and his limbs with some unheard-of kind of punishment? Even though the majesty and goodness of the protecting Lord guarded, when made, the priest whom He willed to be made; yet Cornelius, in what pertains to his devotion and fear, suffered whatever he could suffer, and conquered the tyrant first of all by his priestly office, who was afterwards conquered in arms and in war.

10. But in respect to certain discreditable and malignant things that are bandied about concerning him, I

would not have you wonder when you know that this is always the work of the devil, to wound God's servants with lies, and to defame a glorious name by false opinions, so that they who are bright in the light of their own conscience may be tarnished by the reports of others. Moreover, you are to know that our colleagues have investigated, and have certainly discovered that he has been blemished with no stain of a certificate, as some intimate; neither has he mingled in sacrilegious communion with the bishops who have sacrificed, but has merely associated with us those whose cause had been heard, and whose innocence was approved.

11. For with respect to Trophimus also, of whom you wished tidings to be written to you, the case is not as the report and the falsehood of malignant people had conveyed it to you. For, as our predecessors often did, our dearest brother, in bringing together the brethren, yielded to necessity; and since a very large part of the people had withdrawn with Trophimus, now when Trophimus returned to the Church, and atoned for, and with the penitence of prayer confessed his former error, and with perfect humility and satisfaction recalled the brotherhood whom he had lately taken away, his prayers were heard; and not only Trophimus, but a very great number of brethren who had been with Trophimus, were admitted into the Church of the Lord, who would not all have returned to the Church unless they had come in Trophimus' company. Therefore, the matter being considered there with several colleagues, Trophimus was received, for whom the return of the brethren and salvation restored to many made atonement. Yet Trophimus was admitted in such a manner as only to communicate as a layman, not, according to the

information given to you by the letters of the malignants, in such a way as to assume the place of a priest.

12. But, moreover, in respect of what has been told you, that Cornelius communicates everywhere with those who have sacrificed, this intelligence has also arisen from the false reports of the apostates. For neither can they praise us who depart from us, nor ought we to expect to please them, who, while they displease us, and revolt against the Church, violently persist in soliciting brethren away from the Church. Wherefore, dearest brethren, do not with facility either hear or believe whatever is currently rumored against Cornelius and about me.

13. For if any are seized with sicknesses, help is given to them in danger, as it has been decided. Yet after they have been assisted, and peace has been granted to them in their danger, they cannot be suffocated by us, or destroyed, or by our force or hands urged on to the result of death; as if, because peace is granted to the dying, it were necessary that those who have received peace should die; although the token of divine love and paternal lenity appears more in this way, that they, who in peace given to them receive the pledge of life, are moreover here bound to life by the peace they have received. And therefore, if with peace received, a reprieve is given by God, no one ought to complain of the priests for this, when once it has been decided that brethren are to be aided in peril. Neither must you think, dearest brother, as some do, that those who receive certificates are to be put on a par with those who have sacrificed; since even among those who have sacrificed, the condition and the case are frequently different. For we must not place on a level one who has at once leapt forward with good-will to the abominable sacrifice, and one who, after long struggle and resistance,

has reached that fatal result under compulsion; one who has betrayed both himself and all his connections, and one who, himself approaching the trial in behalf of all, has protected his wife and his children, and his whole family, by himself undergoing the danger; one who has compelled his inmates or friends to the crime, and one who has spared inmates and servants, and has even received many brethren who were departing to banishment and flight, into his house and hospitality; showing and offering to the Lord many souls living and safe to entreat for a single wounded one.

14. Since, then, there is much difference between those who have sacrificed, what a want of mercy it is, and how bitter is the hardship, to associate those who have received certificates, with those who have sacrificed, when he by whom the certificate has been received may say, "I had previously read, and had been made aware by the discourse of the bishop, that we must not sacrifice to idols, that the servant of God ought not to worship images; and therefore, in order that I might not do this which was not lawful, when the opportunity of receiving a certificate was offered, which itself also I should not have received, unless the opportunity had been put before me, I either went or charged some other person going to the magistrate, to say that I am a Christian, that I am not allowed to sacrifice, that I cannot come to the devil's altars, and that I pay a price for this purpose, that I may not do what is not lawful for me to do." Now, however, even he who is stained with having received a certificate,—after he has learnt from our admonitions that he ought not even to have done this, and that although his hand is pure, and no contact of deadly food has polluted his lips, yet his conscience is nevertheless polluted, weeps

when he hears us, and laments, and is now admonished of the thing wherein he has sinned, and having been deceived, not so much by guilt as by error, bears witness that for another time he is instructed and prepared.

15. If we reject the repentance of those who have some confidence in a conscience that may be tolerated; at once with their wife, with their children, whom they had kept safe, they are hurried by the devil's invitation into heresy or schism; and it will be attributed to us in the day of judgment, that we have not cared for the wounded sheep, and that on account of a single wounded one we have lost many sound ones. And whereas the Lord left the ninety and nine that were whole, and sought after the one wandering and weary, and Himself carried it, when found, upon His shoulders, we not only do not seek the lapsed, but even drive them away when they come to us; and while false prophets are not ceasing to lay waste and tear Christ's flock, we give an opportunity to dogs and wolves, so that those whom a hateful persecution has not destroyed, we ruin by our hardness and inhumanity. And what will become, dearest brother, of what the apostle says: "I please all men in all things, not seeking mine own profit, but the profit of many, that they may be saved. Be ye followers of me, as I also am of Christ." And again: "To the weak I became as weak, that I might gain the weak." And again: "Whether one member suffer, all the members suffer with it; or one member rejoice, all the members rejoice with it."

16. The principle of the philosophers and stoics is different, dearest brother, who say that all sins are equal, and that a grave man ought not easily to be moved. But there is a wide difference between Christians and philosophers. And when the apostle says, "Beware, lest

any man spoil you through philosophy and vain deceit," we are to avoid those things which do not come from God's clemency but are begotten of the presumption of a too rigid philosophy. Concerning Moses, moreover, we find it said in the Scriptures, "Now the man Moses was very meek;" and the Lord in His Gospel says, "Be ye merciful, as your Father also had mercy upon you;" and again, "They that be whole need not a physician, but they that are sick." What medical skill can he exercise who says, "I cure the sound only, who have no need of a physician?" We ought to give our assistance, our healing art, to those who are wounded; neither let us think them dead, but rather let us regard them as lying half alive, whom we see to have been wounded in the fatal persecution, and who, if they had been altogether dead, would never from the same men become afterwards both confessors and martyrs.

17. But since in them there is that, which, by subsequent repentance, may be strengthened into faith; and by repentance strength is armed to virtue, which could not be armed if one should fall away through despair; if, hardly and cruelly separated from the Church, he should turn himself to Gentile ways and to worldly works, or, if rejected by the Church, he should pass over to heretics and schismatics; where, although he should afterwards be put to death on account of the name, still, being placed outside the Church, and divided from unity and from charity, he could not in his death be crowned. And therefore it was decided, dearest brother, the case of each individual having been examined into, that the receivers of certificates should in the meantime be admitted, that those who had sacrificed should be assisted at death, because there is no confession in the place of the

departed, nor can anyone be constrained by us to repentance, if the fruit of repentance be taken away. If the battle should come first, strengthened by us, he will be found ready armed for the battle; but if sickness should press hard upon him before the battle, he departs with the consolation of peace and communion.

18. Moreover, we do not prejudge when the Lord is to be the judge; save that if He shall find the repentance of the sinners full and sound, He will then ratify what shall have been here determined by us. If, however, any one should delude us with the pretense of repentance, God, who is not mocked, and who looks into man's heart, will judge of those things which we have imperfectly looked into, and the Lord will amend the sentence of His servants; while yet, dearest brother, we ought to remember that it is written, "A brother that helps a brother shall be exalted;" and that the apostle also has said, "Let all of you severally have regard to yourselves, lest ye also be tempted. Bear ye one another's burdens, and so fulfil the law of Christ;" also that, rebuking the haughty, and breaking down their arrogance, he says in his epistle, "Let him that thinks he stands, take heed lest he fall;" and in another place he says, "Who art thou that judges another man's servant? To his own master he stands or falls; yea, he shall stand, for God is able to make him stand." John also proves that Jesus Christ the Lord is our Advocate and Intercessor for our sins, saying, "My little children, these things write I unto you, that ye sin not. And if any man sin, we have an Advocate with the Father, Jesus Christ the Supporter: and He is the propitiation for our sins." And Paul also, the apostle, in his epistle, has written, "If, while we were yet sinners, Christ died for us; much more, being now justified by His blood, we shall be saved from wrath

through Him."

19. Considering His love and mercy, we ought not to be so bitter, nor cruel, nor inhuman in cherishing the brethren, but to mourn with those that mourn, and to weep with them that weep, and to raise them up as much as we can by the help and comfort of our love; neither being too ungentle and pertinacious in repelling their repentance; nor, again, being too lax and easy in rashly yielding communion. Lo! a wounded brother lies stricken by the enemy in the field of battle. There the devil is striving to slay him whom he has wounded; here Christ is exhorting that he whom He has redeemed may not wholly perish. Whether of the two do we assist? On whose side do we stand? Whether do we favor the devil, that he may destroy, and pass by our prostrate lifeless brother, as in the Gospel did the priest and Levite; or rather, as priests of God and Christ, do we imitate what Christ both taught and did, and snatch the wounded man from the jaws of the enemy, that we may preserve him cured for God the judge?

20. And do not think, dearest brother, that either the courage of the brethren will be lessened, or that martyrdoms will fail for this cause, that repentance is relaxed to the lapsed, and that the hope of peace is offered to the penitent. The strength of the truly believing remains unshaken; and with those who fear and love God with their whole heart, their integrity continues steady and strong. For to adulterers even a time of repentance is granted by us, and peace is given. Yet virginity is not therefore deficient in the Church, nor does the glorious design of continence languish through the sins of others. The Church, crowned with so many virgins, flourishes; and chastity and modesty preserve the tenor of their glory.

Nor is the vigor of continence broken down because repentance and pardon are facilitated to the adulterer. It is one thing to stand for pardon, another thing to attain glory: it is one thing, when cast into prison, not to go out thence until one has paid the uttermost farthing; another thing at once to receive the wages of faith and courage. It is one thing, tortured by long suffering for sins, to be cleansed and long purged by fire; another to have purged all sins by suffering. It is one thing, in fine, to be in suspense till the sentence of God at the day of judgment; another to be at once crowned by the Lord.

21. And, indeed, among our predecessors, some of the bishops here in our province thought that peace was not to be granted to adulterers, and wholly closed the gate of repentance against adultery. Still, they did not withdraw from the assembly of their co-bishops, nor break the unity of the Catholic Church by the persistency of their severity or censure; so that, because by some peace was granted to adulterers, he who did not grant it should be separated from the Church. While the bond of concord remains, and the undivided sacrament of the Catholic Church endures, every bishop disposes and directs his own acts, and will have to give an account of his purposes to the Lord.

22. But I wonder that some are so obstinate as to think that repentance is not to be granted to the lapsed, or to suppose that pardon is to be denied to the penitent, when it is written, "Remember whence thou art fallen, and repent, and do the first works," which certainly is said to him who evidently has fallen, and whom the Lord exhorts to rise up again by his works, because it is written, "Alms do deliver from death," and not, assuredly, from that death which once the blood of Christ

extinguished, and from which the saving grace of baptism and of our Redeemer has delivered us, but from that which subsequently creeps in through sins. Moreover, in another place time is granted for repentance; and the Lord threatens him that does not repent: "I have," saith He, "many things against thee, because thou suffers thy wife Jezebel, which calleth herself a prophetess, to teach and to seduce my servants to commit fornication, and to eat things sacrificed to idols; and I gave her a space to repent, and she will not repent of her fornication. Behold, I will cast her into a bed, and them that commit adultery with her into great tribulation, except they repent of their deeds;" whom certainly the Lord would not exhort to repentance, if it were not that He promises mercy to them that repent. And in the Gospel He says, "I say unto you, that likewise joy shall be in heaven over one sinner that repented, more than over ninety and nine just persons that need no repentance." For since it is written, "God did not make death, neither hath He pleasure in the destruction of the living," assuredly He who wills that none should perish, desires that sinners should repent, and by repentance should return again to life. Thus also He cries by Joel the prophet, and says, "And now, thus saith the Lord your God, Turn ye even to me with all your heart, and with fasting, and with weeping, and with mourning; and rend your heart, and not your garments, and return unto the Lord your God; for He is gracious and merciful, slow to anger, and of great kindness, and repented Him of the evil appointed." In the Psalms, also, we read as well the rebuke as the clemency of God, threatening at the same time as He spares, punishing that He may correct; and when He has corrected, preserving. "I will visit," He says, "their transgressions with the rod, and their iniquity with stripes. Nevertheless, my loving-kindness will I not utterly take from them."

23. The Lord also in His Gospel, setting forth the love of God the Father, says, "What man is there of you, whom, if his son ask bread, will he give him a stone? or if he ask a fish, will he give him a serpent? If ye then, being evil, know how to give good gifts unto your children, how much more shall your heavenly Father give good things to them that ask Him?" The Lord is here comparing the father after the flesh, and the eternal and liberal love of God the Father. But if that evil father upon earth, deeply offended by a sinful and evil son, yet if he should see the same son afterwards reformed, and, the sins of his former life being put away, restored to sobriety and morality and to the discipline of innocence by the sorrow of his repentance, both rejoices and gives thanks, and with the eagerness of a father's exultation, embraces the restored one, whom before he had cast out; how much more does that one and true Father, good, merciful, and loving—yea, Himself Goodness and Mercy and Love—rejoice in the repentance of His own sons! nor threatens punishment to those who are now repenting, or mourning and lamenting, but rather promises pardon and clemency. Whence the Lord in the Gospel calls those that mourn, blessed; because he who mourns calls forth mercy. He who is stubborn and haughty heaps up wrath against himself, and the punishment of the coming judgment. And therefore, dearest brother, we have decided that those who do not repent, nor give evidence of sorrow for their sins with their whole heart, and with manifest profession of their lamentation, are to be absolutely restrained from the hope of communion and peace if they begin to beg for them in the midst of sickness and peril; because it is not

repentance for sin, but the warning of urgent death, that drives them to ask; and he is not worthy to receive consolation in death who has not reflected that he was about to die.

24. In reference, however, to the character of Novatian, dearest brother, of whom you desired that intelligence should be written you what heresy he had introduced; know that, in the first place, we ought not even to be inquisitive as to what he teaches, so long as he teaches out of the pale of unity. Whoever he may be, and whatever he may be, he who is not in the Church of Christ is not a Christian. Although he may boast himself, and announce his philosophy or eloquence with lofty words, yet he who has not maintained brotherly love or ecclesiastical unity has lost even what he previously had been. Unless he seems to you to be a bishop, who—when a bishop has been made in the Church by sixteen co-bishops—strives by bribery to be made an adulterous and extraneous bishop by the hands of deserters; and although there is one Church, divided by Christ throughout the whole world into many members, and also one episcopate diffused through a harmonious multitude of many bishops; in spite of God's tradition, in spite of the combined and everywhere compacted unity of the Catholic Church, is endeavoring to make a human church, and is sending his new apostles through very many cities, that he may establish some new foundations of his own appointment. And although there have already been ordained in each city, and through all the provinces, bishops old in years, sound in faith, proved in trial, proscribed in persecution, (this one) dares to create over these other and false bishops: as if he could either wander over the whole world with the persistence of his new

endeavor, or break asunder the structure of the ecclesiastical body, by the propagation of his own discord, not knowing that schismatics are always fervid at the beginning, but that they cannot increase nor add to what they have unlawfully begun, but that they immediately fail together with their evil emulation. But he could not hold the episcopate, even if he had before been made bishop, since he has cut himself off from the body of his fellow-bishops, and from the unity of the Church; since the apostle admonishes that we should mutually sustain one another, and not withdraw from the unity which God has appointed, and says, "Bearing with one another in love, endeavoring to keep the unity of the Spirit in the bond of peace." He then who neither maintains the unity of the Spirit nor the bond of peace, and separates himself from the band of the Church, and from the assembly of priests, can neither have the power nor the honour of a bishop, since he has refused to maintain either the unity or the peace of the episcopate.

25. Then, moreover, what a swelling of arrogance it is, what oblivion of humility and gentleness, what a boasting of his own arrogance, that any one should either dare, or think that he is able, to do what the Lord did not even grant to the apostles; that he should think that he can discern the tares from the wheat, or, as if it were granted to him to bear the fan and to purge the threshing-floor, should endeavor to separate the chaff from the wheat; and since the apostle says, "But in a great house there are not only vessels of gold and of silver, but also of wood and of earth," should think to choose the vessels of gold and of silver, to despise, to cast away, and to condemn the vessels of wood and of clay; while the vessels of wood are not burnt up except in the day of the Lord by the

flame of the divine burning, and the vessels of clay are only broken by Him to whom is given the rod of iron.

26. Or if he appoints himself a searcher and judge of the heart and reins, let him in all cases judge equally. And as he knows that it is written, "Behold, thou art made whole; sin no more, lest a worse thing happen unto thee," let him separate the fraudulent and adulterers from his side and from his company, since the case of an adulterer is by far both graver and worse than that of one who has taken a certificate, because the latter has sinned by necessity, the former by free will: the latter, thinking that it is sufficient for him that he has not sacrificed, has been deceived by an error; the former, a violator of the matrimonial tie of another, or entering a brothel, into the sink and filthy gulf of the common people, has befouled by detestable impurity a sanctified body and God's temple, as says the apostle: "Every sin that a man does is without the body, but he that commits fornication sins against his own body." And yet to these persons themselves repentance is granted, and the hope of lamenting and atoning is left, according to the saying of the same apostle: "I fear lest, when I come to you, I shall bewail many of those who have sinned already, and have not repented of the uncleanness, and fornication, and lasciviousness which they have committed."

27. Neither let the new heretics flatter themselves in this, that they say that they do not communicate with idolaters; although among them there are both adulterers and fraudulent persons, who are held guilty of the crime of idolatry, according to the saying of the apostle: "For know this with understanding, that no whoremonger, nor unclean person, nor covetous man, whose guilt is that of idolatry, hath any inheritance in the kingdom of Christ

and of God." And again: "Mortify therefore your members which are upon the earth; putting off fornication, uncleanness, and evil concupiscence, and covetousness, which are the service of idols: for which things' sake cometh the wrath of God." For as our bodies are members of Christ, and we are each a temple of God, whosoever violates the temple of God by adultery, violates God; and he who, in committing sins, does the will of the devil, serves demons and idols. For evil deeds do not come from the Holy Spirit, but from the prompting of the adversary, and lusts born of the unclean spirit constrain men to act against God and to obey the devil. Thus it happens that if they say that one is polluted by another's sin, and if they contend, by their own asseveration, that the idolatry of the delinquent passes over to one who is not guilty according to their own word; they cannot be excused from the crime of idolatry, since from the apostolic proof it is evident that the adulterers and defrauders with whom they communicate are idolaters. But with us, according to our faith and the given rule of divine preaching, agrees the principle of truth, that everyone is himself held fast in his own sin; nor can one become guilty for another, since the Lord forewarns us, saying, "The righteousness of the righteous shall be upon him, and the wickedness of the wicked shall be upon him." And again: "The fathers shall not die for the children, and the children shall not die for the fathers. Everyone shall die in his own sin." Reading and observing this, we certainly think that no one is to be restrained from the fruit of satisfaction, and the hope of peace, since we know, according to the faith of the divine Scriptures, God Himself being their author, and exhorting in them, both that sinners are brought back to repentance, and that pardon and mercy are not denied to penitents.

28. And oh, mockery of a deceived fraternity! Oh, vain deception of miserable and senseless mourners! Oh, ineffectual and profitless tradition of heretical institution! to exhort to the repentance of atonement, and to take away the healing from the atonement; to say to our brethren, "Mourn and shed tears, and groan day and night, and labor largely and frequently for the washing away and cleansing of your sin; but, after all these things, you shall die without the pale of the Church. Whatsoever things are necessary to peace, you shall do, but none of that peace which you seek shall you receive!" Who would not perish at once? Who would not fall away from very desperation? Who would not turn away his mind from all design of lamentation? Do you think that the husbandman could labor if you should say, "Till the field with all the skill of husbandry, diligently persevere in its cultivation; but you shall reap no harvest, you shall press no vintage, you shall receive no fruits of your olive-yard, you shall gather no apples from the trees;" or if, urging upon any one the possession and use of ships, you were to say, "Purchase, my brother, material from excellent woods; inweave your keel with the strongest and chosen oak; labor on the rudder, the ropes, the sails, that the ship may be constructed and fitted; but when you have done this, you shall never behold the result from its doings and its voyages?"

29. This is to shut up and to cut off the way of grief and of repentance; so that while in all Scripture the Lord God sooths those who return to Him and repent, repentance itself is taken away by our hardness and cruelty, which intercepts the fruits of repentance. But if we find that none ought to be restrained from repenting,

and that peace may be granted by His priests to those who entreat and beseech the Lord's mercy, inasmuch as He is merciful and loving, the groaning of those who mourn is to be admitted, and the fruit of repentance is not to be denied to those who grieve. And because in the place of the departed there is no confession, neither can confession be made there, they who have repented from their whole heart, and have asked for it, ought to be received within the Church, and to be kept in it for the Lord, who will of a surety judge, when He comes to His Church, those whom He shall find within it. But apostates and deserters, or adversaries and enemies, and those who lay waste the Church of Christ, cannot, even if outside the Church they have been slain for His name, according to the apostle, be admitted to the peace of the Church, since they have neither kept the unity of the spirit nor of the Church.

30. These few things for the present, out of many, dearest brother, I have run over as briefly as I could, that I might thereby both satisfy your desire, and might link you more and more closely to the society of our college and body. But if there should arise to you an opportunity and power of coming to us, we shall be able to confer more fully together, and to consider more fruitfully and more at large the things which make for a salutary agreement. I bid you, dearest brother, ever heartily farewell.

Epistle LII.
To Fortunatus and His Other Colleagues, Concerning Those Who Had Been Overcome by Tortures.
Argument.—Cyprian Being Consulted by His

Colleagues, Whether Certain Lapsed Persons Who Had Been Overpowered by Torture Should Be Admitted to Communion, Replies, that Inasmuch as They Had Already Repented for the Space of Three Years, He Thought They Should Be Received; But as After the Festival of Easter There Would Be a Council of Bishops with Him, He Would Then Consider the Matter with Them.

1. Cyprian to Fortunatus, Ahymnus, Optatus, Privatianus, Donatulus, and Felix, his brethren, greeting. You have written to me, dearest brethren, that when you were in the city of Capsa for the purpose of ordaining a bishop, Superius, our brother and colleague brought before you, that Ninus, Clementianus, and Florus, our brethren, who had been previously laid hold of in the persecution, and confessing the name of the Lord, had overcome the violence of the magistracy, and the attack of a raging populace, afterwards, when they were tortured before the proconsul with severe sufferings, were vanquished by the acuteness of the torments, and fell, through their lengthened agonies, from the degree of glory to which in the full virtue of faith they were tending, and after this grave lapse, incurred not willingly but of necessity, had not yet ceased their repentance for the space of three years: of whom you thought it right to consult whether it was well to receive them now to communion.

2. And indeed, in respect of my own opinion, I think that the Lord's mercy will not be wanting to those who are known to have stood in the ranks of battle, to have confessed the name, to have overcome the violence of the magistrates and the rush of the raging populace with the persistency of unshaken faith, to have suffered

imprisonment, to have long resisted, amidst the threats of the proconsul and the warring of the surrounding people, torments that wrenched and tore them with protracted repetition; so that in the last moment to have been vanquished by the infirmity of the flesh, may be extenuated by the plea of preceding deserts. And it may be sufficient for such to have lost their glory, but that we ought not, moreover, to close the place of pardon to them, and deprive them of their Father's love and of our communion; to whom we think it may be sufficient for entreating the mercy of the Lord, that for three years continually and sorrowfully, as you write, they have lamented with excessive penitential mourning. Assuredly I do not think that peace is incautiously and over-hastily granted to those, who by the bravery of their warfare, have not, we see, been previously wanting to the battle; and who, if the struggle should come on anew, might be able to regain their glory. For when it was decided in the council that penitents in peril of sickness should be assisted, and have peace granted to them, surely those ought to precede in receiving peace whom we see not to have fallen by weakness of mind, but who, having engaged in the conflict, and being wounded, have not been able to sustain the crown of their confession through weakness of the flesh; especially since, in their desire to die, they were not permitted to be slain, but the tortures wrenched their wearied frames long enough, not to conquer their faith, which is unconquerable, but to exhaust the flesh, which is weak.

3. Since, however, you have written for me to give full consideration to this matter with many of my colleagues; and so great a subject claims greater and more careful counsel from the conference of many; and as now

almost all, during the first celebrations of Easter, are dwelling at home with their brethren: when they shall have completed the solemnity to be celebrated among their own people, and have begun to come to me, I will consider it more at large with each one, so that a decided opinion, weighed in the council of many priests, on the subject on which you have consulted me, may be established among us, and may be written to you. I bid you, dearest brethren, ever heartily farewell.

Epistle LIII.
To Cornelius, Concerning Granting Peace to the Lapsed.

Argument.—Cyprian Announces This Decree of the Bishops in the Name of the Whole Synod to Father Cornelius; And Therefore This Letter is Not So Much the Letter of Cyprian Himself, as that of the Entire African Synod. Cyprian, Liberalis, Caldonius, Nicomedes, Cæcilius, Junius, Marrutius, Felix, Successus, Faustinus, Fortunatus, Victor, Saturninus, another Saturninus, Rogatianus, Tertullus, Lucianus, Eutyches, Amplus, Sattius, Secundinus, another Saturninus, Aurelius, Priscus, Herculanus, Victoricus, Quintus, Honoratus, Montanus, Hortensianus, Verianus, Iambus, Donatus, Pompeius, Polycarpus, Demetrius, another Donatus, Privatianus, another Fortunatus, Rogatus and Monulus, to Cornelius their brother, greeting.

1. We had indeed decided some time ago, dearest brother, having mutually taken counsel one with another, that they who, in the fierceness of persecution, had been overthrown by the adversary, and had lapsed, and had polluted themselves with unlawful sacrifices, should undergo a long and full repentance; and if the risk of

sickness should be urgent, should receive peace on the very point of death. For it was not right, neither did the love of the Father nor divine mercy allow, that the Church should be closed to those that knock, or the help of the hope of salvation be denied to those who mourn and entreat, so that when they pass from this world, they should be dismissed to their Lord without communion and peace; since He Himself who gave the law, that things which were bound on earth should also be bound in heaven, allowed, moreover, that things might be loosed there which were here first loosed in the Church. But now, when we see that the day of another trouble is again beginning to draw near, and are admonished by frequent and repeated intimations that we should be prepared and armed for the struggle which the enemy announces to us, that we should also prepare the people committed to us by divine condescension, by our exhortations, and gather together from all parts all the soldiers of Christ who desire arms, and are anxious for the battle within the Lord's camp: under the compulsion of this necessity, we have decided that peace is to be given to those who have not withdrawn from the Church of the Lord, but have not ceased from the first day of their lapse to repent, and to lament, and to beseech the Lord; and we have decided that they ought to be armed and equipped for the battle which is at hand.

2. For we must comply with fitting intimations and admonitions, that the sheep may not be deserted in danger by the shepherds, but that the whole flock may be gathered together into one place, and the Lord's army may be arrived for the contest of the heavenly warfare. For the repentance of the mourners was reasonably prolonged for a more protracted time, help only being

afforded to the sick in their departure, so long as peace and tranquility prevailed, which permitted the long postponement of the tears of the mourners, and late assistance in sickness to the dying. But now indeed peace is necessary, not for the sick, but for the strong; nor is communion to be granted by us to the dying, but to the living, that we may not leave those whom we stir up and exhort to the battle unarmed and naked, but may fortify them with the protection of Christ's body and blood. And, as the Eucharist is appointed for this very purpose that it may be a safeguard to the receivers, it is needful that we may arm those whom we wish to be safe against the adversary with the protection of the Lord's abundance. For how do we teach or provoke them to shed their blood in confession of His name, if we deny to those who are about to enter on the warfare the blood of Christ? Or how do we make them fit for the cup of martyrdom, if we do not first admit them to drink, in the Church, the cup of the Lord by the right of communion?

3. We should make a difference, dearest brother, between those who either have apostatized, and, having returned to the world which they have renounced, are living heathenish lives, or, having become deserters to the heretics, are daily taking up parricidal arms against the Church; and those who do not depart from the Church's threshold, and, constantly and sorrowfully imploring divine and paternal consolation, profess that they are now prepared for the battle, and ready to stand and fight bravely for the name of their Lord and for their own salvation. In these times we grant peace, not to those who sleep, but to those who watch. We grant peace, not amid indulgences, but amid arms. We grant peace, not for rest, but for the field of battle. If, according to what we hear,

and desire, and believe of them, they shall stand bravely, and shall overthrow the adversary with us in the encounter, we shall not repent of having granted peace to men so brave. Yea, it is the great honour and glory of our episcopate to have granted peace to martyrs, so that we, as priests, who daily celebrate the sacrifices of God, may prepare offerings and victims for God. But if—which may the Lord avert from our brethren—any one of the lapsed should deceive, seeking peace by guile, and at the time of the impending struggle receiving peace without any purpose of doing battle, he betrays and deceives himself, hiding one thing in his heart and pronouncing another with his voice. We, so far as it is allowed to us to see and to judge, look upon the face of each one; we are not able to scrutinize the heart and to inspect the mind. Concerning these the Discerner and Searcher of hidden things judges, and He will quickly come and judge of the secrets and hidden things of the heart. But the evil ought not to stand in the way of the good, but rather the evil ought to be assisted by the good. Neither is peace, therefore, to be denied to those who are about to endure martyrdom, because there are some who will refuse it, since for this purpose peace should be granted to all who are about to enter upon the warfare, that through our ignorance he may not be the first one to be passed over, who in the struggle is to be crowned.

4. Nor let anyone say, "that he who accepts martyrdom is baptized in his own blood, and peace is not necessary to him from the bishop, since he is about to have the peace of his own glory, and about to receive a greater reward from the condescension of the Lord." First of all, he cannot be fitted for martyrdom who is not armed for the contest by the Church; and his spirit is deficient

which the Eucharist received does not raise and stimulate. For the Lord says in His Gospel: "But when they deliver you up, take no thought what ye shall speak; for it shall be given you in that hour what ye shall speak. For it is not ye that speak, but the Spirit of your Father which speaks in you." Now, since He says that the Spirit of the Father speaks in those who are delivered up and set in the confession of His name, how can he be found prepared or fit for that confession who has not first, in the reception of peace, received the Spirit of the Father, who, giving strength to His servants, Himself speaks and confesses in us? Then, besides—if, having forsaken everything that he has, a man shall flee, and dwelling in hiding-places and in solitude, shall fall by chance among thieves, or shall die in fever and in weakness, will it not be charged upon us that so good a soldier, who has forsaken all that he hath, and contemning his house, and his parents, and his children, has preferred to follow his Lord, dies without peace and without communion? Will not either inactive negligence or cruel hardness be ascribed to us in the day of judgment, that, pastors though we are, we have neither been willing to take care of the sheep trusted and committed to us in peace, nor to arm them in battle? Would not the charge be brought against us by the Lord, which by His prophet He utters and says? "Behold, ye consume the milk, and ye clothe you with the wool, and ye kill them that are fed; but ye feed not my flock. The weak have ye not strengthened, neither have ye healed that which was sick, neither have ye comforted that which was broken, neither have ye brought again that which strayed, neither have ye sought that which was lost, and that which was strong ye wore out with labor. And my sheep were scattered, because there were no shepherds:

and they became meat to all the beasts of the field; and there was none who sought after them, nor brought them back. Therefore thus saith the Lord, Behold, I am against the shepherds; and I will require my sheep of their hand, and cause them to cease from feeding my sheep; neither shall they feed them any more: and I will deliver my sheep from their mouth, and I will feed them with judgment."

5. Lest, then, the sheep committed to us by the Lord be demanded back from our mouth, wherewith we deny peace, wherewith we oppose to them rather the severity of human cruelty than the benignity of divine and paternal love; we have determined by the suggestion of the Holy Spirit and the admonition of the Lord, conveyed by many and manifest visions, because the enemy is foretold and shown to be at hand, to gather within the camp the soldiers of Christ, to examine the cases of each one, and to grant peace to the lapsed, yea, rather to furnish arms to those who are about to fight. And this, we trust, will please you in contemplation of the paternal mercy. But if there be any (one) of our colleagues who, now that the contest is urgent, thinks that peace should not be granted to our brethren and sisters, he shall give an account to the Lord in the day of judgment, either of his grievous rigour or of his inhuman hardness. We, as befitted our faith and charity and solicitude, have laid before you what was in our own mind, namely, that the day of contest has approached, that a violent enemy will soon rise up against us, that a struggle is coming on, not such as it has been, but much more serious and fierce. This is frequently shown to us from above; concerning this we are often admonished by the providence and mercy of the Lord, of whose help and love we who trust

in Him may be secure, because He who in peace foretells to His soldiers that the battle will come, will give to them when they are warring victory in the encounter. We bid you, dearest brother, ever heartily farewell.

Epistle LIV.
To Cornelius, Concerning Fortunatus and Felicissimus, or Against the Heretics.

Argument.—Cyprian Chiefly Warns Cornelius in This Letter Not to Hear the Calumnies of Felicissimus and Fortunatus Against Him, and Not to Be Frightened by Their Threats, But to Be of a Brave Spirit, as Becomes God's Priests in Opposition to Heretics; Namely, Those Who, After the Custom Prevailing Among Heretics, Began Their Heresy and Schisms with the Contempt of One Bishop in the Church.

1. I have read your letter, dearest brother, which you sent by Saturus our brother the acolyte, abundantly full of fraternal love and ecclesiastical discipline and priestly reproof; in which you signified that Felicissimus, no new enemy of Christ, but long ago excommunicated for his very many and grave crimes, and condemned not only by my judgment, but also by that of very many of my fellow-bishops, has been rejected by you there, and that when he came attended by a band and faction of desperadoes, he was driven from the Church with the full rigour with which it behooves a bishop to act. From which Church long ago he was driven, with others like himself, by the majesty of God and the severity of Christ our Lord and Judge; that the author of schism and disagreement, the fraudulent user of money entrusted to him, the violator of virgins, the destroyer and corrupter of many marriages, should not, by the dishonor of his

presence and his immodest and incestuous contact, violate further the spouse of Christ, hitherto uncorrupt, holy, modest.

2. But yet, when I read your other letter, brother, which you subjoined to your first one, I was considerably surprised at observing that you were in some degree disturbed by the threats and terrors of those who had come, when, according to what you wrote, they had attacked and threatened you with the greatest desperation, that if you would not receive the letters which they had brought, they would read them publicly, and would utter many base and disgraceful things, and such as were worthy of their mouth. But if the matter is thus, dearest brother, that the audacity of the most wicked men is to be dreaded, and that what evil men cannot do rightly and equitably, they may accomplish by daring and desperation, there is an end of the vigor of the episcopacy, and of the sublime and divine power of governing the Church; nor can we continue any longer, or in fact now be Christians, if it is come to this, that we are to be afraid of the threats or the snares of outcasts. For both Gentiles and Jews threaten, and heretics and all those, of whose hearts and minds the devil has taken possession, daily attest their venomous madness with furious voice. We are not, therefore, to yield because they threaten; nor is the adversary and enemy on that account greater than Christ, because he claims for himself and assumes so much in the world. There ought to abide with us, dearest brother, an immoveable strength of faith; and against all the irruptions and onsets of the waves that roar against us, a steady and unshaken courage should plant itself as with the fortitude and mass of a resisting rock. Nor does it matter whence comes the terror or the danger to a bishop,

who lives subject to terrors and dangers, and is nevertheless made glorious by those very terrors and dangers. For we ought not to consider and regard the mere threats of the Gentiles or of the Jews, when we see that the Lord Himself was deserted by His brethren, and was betrayed by him whom He Himself had chosen among His apostles; that also in the beginning of the world it was none other than a brother who slew righteous Abel, and an angry brother pursued the fleeing Jacob, and the youthful Joseph was sold by the act of his brethren. In the Gospel also we read that it was foretold that our foes should rather be of our own household, and that they who have first been associated in the sacrament of unity shall be they who shall betray one another. It makes no difference who delivers up or who rages, since God permits those to be delivered up whom He appoints to be crowned. For it is no ignominy to us to suffer from our brethren what Christ suffered, nor is it glory to them to do what Judas did. But what insolence it is in them, what swelling and inflated and vain boasting on the part of these threateners, there to threaten me in my absence, when here they have me present in their power! I do not fear their reproaches with which they daily wound themselves and their own life; I do not tremble at their clubs and stones and swords, which they brandish with parricidal words: as far as lies in their power such men are homicides before God. Yet they are not able to slay unless the Lord has allowed them to slay; and although I must die but once, yet they daily slay me by their hatred, their words, and their villainies.

3. But, dearest brother, ecclesiastical discipline is not on that account to be forsaken, nor priestly censure to be relaxed, because we are disturbed with reproaches or

are shaken with terrors; since Holy Scripture meets and warns us, saying, "But he who presumes and is haughty, the man who boasts of himself, who hath enlarged his soul as hell, shall accomplish nothing." And again: "And fear not the words of a sinful man, for his glory shall be dung and worms. To-day he is lifted up, and to-morrow he shall not be found, because he is turned into his earth, and his thought shall perish." And again: "I have seen the wicked exalted and raised above the cedars of Libanus: I went by, and, lo, he was not; yea, I sought him, and his place was not found." Exaltation, and puffing up, and arrogant and haughty boastfulness, spring not from the teaching of Christ who teaches humility, but from the spirit of Antichrist, whom the Lord rebukes by His prophet, saying, "For thou hast said in thine heart, I will ascend into heaven, I will place my throne above the stars of God: I will sit on a lofty mountain, above the lofty mountains to the north: I will ascend above the clouds; I will be like the Most High." And he added, saying, "Yet thou shalt descend into hell, to the foundations of the earth; and they that see thee shall wonder at thee." Whence also divine Scripture threatens a like punishment to such in another place, and says, "For the day of the Lord of hosts shall be upon every one that is injurious and proud, and upon every one that is lifted up, and lofty." By his mouth, therefore, and by his words, is every one at once betrayed; and whether he has Christ in his heart, or Antichrist, is discerned in his speaking, according to what the Lord says in His Gospel, "O generation of vipers, how can ye, being evil, speak good things? for out of the abundance of the heart the mouth speaks. A good man out of the good treasure bringeth forth good things; and an evil man out of the evil treasure bringeth forth evil things." Whence also that rich sinner who implores help from Lazarus, then laid in Abraham's bosom, and established in a place of comfort, while he, writhing in torments, is consumed by the heats of burning flame, suffers most punishment of all parts of his body in his mouth and his tongue, because doubtless in his mouth and his tongue he had most sinned.

4. For since it is written, "Neither shall revilers inherit the kingdom of God," and again the Lord says in His Gospel, "Whosoever shall say to his brother, Thou fool; and whosoever shall say, Raca, shall be in danger of the Gehenna of fire," how can they evade the rebuke of the Lord the avenger, who heap up such expressions, not only on their brethren, but also on the priests, to whom is granted such honour of the condescension of God, that whosoever should not obey his priest, and him that judges here for the time, was immediately to be slain? In Deuteronomy the Lord God speaks, saying, "And the man that will do presumptuously, and will not hearken unto the priest or to the judge, whosoever he shall be in those days, that man shall die; and all the people, when they hear, shall fear, and shall do no more wickedly." Moreover, to Samuel when he was despised by the Jews, God says; "They have not despised thee, but they have despised me." And the Lord also in the Gospel says, "He that heareth you, heareth me, and Him that sent me; and he that rejected you, rejected me; and he that rejected me, rejected Him that sent me." And when he had cleansed the leprous man, he said, "Go, show thyself to the priest." And when afterwards, in the time of His passion, He had received a buffet from a servant of the priest, and the servant said to Him, "Answer thou the high priest so?" the Lord said nothing reproachfully against the high priest,

nor detracted anything from the priest's honour; but rather asserting His own innocence, and showing it, He says, "If I have spoken evil, bear witness of the evil; but if well, why smites thou me?" Also subsequently, in the Acts of the Apostles, the blessed Apostle Paul, when it was said to him, "Reviles thou God's priest?"—although they had begun to be sacrilegious, and impious, and bloody, the Lord having already been crucified, and had no longer retained anything of the priestly honour and authority—yet Paul, considering the name itself, however empty, and the shadow, as it were, of the priest, said, "I wist not, brethren, that he was the high priest: for it is written, Thou shalt not speak evil of the ruler of thy people."

5. When, then, such and so great examples, and many others, are precedents whereby the priestly authority and power by the divine condescension is established, what kind of people, think you, are they who, being enemies of the priests, and rebels against the Catholic Church, are frightened neither by the threatening of a forewarning Lord, nor by the vengeance of coming judgment? For neither have heresies arisen, nor have schisms originated, from any other source than from this, that God's priest is not obeyed; nor do they consider that there is one person for the time priest in the Church, and for the time judge in the stead of Christ; whom, if, according to divine teaching, the whole fraternity should obey, no one would stir up anything against the college of priests; no one, after the divine judgment, after the suffrage of the people, after the consent of the co-bishops, would make himself a judge, not now of the bishop, but of God. No one would rend the Church by a division of the unity of Christ. No one, pleasing himself, and swelling with arrogance, would found a new heresy, separate and

without, unless anyone be of such sacrilegious daring and abandoned mind, as to think that a priest is made without God's judgment, when the Lord says in His Gospel, "Are not two sparrows sold for a farthing? and one of them does not fall to the ground without the will of your Father." When He says that not even the least things are done without God's will, does anyone think that the highest and greatest things are done in God's Church either without God's knowledge or permission, and that priests—that is, His stewards—are not ordained by His decree? This is not to have faith, whereby we live; this is not to give honour to God, by whose direction and decision we know and believe that all things are ruled and governed. Undoubtedly there are bishops made, not by the will of God, but they are such as are made outside of the Church—such as are made contrary to the ordinance and tradition of the Gospel, as the Lord Himself in the twelve prophets asserts, saying, "They have set up a king for themselves, and not by me." And again: "Their sacrifices are as the bread of mourning; all that eat thereof shall be polluted." And the Holy Spirit also cries by Isaiah, and says, "Woe unto you, children that are deserters. Thus, saith the Lord, Ye have taken counsel, but not of me; and ye have made a covenant, but not of my Spirit, that ye may add sin to sin."

6. But—I speak to you as being provoked; I speak as grieving; I speak as con☐strained—when a bishop is appointed into the place of one deceased, when he is chosen in time of peace by the suffrage of an entire people, when he is protected by the help of God in persecution, faithfully linked with all his colleagues, approved to his people by now four years' experience in his episcopate; observant of discipline in time of peace; in

time of disturbance, proscribed with the name of his episcopate applied and attached to him; so often asked for in the circus "for the lions;" in the amphitheater, honoured with the testimony of the divine condescension; even in these very days on which I have written this letter to you, on account of the sacrifices which, by proclaimed edict, the people were commanded to celebrate, demanded anew in the circus "for the lions" by the clamor of the populace;—when such a one, dearest brother, is seen to be assailed by some desperate and reckless men, and by those who have their place outside the Church, it is manifest who assails him: not assuredly Christ, who either appoints or protects his priests; but he who, as the adversary of Christ and the foe to His Church, for this purpose persecutes with his malice the ruler of the Church, that when the pilot is removed, he may rage more atrociously and more violently with a view to the Church's dispersion.

7. Nor ought it, my dearest brother, to disturb anyone who is faithful and mindful of the Gospel, and retains the commands of the apostle who forewarns us; if in the last days certain persons, proud, contumacious, and enemies of God's priests, either depart from the Church or act against the Church, since both the Lord and His apostles have previously foretold that there should be such. Nor let any one wonder that the servant placed over them should be forsaken by some, when His own disciples forsook the Lord Himself, who performed such great and wonderful works, and illustrated the attributes of God the Father by the testimony of His doings. And yet He did not rebuke them when they went away, nor even severely threaten them; but rather, turning to His apostles, He said, "Will ye also go away?" manifestly observing

the law whereby a man left to his own liberty, and established in his own choice, himself desires for himself either death or salvation. Nevertheless, Peter, upon whom by the same Lord the Church had been built, speaking one for all, and answering with the voice of the Church, says, "Lord, to whom shall we go? Thou hast the words of eternal life; and we believe, and are sure that Thou art the Christ, the Son of the living God:" signifying, doubtless, and showing that those who departed from Christ perished by their own fault, yet that the Church which believes on Christ, and holds that which it has once learned, never departs from Him at all, and that those are the Church who remain in the house of God; but that, on the other hand, they are not the plantation planted by God the Father, whom we see not to be established with the stability of wheat, but blown about like chaff by the breath of the enemy scattering them, of whom John also in his epistle says, "They went out from us, but they were not of us; for if they had been of us, no doubt they would have continued with us." Paul also warns us, when evil men perish out of the Church, not to be disturbed, nor to let our faith be lessened by the departure of the faithless. "For what," he says, "if some of them have departed from the faith? Hath their unbelief made the faith of God of none effect? God forbid! For God is true, but every man a liar."

    8. For our own part, it befits our conscience, dearest brother, to strive that none should perish going out of the Church by our fault; but if any one, of his own accord and by his own sin, should perish, and should be unwilling to repent and to return to the Church, that we who are anxious for their well-being should be blameless in the day of judgment, and that they alone should remain

in punishment who refused to be healed by the wholesomeness of our advice. Nor ought the reproaches of the lost to move us in any degree to depart from the right path and from the sure rule, since also the apostle instructs us, saying, "If I should please men, I should not be the servant of Christ." There is a great difference whether one desires to deserve well of men or of God. If we seek to please men, the Lord is offended. But if we strive and labor that we may please God, we ought to contemn human reproaches and abuse.

9. But that I did not immediately write to you, dearest brother, about Fortunatus, that pseudo-bishop, constituted by a few, and those, inveterate heretics, the matter was not such as ought at once and hastily to be brought under your notice, as if it were great or to be feared; especially since you already know well enough the name of Fortunatus, who is one of the five presbyters who some time back deserted from the Church, and were lately excommunicated by the judgment of our fellow-bishops, men both numerous and entitled to the greatest respect, who on this matter wrote to you last year. Also, you would recognize Felicissimus, the standard-bearer of sedition, who himself also is comprised in those same letters long ago written to you by our co-bishops, and who not only was excommunicated by them here, but moreover was lately driven from the Church by you there. Since I was confident that these things were in your knowledge and knew for certain that they abode in your memory and discipline, I did not think it necessary that the follies of heretics should be told you quickly and urgently. For indeed it ought not to pertain to the majesty or the dignity of the Catholic Church, to concern itself with what the audacity of heretics and schismatics may

attempt among themselves. For Novatian's party is also said to have now made Maximus the presbyter—who was lately sent to us as an ambassador for Novatian, and rejected from communion with us—their false bishop in that place; and yet I had not written to you about this, since all these things are slighted by us; and I had sent to you lately the names of the bishops appointed there, who with wholesome and sound discipline govern the brethren in the Catholic Church. And this certainly, therefore, it was decided by the advice of all of us to write to you, that there might be found a short method of destroying error and of finding out truth, that you and our colleagues might know to whom to write, and reciprocally, from whom it behooved you to receive letters; but if any one, except those whom we have comprised in our letter, should dare to write to you, you would know either that he was polluted by sacrifice, or by receiving a certificate, or that he was one of the heretics, and therefore perverted and profane. Nevertheless, having gained an opportunity, by means of a very great friend and a clerk, I have written to you by Felicianus the acolyte, whom you had sent with Perseus our colleague, among other matters which were to be brought under your notice from their party, about that Fortunatus also. But while our brother Felicianus is either retarded there by the wind or is detained by receiving other letters from us, he has been forestalled by Felicissimus hastening to you. For thus wickedness always hastens, as if by its speed it could prevail against innocence.

   10. But I intimated to you, my brother, by Felicianus, that there had come to Carthage, Privatus, an old heretic in the colony of Lambesa, many years ago condemned for many and grave crimes by the judgment

of ninety bishops, and severely remarked upon in the letters of Fabian and Donatus, also our predecessors, as is not hidden from your knowledge; who, when he said that he wished to plead his cause before us in the council which we held on the Ides of May then past, and was not permitted, made for himself that Fortunatus a pretended bishop, worthy of his college. And there had also come with him a certain Felix, whom he himself had formerly appointed a pseudo-bishop outside the Church, in heresy. But Jovinus also, and Maximus, were present as companions with the proved heretic, condemned for wicked sacrifices and crimes proved against them by the judgment of nine bishops, our colleagues, and again excommunicated also by many of us last year in a council. And with these four was also joined Repostus of Suturnica, who not only fell himself in the persecution, but cast down by sacrilegious persuasion the greatest part of his people. These five, with a few who either had sacrificed, or had evil consciences, concurred in desiring Fortunatus as a false bishop for themselves, that so, their crimes agreeing, the ruler should be such as those who are ruled.

11. Hence also, dearest brother, you may now know the other falsehoods which desperate and abandoned men have there spread about, that although, of the sacrificers, or of the heretics, there were not more than five false bishops who came to Carthage, and appointed Fortunatus as the associate of their madness; yet they, as children of the devil, and full of lies, dared, as you write, to boast that there were present twenty-five bishops; which falsehood they boasted here also before among our brethren, saying that twenty-five bishops would come from Numidia to make a bishop for them. After they were

detected and confounded in this their lie (only five who had made shipwreck coming together, and these being excommunicated by us), they sailed to Rome with the reward of their lies, as if the truth could not sail after them, and convict their lying tongues by proof of the certainty. And this, my brother, is real madness, not to think nor to know that lies do not long deceive, that the night only lasts so long as until the day brightens; but that when the day is clear and the sun has arisen, the darkness and gloom give place to light, and the robberies which were going on through the night cease. In fine, if you were to seek the names from them, they would have none which they could even falsely give. For such among them is the penury even of wicked men, that neither of sacrificers nor of heretics can there be collected twenty-five for them; and yet, for the sake of deceiving the ears of the simple and the absent, the number is exaggerated by a lie, as if, even if this number were true, either the Church would be overcome by heretics, or righteousness by the unrighteous.

12. Nor does it behoove me, dearest brother, to do like things to them, and to go through in my discourse those things which they have committed, and still commit, since we have to consider what it becomes God's priests to utter and to write. Nor ought grief to speak among us so much as shame, and I ought not to seem provoked rather to heap together reproaches than crimes and sins. Therefore, I am silent upon the deceits practiced in the Church. I pass over the conspiracies and adulteries, and the various kinds of crimes. That circumstance alone, however, of their wickedness, in which the cause is not mine, nor man's, but God's, I do not think must be withheld; that from the very first day of the persecution,

while the recent crimes of the guilty were still hot, and not only the devil's altars, but the very hands and the mouths of the lapsed, were still smoking with the abominable sacrifices, they did not cease to communicate with the lapsed, and to interfere with their repentance. God cries, "He that sacrificed unto any gods, save unto the Lord only, shall be rooted out." And in the Gospel the Lord says, "Whosoever shall deny me, him will I deny." And in another place the divine indignation and anger are not silent, saying, "To them hast thou poured out a drink-offering, and to them hast thou offered a meat-offering. Shall I not be angry with these things? saith the Lord." And they interfere that God may not be entreated, who Himself declares that He is angry; they interpose that Christ may not be besought with prayers and satisfactions, who professes that him who denies Him He will deny.

13. In the very time of persecution we wrote letters on this matter, but we were not attended to. A full council being held, we decreed, not only with our consent, but also with our threatening, that the brethren should repent, and that none should rashly grant peace to those who did not repent. And those sacrilegious persons rush with impious madness against God's priests, departing from the Church; and raising their parricidal arms against the Church, in order that the malice of the devil may consummate their work, take pains that the divine clemency may not heal the wounded in His Church. They corrupt the repentance of the wretched men by the deceitfulness of their lies, that it may not satisfy an offended God—that he who has either blushed or feared to be a Christian before, may not afterwards seek Christ his Lord, nor he return to the Church who had departed from the Church. Efforts are used that the sins may not be

atoned for with just satisfactions and lamentations, that the wounds may not be washed away with tears. True peace is done away by the falsehood of a false peace; the healthful bosom of a mother is closed by the interference of the stepmother, that weeping and groaning may not be heard from the breast and from the lips of the lapsed. And beyond this, the lapsed are compelled with their tongues and lips, in the Capitol wherein before they had sinned, to reproach the priests—to assail with contumelies and with abusive words the confessors and virgins, and those righteous men who are most eminent for the praise of the faith, and most glorious in the Church. By which things, indeed, it is not so much the modesty and the humility and the shame of our people that are smitten, as their own hope and life that are lacerated. For neither is it he who hears, but he who utters the reproach, that is wretched; nor is it he who is smitten by his brother, but he who smites a brother, that is a sinner under the law; and when the guilty do a wrong to the innocent, they suffer the injury who think that they are doing it. Finally, their mind is smitten by these things, and their spirit is dull, and their sense of right is estranged: it is God's wrath that they do not perceive their sins, lest repentance should follow as it is written, "And God gave them the spirit of torpor," that is, that they may not return and be healed, and be made whole after their sins by just prayers and satisfactions. Paul the apostle in his epistle lays it down, and says, "They received not the love of the truth, that they might be saved. And for this cause God shall send them strong delusion, that they should believe a lie: that they all might be judged who believed not the truth but had pleasure in unrighteousness." The highest degree of happiness is, not to sin; the second, to acknowledge our sins. In the former, innocence flows pure and unstained to preserve us; in the latter, there comes a medicine to heal us. Both of these they have lost by offending God, both because the grace is lost which is received from the sanctification of baptism, and repentance comes not to their help, whereby the sin is healed. Think you, brother, that their wickednesses against God are trifling, their sins small and moderate—since by their means the majesty of an angry God is not besought, since the anger and the fire and the day of the Lord is not feared—since, when Antichrist is at hand the faith of the militant people is disarmed by the taking away of the power of Christ and His fear? Let the laity see to it how they may amend this. A heavier labor is incumbent on the priests in asserting and maintaining the majesty of God, that we seem not to neglect anything in this respect, when God admonishes us, and says, "And now, O ye priests, this commandment is for you. If ye will not hear, and if ye will not lay it to heart, to give glory unto my name, saith the Lord, I will even send a curse upon you, and I will curse your blessing." Is honour, then, given to God when the majesty and decree of God are so condemned, that when He declares that He is indignant and angry with those who sacrifice, and when He threatens eternal penalties and perpetual punishments, it is proposed by the sacrilegious, and said, Let not the wrath of God be considered, let not the judgment of the Lord be feared, let not any knock at the Church of Christ; but repentance being done away with, and no confession of sin being made, the bishops being despised and trodden under foot, let peace be proclaimed by the presbyters in deceitful words; and lest the lapsed should rise up, or those placed without should return to the Church, let communion be offered to those who are not in communion?

14. To these also it was not sufficient that they had withdrawn from the Gospel, that they had taken away from the lapsed the hope of satisfaction and repentance, that they had taken away those involved in frauds or stained with adulteries, or polluted with the deadly contagion of sacrifices, lest they should entreat God, or make confession of their crimes in the Church, from all feeling and fruit of repentance; that they had set up outside for themselves—outside the Church, and opposed to the Church, a conventicle of their abandoned faction, when there had flowed together a band of creatures with evil consciences, and unwilling to entreat and to satisfy God. After such things as these, moreover, they still dare—a false bishop having been appointed for them by heretics—to set sail and to bear letters from schismatic and profane persons to the throne of Peter, and to the chief church whence priestly unity takes its source; and not to consider that these were the Romans whose faith was praised in the preaching of the apostle, to whom faithlessness could have no access. But what was the reason of their coming and announcing the making of the pseudo-bishop in opposition to the bishops? For either they are pleased with what they have done, and persist in their wickedness; or, if they are displeased and retreat, they know whither they may return. For, as it has been decreed by all of us—and is equally fair and just—that the case of every one should be heard there where the crime has been committed; and a portion of the flock has been assigned to each individual pastor, which he is to rule and govern, having to give account of his doing to the Lord; it certainly behooves those over whom we are placed not to run about nor to break up the harmonious agreement of

the bishops with their crafty and deceitful rashness, but there to plead their cause, where they may be able to have both accusers and witnesses of their crime; unless perchance the authority of the bishops constituted in Africa seems to a few desperate and abandoned men to be too little, who have already judged concerning them, and have lately condemned, by the gravity of their judgment, their conscience bound in many bonds of sins. Already their case has been examined, already sentence concerning them has been pronounced; nor is it fitting for the dignity of priests to be blamed for the levity of a changeable and inconstant mind, when the Lord teaches and says, "Let your communication be, Yea, yea; Nay, nay."

15. If the number of those who judged concerning them last year be reckoned with the presbyters and deacons, then there were more present to the judgment and hearing than are those very same persons who now seem to be associated with Fortunatus. For you ought to know, dearest brother, that after he was made a pseudo-bishop by the heretics, he was at once deserted by almost all. For those to whom in past time delusions were offered, and deceitful words were given, to the effect that they were to return to the Church together; after they saw that a false bishop was made there, learned that they had been fooled and deceived, and are daily returning and knocking at the door of the Church; while we, meanwhile, by whom account is to be given to the Lord, are anxiously weighing and carefully examining who ought to be received and admitted into the Church. For some are either hindered by their crimes to such a degree, or they are so obstinately and firmly opposed by their brethren, that they cannot be received at all except with offence and

risk to a great many. For neither must some putridity be so collected and brought together, that the parts which are sound and whole should be injured; nor is that pastor serviceable or wise who so mingles the diseased and affected sheep with his flock as to contaminate the whole flock with the infection of the clinging evil. (Do not pay attention to their number. For one who fears God is better than a thousand impious sons, as the Lord spoke by the prophet, saying, "O son, do not delight in ungodly sons, though they multiply to thee, except the fear of the Lord be with them.") Oh, if you could, dearest brother, be with us here when those evil and perverse men return from schism, you would see what labor is mine to persuade patience to our brethren, that they should calm their grief of mind, and consent to receive and heal the wicked. For as they rejoice and are glad when those who are endurable and less guilty return, so, on the other hand, they murmur and are dissatisfied as often as the incorrigible and violent, and those who are contaminated either by adulteries or by sacrifices, and who, in addition to this, are proud besides, so return to the Church, as to corrupt the good dispositions within it. Scarcely do I persuade the people; nay, I extort it from them, that they should suffer such to be admitted. And the grief of the fraternity is made the more just, from the fact that one and another who, notwithstanding the opposition and contradiction of the people, have been received by my facility, have proved worse than they had been before, and have not been able to keep the faith of their repentance, because they had not come with true repentance.

16. But what am I to say of those who have now sailed to you with Felicissimus, guilty of every crime, as ambassadors sent by Fortunatus the pseudo-bishop,

bringing to you letters as false as he himself is false, whose letters they bring, as his conscience is full of sins, as his life is execrable, as it is disgraceful; so that, even if they were in the Church, such people ought to be expelled from the Church. In addition, since they have known their own conscience, they do not dare to come to us or to approach to the threshold of the Church, but wander about, without her, through the province, for the sake of circumventing and defrauding the brethren; and now, being sufficiently known to all, and everywhere excluded for their crimes, they sail thither also to you. For they cannot have the face to approach to us, or to stand before us, since the crimes which are charged upon them by the brethren are most grievous and grave. If they wish to undergo our judgment, let them come. Finally, if they can find any excuse or defense, let us see what thought they have of making satisfaction, what fruit of repentance they bring forward. The Church is neither closed here to anyone, nor is the bishop denied to any. Our patience, and facility, and humanity are ready for those who come. I entreat all to return into the Church. I beg all our fellow-soldiers to be included within the camp of Christ, and the dwelling-place of God the Father. I remit everything. I shut my eyes to many things, with the desire and the wish to gather together the brotherhood. Even those things which are committed against God I do not investigate with the full judgment of religion. I almost sin myself, in remitting sins more than I ought. I embrace with prompt and full love those who return with repentance, confessing their sin with lowly and unaffected atonement.

17. But if there are some who think that they can return to the Church not with prayers but with threats, or suppose that they can make a way for themselves, not

with lamentation and atonements, but with terrors, let them take it for certain that against such the Church of the Lord stands closed; nor does the camp of Christ, unconquered and firm with the Lord's protection, yield to threats. The priest of God holding fast the Gospel and keeping Christ's precepts may be slain; he cannot be conquered. Zacharias, God's priest, suggests and furnishes to us examples of courage and faith, who, when he could not be terrified with threats and stoning, was slain in the temple of God, at the same time crying out and saying, what we also cry out and say against the heretics, "Thus saith the Lord, Ye have forsaken the ways of the Lord, and the Lord will forsake you." For because a few rash and wicked men forsake the heavenly and wholesome ways of the Lord, and not doing holy things are deserted by the Holy Spirit, we also ought not therefore to be unmindful of the divine tradition, so as to think that the crimes of madmen are greater than the judgments of priests; or conceive that human endeavors can do more to attack, than divine protection avails to defend.

18. Is the dignity of the Catholic Church, dearest brother, to be laid aside, is the faithful and uncorrupted majesty of the people placed within it, and the priestly authority and power also, all to be laid aside for this, that those who are set without the Church may say that they wish to judge concerning a prelate in the Church? heretics concerning a Christian? wounded men about a whole man? maimed concerning a sound man? lapsed concerning one who stands fast? guilty concerning their judge? sacrilegious men concerning a priest? What is left but that the Church should yield to the Capitol, and that, while the priests depart and remove the Lord's altar, the

images and idols should pass over with their altars into the sacred and venerable assembly of our clergy, and a larger and fuller material for declaiming against us and abusing us be afforded to Novatian; if they who have sacrificed and have publicly denied Christ should begin not only to be entreated and admitted without penance done, but, moreover, in addition, to domineer by the power of their terror?

19. If they desire peace, let them lay aside their arms. If they make atonement, why do they threaten? or if they threaten, let them know that they are not feared by God's priests. For even Antichrist, when he shall begin to come, shall not enter into the Church because he threatens; neither shall we yield to his arms and violence, because he declares that he will destroy us if we resist. Heretics arm us when they think that we are terrified by their threatening; nor do they cast us down on our face, but rather they lift us up and inflame us, when they make peace itself worse to the brethren than persecution. And we desire, indeed, that they may not fill up with crime what they speak in madness, that they who sin with perfidious and cruel words may not also sin in deeds. We pray and beseech God, whom they do not cease to provoke and exasperate, that He will soften their hearts, that they may lay aside their madness, and return to soundness of mind; that their breasts, covered over with the darkness of sins, may acknowledge the light of repentance, and that they may rather seek that the prayers and supplications of the priest may be poured out on their behalf, than themselves pour out the blood of the priest. But if they continue in their madness, and cruelly persevere in these their parricidal deceits and threats, no priest of God is so weak, so prostrate, and so abject, so

inefficient by the weakness of human infirmity, as not to be aroused against the enemies and impugners of God by strength from above; as not to find his humility and weakness animated by the vigor and strength of the Lord who protects him. It matters nothing to us by whom, or when we are slain, since we shall receive from the Lord the reward of our death and of our blood. Their concision is to be mourned and lamented, whom the devil so blinds, that, without considering the eternal punishments of Gehenna, they endeavor to imitate the coming of Antichrist, who is now approaching.

20. And although I know, dearest brother, from the mutual love which we owe and manifest one towards another, that you always read my letters to the very distinguished clergy who preside with you there, and to your very holy and large congregation, yet now I both warn and ask you to do by my request what at other times you do of your own accord and courtesy; that so, by the reading of this my letter, if any contagion of envenomed speech and of pestilent propagation has crept in there, it may be all purged out of the ears and of the hearts of the brethren, and the sound and sincere affection of the good may be cleansed anew from all the filth of heretical disparagement.

21. But for the rest, let our most beloved brethren firmly decline, and avoid the words and conversations of those whose word creeps onwards like a cancer; as the apostle says, "Evil communications corrupt good manners." And again: "A man that is a heretic, after one admonition, reject: knowing that he is such is subverted, and sinned, being condemned of himself." And the Holy Spirit speaks by Solomon, saying, "A perverse man carries perdition in his mouth; and in his lips he

hides a fire." Also again, he warns us, and says, "Hedge in thy ears with thorns, and hearken not to a wicked tongue." And again: "A wicked doer giveth heed to the tongue of the unjust; but a righteous man does not listen to lying lips." And although I know that our brotherhood there, assuredly fortified by your foresight, and besides sufficiently cautious by their own vigilance, cannot be taken nor deceived by the poisons of heretics, and that the teachings and precepts of God prevail with them only in proportion as the fear of God is in them; yet, even although needlessly, either my solicitude or my love persuaded me to write these things to you, that no commerce should be entered into with such; that no banquets nor conferences be entertained with the wicked; but that we should be as much separated from them, as they are deserters from the Church; because it is written, "If he shall neglect to hear the Church, let him be unto thee as a heathen man and a publican." And the blessed apostle not only warns, but also commands us to withdraw from such. "We command you," he says, "in the name of Jesus Christ our Lord, that ye withdraw yourselves from every brother that walketh disorderly, and not after the tradition which he received of us." There can be no fellowship between faith and faithlessness. He who is not with Christ, who is an adversary of Christ, who is hostile to His unity and peace, cannot be associated with us. If they come with prayers and atonements, let them be heard; if they heap together curses and threats, let them be rejected. I bid you, dearest brother, ever heartily farewell.

Epistle LV.
To the People of Thibaris, Exhorting Martyrdom.
Argument.—Cyprian First of All Excuses Himself to the Thibaritans that He Had Not Been to Visit Them, and Gives Them Warning of the Persecution at Hand; He Then Furnishes Inducements Readily to Undergo Martyrdom.

1. Cyprian to the people abiding at Thibaris, greeting. I had indeed thought, beloved brethren, and prayerfully desired—if the state of things and the condition of the times permitted, in conformity with what you frequently desired—myself to come to you; and being present with you, then to strengthen the brotherhood with such moderate powers of exhortation as I possess. But since I am detained by such urgent affairs, that I have not the power to travel far from this place, and to be long absent from the people over whom by divine mercy I am placed, I have written in the meantime this letter, to be to you in my stead. For as, by the condescension of the Lord instructing me, I am very often instigated and warned, I ought to bring unto your conscience also the anxiety of my warning. For you ought to know and to believe, and hold it for certain, that the day of affliction has begun to hang over our heads, and the end of the world and the time of Antichrist to draw near, so that we must all stand prepared for the battle; nor consider anything but the glory of life eternal, and the crown of the confession of the Lord; and not regard those things which are coming as being such as were those which have passed away. A severer and a fiercer fight is now threatening, for which the soldiers of Christ ought to prepare themselves with uncorrupted faith and robust courage, considering that they drink the cup of Christ's blood daily, for the reason

that they themselves also may be able to shed their blood for Christ. For this is to wish to be found with Christ, to imitate that which Christ both taught and did, according to the Apostle John, who said, "He that says he abides in Christ, ought himself also so to walk even as He walked."

Moreover, the blessed Apostle Paul exhorts and teaches, saying, "We are God's children; but if children, then heirs of God, and joint heirs with Christ; if so be that we suffer with Him, that we may also be glorified together."

2. Which things must all now be considered by us, that no one may desire anything from the world that is now dying, but may follow Christ, who both lives forever, and quickens His servants, who are established in the faith of His name. For there comes the time, beloved brethren, which our Lord long ago foretold and taught us was approaching, saying, "The time cometh, that whosoever kills you will think that he doeth God service. And these things they will do unto you, because they have not known the Father nor me. But these things have I told you, that when the time shall come, ye may remember that I told you of them." Nor let any one wonder that we are harassed with constant persecutions, and continually tried with increasing afflictions, when the Lord before predicted that these things would happen in the last times, and has instructed us for the warfare by the teaching and exhortation of His words. Peter also, His apostle, has taught that persecutions occur for the sake of our being proved, and that we also should, by the example of righteous men who have gone before us, be joined to the love of God by death and sufferings. For he wrote in his epistle, and said, "Beloved, think it not strange concerning the fiery trial which is to try you, nor do ye fall away, as if some new thing happened unto you; but as

often as ye partake in Christ's sufferings, rejoice in all things, that when His glory shall be revealed, ye may be glad also with exceeding joy. If ye be reproached in the name of Christ, happy are ye; for the name of the majesty and power of the Lord rested on you, which indeed on their part is blasphemed, but on our part is glorified." Now the apostles taught us those things which they themselves also learnt from the Lord's precepts and the heavenly commands, the Lord Himself thus strengthening us, and saying, "There is no man that hath left house, or land, or parents, or brethren, or sisters, or wife, or children, for the kingdom of God's sake, who shall not receive sevenfold more in this present time, and in the world to come life everlasting." And again, He says, "Blessed are ye when men shall hate you, and shall separate you from their company, and shall cast you out, and shall reproach your name as evil for the Son of man's sake. Rejoice ye in that day, and leap for joy; for, behold your reward is great in heaven."

    3. The Lord desired that we should rejoice and leap for joy in persecutions, because, when persecutions occur, then are given the crowns of faith, then the soldiers of God are proved, then the heavens are opened to martyrs. For we have not in such a way given our name to warfare that we ought only to think about peace and draw back from and refuse war, when in this very warfare the Lord walked first—the Teacher of humility, and endurance, and suffering—so that what He taught to be done, He first of all did, and what He exhorts to suffer, He Himself first suffered for us. Let it be before your eyes beloved brethren, that He who alone received all judgment from the Father, and who will come to judge, has already declared the decree of His judgment and of

His future recognition, foretelling and testifying that He will confess those before His Father who confess Him, and will deny those who deny Him. If we could escape death, we might reasonably fear to die. But since, on the other hand, it is necessary that a mortal man should die, we should embrace the occasion that comes by the divine promise and condescension, and accomplish the ending provided by death with the reward of immortality; nor fear to be slain, since we are sure when we are slain to be crowned.

4. Nor let anyone, beloved brethren, when he beholds our people driven away and scattered by the fear of persecution, be disturbed at seeing the brotherhood gathered together, nor the bishops discoursing. All are not able to be there together, who may not kill, but who must be killed. Wherever, in those days, each one of the brethren shall be separated from the flock for a time, by the necessity of the season, in body, not in spirit, let him not be moved at the terror of that flight; nor, if he withdraw and be concealed, let him be alarmed at the solitude of the desert place. He is not alone, whose companion in flight Christ is; he is not alone who, keeping God's temple wheresoever he is, is not without God. And if a robber should fall upon you, a fugitive in the solitude or in the mountains; if a wild beast should attack you; if hunger, or thirst, or cold should distress you, or the tempest and the storm should overwhelm you hastening in a rapid voyage over the seas, Christ everywhere looks upon His soldier fighting; and for the sake of persecution, for the honour of His name, gives a reward to him when he dies, as He has promised that He will give in the resurrection. Nor is the glory of martyrdom less that he has not perished publicly and

before many, since the cause of perishing is to perish for Christ. That Witness who proves martyrs, and crowns them, suffices for a testimony of his martyrdom.

5. Let us, beloved brethren, imitate righteous Abel, who initiated martyrdoms, he first being slain for righteousness' sake. Let us imitate Abraham, the friend of God, who did not delay to offer his son as a victim with his own hands, obeying God with a faith of devotion. Let us imitate the three children Ananias, Azarias, and Misael, who, neither frightened by their youthful age nor broken down by captivity, Judea, being conquered and Jerusalem taken, overcame the king by the power of faith in his own kingdom; who, when bidden to worship the image which Nebuchadnezzar the king had made, stood forth stronger both than the king's threats and the flames, calling out and attesting their faith by these words: "O king Nebuchadnezzar, we are not careful to answer thee in this matter. For the God whom we serve is able to deliver us from the burning fiery furnace; and He will deliver us out of thine hands, O king. But if not, be it known unto thee, that we do not serve thy gods, nor worship the golden image which thou hast set up." They believed that they might escape according to their faith, but they added, "and if not," that the king might know that they could also die for the God they worshipped. For this is the strength of courage and of faith, to believe and to know that God can deliver from present death, and yet not to fear death nor to give way, that faith may be the more mightily proved. The uncorrupted and unconquered might of the Holy Spirit broke forth by their mouth, so that the words which the Lord in His Gospel spoke are seen to be true: "But when they shall seize you, take no thought what ye shall speak; for it shall be given you in

that hour what ye shall speak. For it is not ye that speak, but the Spirit of your Father which speaks in you." He said that what we are able to speak and to answer is given to us in that hour from heaven, and supplied; and that it is not then we who speak, but the Spirit of God our Father, who, as He does not depart nor is separated from those who confess Him, Himself both speaks and is crowned in us. So Daniel, too, when he was required to worship the idol Bel, which the people and the king then worshipped, in asserting the honour of his God, broke forth with full faith and freedom, saying, "I worship nothing but the Lord my God, who created the heaven and the earth."

6. What shall we say of the cruel tortures of the blessed martyrs in the Maccabees, and the multiform sufferings of the seven brethren, and the mother comforting her children in their agonies, and herself dying also with her children? Do not they witness the proofs of great courage and faith, and exhort us by their sufferings to the triumphs of martyrdom? What of the prophets whom the Holy Spirit quickened to the foreknowledge of future events? What of the apostles whom the Lord chose? Since these righteous men were slain for righteousness' sake, have they not taught us also to die? The nativity of Christ witnessed at once the martyrdom of infants, so that they who were two years old and under were slain for His name's sake. An age not yet fitted for the battle appeared fit for the crown. That it might be manifest that they who are slain for Christ's sake are innocent, innocent infancy was put to death for His name's sake. It is shown that none is free from the peril of persecution, when even these accomplished martyrdoms. But how grave is the case of a Christian man, if he, a servant, is unwilling to suffer, when his Master first

suffered; and that we should be unwilling to suffer for our own sins, when He who had no sin of His own suffered for us! The Son of God suffered that He might make us sons of God, and the son of man will not suffer that he may continue to be a son of God! If we suffer from the world's hatred, Christ first endured the world's hatred. If we suffer reproaches in this world, if exile, if tortures, the Maker and Lord of the world experienced harder things than these, and He also warns us, saying, "If the world hate you, remember that it hated me before you. If ye were of the world, the world would love its own: but because ye are not of the world, but I have chosen you out of the world, therefore the world hates you. Remember the word that I said unto you, The servant is not greater than his lord. If they have persecuted me, they will also persecute you." Whatever our Lord and God taught, He also did, that the disciple might not be excused if he learns and does not.

  7. Nor let any one of you, beloved brethren, be so terrified by the fear of future persecution, or the coming of the threatening Antichrist, as not to be found armed for all things by the evangelical exhortations and precepts, and by the heavenly warnings. Antichrist is coming, but above him comes Christ also. The enemy goes about and rages, but immediately the Lord follows to avenge our sufferings and our wounds. The adversary is enraged and threatens, but there is One who can deliver us from his hands. He is to be feared whose anger no one can escape, as He Himself forewarns, and says: "Fear not them which kill the body but are not able to kill the soul; but rather fear Him which is able to destroy both body and soul in hell." And again: "He that loveth his life, shall lose it; and he that hates his life in this world, shall keep it unto life

eternal." And in the Apocalypse He instructs and forewarns, saying, "If any man worship the beast and his image, and receive his mark in his forehead or in his hand, the same also shall drink of the wine of the wrath of God, mixed in the cup of His indignation, and he shall be tormented with fire and brimstone in the presence of the holy angels, and in the presence of the Lamb; and the smoke of their torments shall ascend up for ever and ever; and they shall have no rest day nor night, who worship the beast and his image."

8. For the secular contest men are trained and prepared and reckon it a great glory of their honour if it should happen to them to be crowned in the sight of the people, and in the presence of the emperor. Behold a lofty and great contest, glorious also with the reward of a heavenly crown, inasmuch as God looks upon us as we struggle, and, extending His view over those whom He has condescended to make His sons, He enjoys the spectacle of our contest. God looks upon us in the warfare and fighting in the encounter of faith; His angels look on us, and Christ looks on us. How great is the dignity, and how great the happiness of the glory, to engage in the presence of God, and to be crowned, with Christ for a judge! Let us be armed, beloved brethren, with our whole strength, and let us be prepared for the struggle with an uncorrupted mind, with a sound faith, with a devoted courage. Let the camp of God go forth to the battlefield which is appointed to us. Let the sound ones be armed, lest he that is sound should lose the advantage of having lately stood; let the lapsed also be armed, that even the lapsed may regain what he has lost: let honour provoke the whole; let sorrow provoke the lapsed to the battle. The Apostle Paul teaches us to be armed and prepared, saying,

"We wrestle not against flesh and blood, but against powers, and the princes of this world and of this darkness, against spirits of wickedness in high places. Wherefore put on the whole armor, that ye may be able to withstand in the most evil day, that when ye have done all ye may stand; having your loins girt about with truth, and having put on the breastplate of righteousness; and your feet shod with the preparation of the Gospel of peace; taking the shield of faith, wherewith ye shall be able to quench all the fiery darts of the wicked one; and the helmet of salvation, and the sword of the Spirit, which is the word of God."

9. Let us take these arms, let us fortify ourselves with these spiritual and heavenly safe guards, that in the most evil day we may be able to withstand, and to resist the threats of the devil: let us put on the breastplate of righteousness, that our breast may be fortified and safe against the darts of the enemy: let our feet be shod with evangelical teaching, and armed, so that when the serpent shall begin to be trodden and crushed by us, he may not be able to bite and trip us up: let us bravely bear the shield of faith, by the protection of which, whatever the enemy darts at us may be extinguished: let us take also for protection of our head the helmet of salvation, that our ears may be guarded from hearing the deadly edicts; that our eyes may be fortified, that they may not see the odious images; that our brow may be fortified, so as to keep safe the sign of God; that our mouth may be fortified, that the conquering tongue may confess Christ its Lord: let us also arm the right hand with the sword of the Spirit, that it may bravely reject the deadly sacrifices; that, mindful of the Eucharist, the hand which has received the Lord's body may embrace the Lord Himself,

hereafter to receive from the Lord the reward of heavenly crowns.

10. Oh, what and how great will that day be at its coming, beloved brethren, when the Lord shall begin to count up His people, and to recognize the deservings of each one by the inspection of His divine knowledge, to send the guilty to Gehenna, and to set on fire our persecutors with the perpetual burning of a penal fire, but to pay to us the reward of our faith and devotion! What will be the glory and how great the joy to be admitted to see God, to be honored to receive with Christ, thy Lord God, the joy of eternal salvation and light—to greet Abraham, and Isaac, and Jacob, and all the patriarchs, and prophets, and apostles, and martyrs—to rejoice with the righteous and the friends of God in the kingdom of heaven, with the pleasure of immortality given to us—to receive there what neither eye hath seen, nor ear heard, neither hath entered into the heart of man! For the apostle announces that we shall receive greater things than anything that we here either do or suffer, saying, "The sufferings of this present time are not worthy to be compared with the glory to come hereafter which shall be revealed in us." When that revelation shall come, when that glory of God shall shine upon us, we shall be as happy and joyful, honored with the condescension of God, as they will remain guilty and wretched, who, either as deserters from God or rebels against Him, have done the will of the devil, so that it is necessary for them to be tormented with the devil himself in unquenchable fire.

11. Let these things, beloved brethren, take hold of our hearts; let this be the preparation of our arms, this our daily and nightly meditation, to have before our eyes and ever to revolve in our thoughts and feelings the

punishments of the wicked and the rewards and the deserving of the righteous: what the Lord threatens by way of punishment against those that deny Him; what, on the other hand, He promises by way of glory to those that confess Him. If, while we think and meditate on these things, there should come to us a day of persecution, the soldier of Christ instructed in His precepts and warnings is not fearful for the battle but is prepared for the crown. I bid you, dearest brethren, ever heartily farewell.

Epistle LVI.
To Cornelius in Exile, Concerning His Confession.
Argument.—Cyprian Praises in Cornelius and His People Their Confession of the Name of Christ Even to Banishment; And Exhorts Them to Constancy and to Mutual Prayer for One Another, as Well in Respect of the Approaching Day of Struggle in This Life, as After Death.

1. Cyprian to Cornelius his brother, greeting. We have been made acquainted, dearest brother, with the glorious testimonies of your faith and courage, and have received with such exultation the honour of your confession, that we count ourselves also sharers and companions in your merits and praises. For as we have one Church, a mind united, and a concord undivided, what priest does not congratulate himself on the praises of his fellow priest as if on his own; or what brotherhood would not rejoice in the joy of its brethren? It cannot be sufficiently declared how great was the exultation and how great the joy here, when we had heard of your success and bravery, that you had stood forth as a leader of confession to the brethren there; and, moreover, that

the confession of the leader had increased by the consent of the brethren; so that, while you precede them to glory, you have made many your companions in glory, and have persuaded the people to become a confessor by being first prepared to confess on behalf of all; so that we are at a loss what we ought first of all to commend in you, whether your prompt and decided faith, or the inseparable love of the brethren. Among you the courage of the bishop going before has been publicly proved, and the unitedness of the brotherhood following has been shown. As with you there is one mind and one voice, the whole Roman Church has confessed.

2. The faith, dearest brethren, which the blessed apostle commended in you has shone brightly. He even then in the spirit foresaw this praise of courage and firmness of strength; and, attesting your merits by the commendation of your future doings, in praising the parents he provokes the children. While you are thus unanimous, while you are thus brave, you have given great examples both of unanimity and of bravery to the rest of the brethren. You have taught them deeply to fear God, firmly to cling to Christ; that the people should be associated with the priests in peril; that the brethren should not be separated from brethren in persecution; that a concord, once established, can by no means be overcome; that whatsoever is at the same time sought for by all, the God of peace will grant to the peaceful. The adversary had leapt forth to disturb the camp of Christ with violent terror; but, with the same impetuosity with which he had come, he was beaten back and conquered; and as much fear and terror as he had brought, so much bravery and strength he also found. He had thought that he could again overthrow the servants of God, and agitate

them in his accustomed manner, as if they were novices and inexperienced—as if little prepared and little cautious. He attacked one first, as a wolf had tried to separate the sheep from the flock, as a hawk to separate the dove from the flying troop; for he who has not sufficient strength against all, seeks to gain advantage from the solitude of individuals. But when beaten back as well by the faith as by the vigor of the combined army, he perceived that the soldiers of Christ are now watching, and stand sober and armed for the battle; that they cannot be conquered, but that they can die; and that by this very fact they are invincible, that they do not fear death; that they do not in turn assail their assailants, since it is not lawful for the innocent even to kill the guilty; but that they readily deliver up both their lives and their blood; that since such malice and cruelty rages in the world, they may the more quickly withdraw from the evil and cruel. What a glorious spectacle was that under the eyes of God! what a joy of His Church in the sight of Christ, that not single soldiers, but the whole camp, at once went forth to the battle which the enemy had tried to begin! For it is plain that all would have come if they could have heard, since whoever heard ran hastily and came. How many lapsed were there restored by a glorious confession! They bravely stood, and by the very suffering of repentance were made braver for the battle, that it might appear that lately they had been taken at unawares, and had trembled at the fear of a new and unaccustomed thing, but that they had afterwards returned to themselves; that true faith and their strength, gathered from the fear of God, had constantly and firmly strengthened them to all endurance; and that now they do not stand for pardon of their crime, but for the crown of their suffering.

3. What does Novatian say to these things, dearest brother? Does he yet lay aside his error? Or, indeed, as is the custom of foolish men, is he more driven to fury by our very benefits and prosperity; and in proportion as the glory of love and faith grows here more and more, does the madness of dissension and envy break out anew there? Does the wretched man not cure his own wound, but wound both himself and his friends still more severely, clamoring with his tongue to the ruin of the brethren, and hurling darts of poisonous eloquence, more severe in accordance with the wickedness of a secular philosophy than peaceable with the gentleness of the Lord's wisdom,—a deserter of the Church, a foe to mercy, a destroyer of repentance, a teacher of arrogance, a corrupter of truth, a murderer of love? Does he now acknowledge who is the priest of God; which is the Church and the house of Christ; who are God's servants, whom the devil molests; who the Christians, whom Antichrist attacks? For neither does he seek those whom he has already subdued, nor does he take the trouble to overthrow those whom he has already made his own. The foe and enemy of the Church despises and passes by those whom he has alienated from the Church and led without as captives and conquered; he goes on to harass those in whom he sees Christ dwell.

4. Even although any one of such should have been seized, there is no reason for his flattering himself, as if in the confession of the name; since it is manifest that, if people of this sort should be put to death outside the Church, it is no crown of faith, but is rather a punishment of treachery. Nor will those dwell in the house of God among those that are of one mind, whom we see to have withdrawn by the madness of discord from

the peaceful and divine household.

5. We earnestly exhort as much as we can, dearest brother, for the sake of the mutual love by which we are joined one to another, that since we are instructed by the providence of the Lord, who warns us, and are admonished by the wholesome counsels of divine mercy, that the day of our contest and struggle is already approaching, we should not cease to be instant with all the people in fasting, in watchings, in prayers. Let us be urgent, with constant groanings and frequent prayers. For these are our heavenly arms, which make us to stand fast and bravely to persevere. These are the spiritual defenses and divine weapons which defend us. Let us remember one another in concord and unanimity. Let us on both sides always pray for one another. Let us relieve burdens and afflictions by mutual love, that if any one of us, by the swiftness of divine condescension, shall go hence the first, our love may continue in the presence of the Lord, and our prayers for our brethren and sisters not cease in the presence of the Father's mercy. I bid you, dearest brother, ever heartily farewell.

Epistle LVII.
To Lucius The Bishop of Rome, Returned from Banishment.
Argument.—Cyprian, with His Colleagues, Congratulates Lucius on His Return from Exile, Reminding Him that Martyrdom Deferred Does Not Make the Glory Less. Then, Pointing Out that the Martyrdom of Cornelius and the Banishment of Lucius Had Happened by Divine Direction, for the Confusion of the Novatians, He Foretells to Him His Own Impending

Martyrdom, God So Ordaining It that It Should Be Consummated Not Away from Home, But Among His Own People.

1. Cyprian, with his colleagues, to Lucius his brother, greeting. We had lately also congratulated you indeed, dearest brother, when the divine condescension, by a double honour, appointed you in the administration of God's Church, as well a confessor as a priest. But now also we no less congratulate you and your companions, and the whole fraternity, that the benignant and liberal protection of the Lord has brought you back again to His own with the same glory, and with praises to you; that so the shepherd might be restored to feed his flock, and the pilot to manage the ship, and the ruler to govern the people; and that it might appear that your banishment was so divinely arranged, not that the bishop banished and driven away should be wanting to the Church, but that he should return to the Church greater than he had left it.

2. For the dignity of martyrdom was not the less in the case of the three youths, because, their death being frustrated, they came forth safe from the fiery furnace; nor did Daniel stand forth uncompleted in the praise he deserved, because, when he had been sent to the lions for a prey, he was protected by the Lord, and lived to glory. Among confessors of Christ, martyrdoms deferred do not diminish the merits of confession, but show forth the greatness of divine protection. We see represented in you what the brave and illustrious youths announced before the king, that they indeed were prepared to be burnt in the flames, that they might not serve his gods, nor worship the image which he had made; but that the God whom they worshipped, and whom we also worship, was able even to rescue them from the fiery furnace, and to deliver

them from the hands of the king, and from imminent sufferings. This we now find carried out in the faith of your confession, and in the Lord's protection over you; so that while you were prepared and ready to undergo all punishment, yet the Lord withdrew you from punishment, and preserved you for the Church. In your return the dignity of his confession has not been abridged in the bishop, but the priestly authority has rather increased; so that a priest is assisting at the altar of God, who exhorts the people to take up the arms of confession, and to submit to martyrdom, not by his words, but by his deeds; and, now that Antichrist is near, prepares the soldiers for the battle, not only by the urgency of his speech and his words, but by the example of his faith and courage.

3. We understand, dearest brother, and we perceive with the whole light of our heart, the salutary and holy plans of the divine majesty, whence the sudden persecution lately arose there—whence the secular power suddenly broke forth against the Church of Christ and the bishop Cornelius, the blessed martyr, and all of you; so that, for the confusion and beating down of heretics, the Lord might show which was the Church—which is its one bishop chosen by divine appointment—which presbyters are associated with the bishop in priestly honour—which is the united and true people of Christ, linked together in the love of the Lord's flock—who they were whom the enemy would harass; whom, on the other hand, the devil would spare as being his own. For Christ's adversary does not persecute and attack any except Christ's camp and soldiers; heretics, once prostrated and made his own, he despises and passes by. He seeks to cast down those whom he sees to stand.

4. And I wish, dearest brother, that the power were

now given us to be with you there on your return, that we ourselves, who love you with mutual love, might, being present with the rest, also receive the very joyous fruit of your coming. What exultation among all the brethren there; what running together and embracing of each one as they arrive! Scarcely can you be satisfied with the kisses of those who cling to you; scarcely can the very faces and eyes of the people be satiated with seeing. At the joy of your coming the brotherhood there has begun to recognize what and how great a joy will follow when Christ shall come. For because His advent will quickly approach, a kind of representation has now gone before in you; that just as John, His forerunner and preparer of His way, came and preached that Christ had come, so, now that a bishop returns as a confessor of the Lord, and His priest, it appears that the Lord also is now returning. But I and my colleagues, and all the brotherhood, send this letter to you in the stead of us, dearest brother; and setting forth to you by our letter our joy, we express the faithful inclination of our love here also in our sacrifices and our prayers, not ceasing to give thanks to God the Father, and to Christ His Son our Lord; and as well to pray as to entreat, that He who is perfect, and makes perfect, will keep and perfect in you the glorious crown of your confession, who perchance has called you back for this purpose, that your glory should not be hidden, if the martyrdom of your confession should be consummated away from home. For the victim which affords an example to the brotherhood both of courage and of faith, ought to be offered up when the brethren are present. We bid you, dearest brother, ever heartily farewell.

Epistle LVIII.

To Fidus, on the Baptism of Infants.

Argument.—In This Letter Cyprian is Not Establishing Any New Decree; But Keeping Most Firmly the Faith of the Church, for the Correction of Those Who Thought that an Infant Must Not Be Baptized Before the Eighth Day After Its Birth, He Decreed with Some of His Fellow-Bishops, that as Soon as It Was Born It Might Properly Be Baptized. He Takes Occasion, However, to Refuse to Recall the Peace that Had Been Granted to One Victor, Although It Had Been Granted Against the Decrees of Synods Concerning the Lapsed; But Forbids Therapius the Bishop to Do It in Other Cases.

1. Cyprian, and others his colleagues who were present in council, in number sixty-six, to Fidus their brother, greeting. We have read your letter, dearest brother, in which you intimated concerning Victor, formerly a presbyter, that our colleague Therapius, rashly at a too early season, and with over-eager haste, granted peace to him before he had fully repented, and had satisfied the Lord God, against whom he had sinned; which thing rather disturbed us, that it was a departure from the authority of our decree, that peace should be granted to him before the legitimate and full time of satisfaction, and without the request and consciousness of the people—no sickness rendering it urgent, and no necessity compelling it. But the judgment being long weighed among us, it was considered sufficient to rebuke Therapius our colleague for having done this rashly, and to have instructed him that he should not do the like with any other. Yet we did not think that the peace once granted in any wise by a priest of God was to be taken away, and for this reason have allowed Victor to avail himself of the communion granted to him.

2. But in respect of the case of the infants, which you say ought not to be baptized within the second or third day after their birth, and that the law of ancient circumcision should be regarded, so that you think that one who is just born should not be baptized and sanctified within the eighth day, we all thought very differently in our council. For in this course which you thought was to be taken, no one agreed; but we all rather judge that the mercy and grace of God is not to be refused to anyone born of man. For as the Lord says in His Gospel, "The Son of man is not come to destroy men's lives, but to save them," as far as we can, we must strive that, if possible, no soul be lost. For what is wanting to him who has once been formed in the womb by the hand of God? To us, indeed, and to our eyes, according to the worldly course of days, they who are born appear to receive an increase. But whatever things are made by God, are completed by the majesty and work of God their Maker.

3. Moreover, belief in divine Scripture declares to us, that among all, whether infants or those who are older, there is the same equality of the divine gift. Elisha, beseeching God, so laid himself upon the infant son of the widow, who was lying dead, that his head was applied to his head, and his face to his face, and the limbs of Elisha were spread over and joined to each of the limbs of the child, and his feet to his feet. If this thing be considered with respect to the inequality of our birth and our body, an infant could not be made equal with a person grown up and mature, nor could its little limbs fit and be equal to the larger limbs of a man. But in that is expressed the divine and spiritual equality, that all men are like and equal, since they have once been made by God; and our age may have a difference in the increase of our bodies,

according to the world, but not according to God; unless that very grace also which is given to the baptized is given either less or more, according to the age of the receivers, whereas the Holy Spirit is not given with measure, but by the love and mercy of the Father alike to all. For God, as He does not accept the person, so does not accept the age; since He shows Himself Father to all with well-weighed equality for the attainment of heavenly grace.

4. For, with respect to what you say, that the aspect of an infant in the first days after its birth is not pure, so that any one of us would still shudder at kissing it, we do not think that this ought to be alleged as any impediment to heavenly grace. For it is written, "To the pure all things are pure." Nor ought any of us to shudder at that which God hath condescended to make. For although the infant is still fresh from its birth, yet it is not such that any one should shudder at kissing it in giving grace and in making peace; since in the kiss of an infant every one of us ought for his very religion's sake, to consider the still recent hands of God themselves, which in some sort we are kissing, in the man lately formed and freshly born, when we are embracing that which God has made. For in respect of the observance of the eighth day in the Jewish circumcision of the flesh, a sacrament was given beforehand in shadow and in usage; but when Christ came, it was fulfilled in truth. For because the eighth day, that is, the first day after the Sabbath, was to be that on which the Lord should rise again, and should quicken us, and give us circumcision of the spirit, the eighth day, that is, the first day after the Sabbath, and the Lord's day, went before in the figure; which figure ceased when by and by the truth came, and spiritual

circumcision was given to us.

5. For which reason we think that no one is to be hindered from obtaining grace by that law which was already ordained, and that spiritual circumcision ought not to be hindered by carnal circumcision, but that absolutely every man is to be admitted to the grace of Christ, since Peter also in the Acts of the Apostles speaks, and says, "The Lord hath said to me that I should call no man common or unclean." But if anything could hinder men from obtaining grace, their more heinous sins might rather hinder those who are mature and grown up and older. But again, if even to the greatest sinners, and to those who had sinned much against God, when they subsequently believed, remission of sins is granted—and nobody is hindered from baptism and from grace—how much rather ought we to shrink from hindering an infant, who, being lately born, has not sinned, except in that, being born after the flesh according to Adam, he has contracted the contagion of the ancient death at its earliest birth, who approaches the more easily on this very account to the reception of the forgiveness of sins—that to him are remitted, not his own sins, but the sins of another. 6. And therefore, dearest brother, this was our opinion in council, that by us no one ought to be hindered from baptism and from the grace of God, who is merciful and kind and loving to all. Which, since it is to be observed and maintained in respect of all, we think is to be even more observed in respect of infants and newly-born persons, who on this very account deserve more from our help and from the divine mercy, that immediately, on the very beginning of their birth, lamenting and weeping, they do nothing else but entreat. We bid you, dearest brother, ever heartily farewell.

Epistle LIX.

To the Numidian Bishops, on the Redemption of Their Brethren from Captivity Among the Barbarians.

Argument.—Cyprian Begins by Deploring the Captivity of the Brethren, of Which He Had Heard from the Numidian Bishops, and Says that He is Sending Them a Hundred Thousand Sesterces, Contributed by Brethren and Sisters and Colleagues.

1. Cyprian to Januarius, Maximus, Proculus, Victor, Modianus, Nemesianus, Nampulus, and Honoratus, his brethren, greeting. With excessive grief of mind, and not without tears, dearest brethren, I have read your letter which you wrote to me from the solicitude of your love, concerning the captivity of our brethren and sisters. For who would not grieve at misfortunes of that kind, or who would not consider his brother's grief his own, since the Apostle Paul speaks, saying, "Whether one member suffer, all the members suffer with it; or one member rejoice, all the members rejoice with it;" and in another place he says, "Who is weak, and I am not weak?" Wherefore now also the captivity of our brethren must be reckoned as our captivity, and the grief of those who are endangered is to be esteemed as our grief, since indeed there is one body of our union; and not love only, but also religion, ought to instigate and strengthen us to redeem the members of the brethren.

2. For inasmuch as the Apostle Paul says again, "Know ye not that ye are the temple of God, and that the Spirit of God dwelleth in you?"—even although love urged us less to bring help to the brethren, yet in this place we must have considered that it was the temples of God which were taken captive, and that we ought not by

long inactivity and neglect of their suffering to allow the temples of God to be long captive, but to strive with what powers we can, and to act quickly by our obedience, to deserve well of Christ our Judge and Lord and God. For as the Apostle Paul says, "As many of you as have been baptized into Christ have put on Christ," Christ is to be contemplated in our captive brethren, and He is to be redeemed from the peril of captivity who redeemed us from the peril of death; so that He who took us out of the jaws of the devil, who abides and dwells in us, may now Himself be rescued and redeemed from the hands of barbarians by a sum of money—who redeemed us by His cross and blood—who suffers these things to happen for this reason, that our faith may be tried, whether each one of us will do for another what he would wish to be done for himself, if he himself were held captive among barbarians. For who that is mindful of humanity, and reminded of mutual love, if he be a father, will not now consider that his sons are there; if he be a husband, will not think that his wife is there kept captive, with as much grief as shame for the marriage tie? But how great is the general grief among all of us, and suffering concerning the peril of virgins who are kept there, on whose behalf we must bewail not only the loss of liberty, but of modesty; and must lament the bonds of barbarians less than the violence of seducers and abominable places, lest the members dedicated to Christ, and devoted forever in honour of continence by modest. virtue, should be sullied by the lust and contagion of the insulter.

3. Our brotherhood, considering all these things according to your letter, and sorrowfully examining, have all promptly and willingly and liberally gathered together supplies of money for the brethren, being always indeed,

according to the strength of their faith, prone to the work of God, but now even more stimulated to salutary works by the consideration of so great a suffering. For since the Lord in His Gospel says, "I was sick, and ye visited me," with how much greater reward for our work will He say now, "I was captive, and ye redeemed me!" And since again He says, "I was in prison, and ye came unto me," how much more will it be when He begins to say, "I was in the dungeon of captivity, and I lay shut up and bound among barbarians, and from that prison of slavery you delivered me," being about to receive a reward from the Lord when the day of judgment shall come! Finally, we give you the warmest thanks that you have wished us to be sharers in your anxiety, and in so great and necessary a work—that you have offered us fruitful fields in which we might cast the seeds of our hope, with the expectation of a harvest of the most abundant fruits which will proceed from this heavenly and saving operation. We have then sent you a sum of one hundred thousand sesterces, which have been collected here in the Church over which by the Lord's mercy we preside, by the contributions of the clergy and people established with us, which you will there dispense with what diligence you may.

4. And we wish, indeed, that nothing of such a kind may happen again, and that our brethren, protected by the majesty of the Lord, may be preserved safe from perils of this kind. If, however, for the searching out of the love of our mind, and for the testing of the faith of our heart, any such thing should happen, do not delay to tell us of it in your letters, counting it for certain that our church and the whole fraternity here beseech by their prayers that these things may not happen again; but if they

happen, that they will willingly and liberally render help. But that you may have in mind in your prayers our brethren and sisters who have labored so promptly and liberally for this needful work, that they may always labor; and that in return for their good work you may present them in your sacrifices and prayers, I have subjoined the names of each one; and moreover also I have added the names of my colleagues and fellow-priests, who themselves also, as they were present, contributed some little according to their power, in their own names and the name of their people. And besides our own amount, I have intimated and sent their small sums, all of whom, in conformity with the claims of faith and charity, you ought to remember in your supplications and prayers. We bid you, dearest brethren, ever heartily farewell, and remember us.

    Epistle LX.
    To Euchratius, About an Actor.
    Argument.—He Forbids an Actor, If He Continue in His Disgraceful Calling, from Communicating in the Church. Neither Does He Allow It to Be an Excuse for Him, that He Himself Does Not Practice the Histrionic Art, So Long as He Teaches It to Others; Neither Does He Excuse It Because of the Want of Means, Since Necessaries May Be Supplied to Him from the Resources of the Church; And Therefore, If the Means of the Church There are Not Sufficient, He Recommends Him to Come to Carthage.

    1. Cyprian to Euchratius his brother, greeting. From our mutual love and your reverence for me you have thought that I should be consulted, dearest brother, as to my opinion concerning a certain actor, who, being

settled among you, still persists in the discredit of the same art of his; and as a master and teacher, not for the instruction, but for the destruction of boys, that which he has unfortunately learnt he also imparts to others: you ask whether such a one ought to communicate with us. This, I think, neither befits the divine majesty nor the discipline of the Gospel, that the modesty and credit of the Church should be polluted by so disgraceful and infamous a contagion. For since, in the law, men are forbidden to put on a woman's garment, and those that offend in this manner are judged accursed, how much greater is the crime, not only to take women's garments, but also to express base and effeminate and luxurious gestures, by the teaching of an immodest art.

2. Nor let anyone excuse himself that he himself has given up the theatre, while he is still teaching the art to others. For he cannot appear to have given it up who substitutes others in his place, and who, instead of himself alone, supplies many in his stead; against God's appointment, instructing and teaching in what way a man may be broken down into a woman, and his sex changed by art, and how the devil who pollutes the divine image may be gratified by the sins of a corrupted and enervated body. But if such a one alleges poverty and the necessity of small means, his necessity also can be assisted among the rest who are maintained by the support of the Church; if he be content, that is, with very frugal but innocent food. And let him not think that he is redeemed by an allowance to cease from sinning, since this is an advantage not to us, but to himself. What more he may wish he must seek thence, from such gain as takes men away from the banquet of Abraham, and Isaac, and Jacob, and leads them down, sadly and perniciously fattened in

this world, to the eternal torments of hunger and thirst; and therefore, as far as you can, recall him from this depravity and disgrace to the way of innocence, and to the hope of eternal life, that he may be content with the maintenance of the Church, sparing indeed, but wholesome. But if the Church with you is not sufficient for this, to afford support for those in need, he may transfer himself to us, and here receive what may be necessary to him for food and clothing, and not teach deadly things to others without the Church, but himself learn wholesome things in the Church. I bid you, dearest brother, ever heartily farewell.

Epistle LXI.
To Pomponius, Concerning Some Virgins.
Argument.—Cyprian, with Some of His Colleagues, Replies to His Colleague Pomponius, that Virgins Who Had Determined to Maintain Their State with Continency and Firmness, But Who Had Yet Subsequently Been Found in the Same Bed with Men, If They Were Still Found to Be Virgins, Should Be Received into Communion and Admitted to the Church. But If Otherwise, Since They are Adulterous Towards Christ, They Should Be Compelled to Full Repentance, and Those Who Should Obstinately Persevere Should Be Ejected from the Church.

1. Cyprian, Cæcilius, Victor, Sedatus, Tertullus, with the presbyters who were present with them, to Pomponius their brother, greeting. We have read, dearest brother, your letter which you sent by Paconius our brother, asking and desiring us to write again to you, and say what we thought of those virgins who, after having once determined to continue in their condition, and firmly

to maintain their continency, have afterwards been found to have remained in the same bed side by side with men; of whom you say that one is a deacon; and yet that the same virgins who have confessed that they have slept with men declare that they are chaste. Concerning which matters, since you have desired our advice, know that we do not depart from the traditions of the Gospel and of the apostles, but with constancy and firmness take counsel for our brethren and sisters, and maintain the discipline of the Church by all the ways of usefulness and safety, since the Lord speaks, saying, "And I will give you pastors according to mine heart, and they shall feed you with discipline." And again it is written, "Whoso despises discipline is miserable; and in the Psalms also the Holy Spirit admonishes and instructs us, saying, "Keep discipline, lest haply the Lord be angry, and ye perish from the right way, when His anger shall quickly burn against you."

2. In the first place, therefore, dearest brother, both by overseers and people nothing is to be more eagerly sought after, than that we who fear God should keep the divine precepts with every observation of discipline, and should not suffer our brethren to stray, and to live according to their own fancy and lust; but that we should faithfully consult for the life of each one, and not suffer virgins to dwell with men,—I do not say to sleep together, but to live together—since both their weak sex and their age, still critical, ought to be bridled in all things and ruled by us, lest an occasion should be given to the devil who ensnares us, and desires to rage over us, to hurt them, since the apostle also says, "Do not give place to the devil." The ship is watchfully to be delivered from perilous places, that it may not be broken among the rocks

and cliffs; the baggage must swiftly be taken out of the fire, before it is burnt up by the flames reaching it. No one who is near to danger is long safe, nor will the servant of God be able to escape the devil if he has entangled himself in the devil's nets. We must interfere at once with such as these, that they may be separated while yet they can be separated in innocence; because by and by they will not be able to be separated by our interference, after they have become joined together by a very guilty conscience. Moreover, what a number of serious mischiefs we see to have arisen hence; and what a multitude of virgins we behold corrupted by unlawful and dangerous conjunctions of this kind, to our great grief of mind! But if they have faithfully dedicated themselves to Christ, let them persevere in modesty and chastity, without incurring any evil report, and so in courage and steadiness await the reward of virginity. But if they are unwilling or unable to persevere, it is better that they should marry, than that by their crimes they should fall into the fire. Certainly let them not cause a scandal to the brethren or sisters, since it is written, "If meat cause my brother to offend, I will eat no flesh while the world stands, lest I make my brother to offend."

3. Nor let anyone think that she can be defended by this excuse, that she may be examined and proved whether she be a virgin; since both the hands and the eyes of the midwives are often deceived; and if she be found to be a virgin in that particular in which a woman may be so, yet she may have sinned in some other part of her body, which may be corrupted and yet cannot be examined. Assuredly the mere lying together, the mere embracing, the very talking together, and the act of kissing, and the disgraceful and foul slumber of two persons lying

together, how much of dishonor and crime does it confess! If a husband come upon his wife, and see her lying with another man, is he not angry and raging, and by the passion of his rage does he not perhaps take his sword into his hand? And what shall Christ and our Lord and Judge think, when He sees His virgin, dedicated to Him, and destined for His holiness, lying with another? How indignant and angry is He, and what penalties does He threaten against such unchaste connections! whose spiritual sword and the coming day of judgment, that every one of the brethren may be able to escape, we ought with all our counsel to provide and to strive. And since it behooves all by all means to keep discipline, much more is it right that overseers and deacons should be careful for this, that they may afford an example and instruction to others concerning their conversation and character. For how can they direct the integrity and continence of others, if the corruptions and teachings of sin begin to proceed from themselves?

4. And therefore you have acted advisedly and with vigor, dearest brother, in excommunicating the deacon who has often abode with a virgin; and, moreover, the others who had been used to sleep with virgins. But if they have repented of this their unlawful lying together, and have mutually withdrawn from one another, let the virgins meantime be carefully inspected by midwives; and if they should be found virgins, let them be received to communion, and admitted to the Church; yet with this threatening, that if subsequently they should return to the same men, or if they should dwell together with the same men in one house or under the same roof, they should be ejected with a severer censure, nor should such be afterwards easily received into the Church. But if any one

of them be found to be corrupted, let her abundantly repent, because she who has been guilty of this crime is an adulteress, not (indeed) against a husband, but against Christ; and therefore, a due time being appointed, let her afterwards, when confession has been made, return to the Church. But if they obstinately persevere, and do not mutually separate themselves, let them know that, with this their immodest obstinacy, they can never be admitted by us into the Church, lest they should begin to set an example to others to go to ruin by their crimes. Nor let them think that the way of life or of salvation is still open to them, if they have refused to obey the bishops and priests, since in Deuteronomy the Lord God says, "And the man that will do presumptuously, and will not hearken unto the priest or judge, whosoever he shall be in those days, that man shall die, and all the people shall hear and fear, and do no more presumptuously." God commanded those who did not obey His priests to be slain, and those who did not hearken to His judges who were appointed for the time. And then indeed they were slain with the sword, when the circumcision of the flesh was yet in force; but now that circumcision has begun to be of the spirit among God's faithful servants, the proud and contumacious are slain with the sword of the Spirit, in that they are cast out of the Church. For they cannot live out of it, since the house of God is one, and there can be no salvation to any except in the Church. But the divine Scripture testifies that the undisciplined perish, because they do not listen to, nor obey wholesome precepts; for it says, "An undisciplined man loveth not him that corrected him. But they who hate reproof shall be consumed with disgrace."

5. Therefore, dearest brother, endeavor that the

undisciplined should not be consumed and perish, that as much as you can, by your salutary counsels, you should rule the brotherhood, and take counsel of each one with a view to his salvation. Straight and narrow is the way through which we enter into life, but excellent and great is the reward when we enter into glory. Let those who have once made themselves eunuchs for the kingdom of heaven please God in all things, and not offend God's priests nor the Lord's Church by the scandal of their wickedness. And if, for the present, certain of our brethren seem to be made sorry by us, let us nevertheless remain in our wholesome persuasion, knowing that an apostle also has said, "Am I therefore become your enemy because I tell you the truth?" But if they shall obey us, we have gained our brethren, and have formed them as well to salvation as to dignity by our address. But if some of the perverse persons refuse to obey, let us follow the same apostle, who says, "If I please men, I should not be the servant of Christ." If we cannot please some, so as to make them please Christ, let us assuredly, as far as we can, please Christ our Lord and God, by observing His precepts. I bid you, brother beloved and much longed-for, heartily farewell in the Lord.

Epistle LXII.
Cæcilius, on the Sacrament of the Cup of the Lord.
Argument.—Cyprian Teaches, in Opposition to Those Who Used Water in the Lord's Supper, that Not Water Alone, But Wine Mixed with Water, Was to Be Offered; That by Water Was Designated in Scripture, Baptism, But Certainly Not the Eucharist. By Types Drawn from the Old Testament, the Use of Wine in the

Sacrament of the Lord's Body is Illustrated; And It is Declared that by the Symbol of Water is Understood the Christian Congregation.

1. Cyprian to Cæcilius his brother, greeting. Although I know, dearest brother, that very many of the bishops who are set over the churches of the Lord by divine condescension, throughout the whole world, maintain the plan of evangelical truth, and of the tradition of the Lord, and do not by human and novel institution depart from that which Christ our Master both prescribed and did; yet since some, either by ignorance or simplicity in sanctifying the cup of the Lord, and in ministering to the people, do not do that which Jesus Christ, our Lord and God, the founder and teacher of this sacrifice, did and taught, I have thought it as well a religious as a necessary thing to write to you this letter, that, if anyone is still kept in this error, he may behold the light of truth, and return to the root and origin of the tradition of the Lord. Nor must you think, dearest brother, that I am writing my own thoughts or man's; or that I am boldly assuming this to myself of my own voluntary will, since I always hold my mediocrity with lowly and modest moderation. But when anything is prescribed by the inspiration and command of God, it is necessary that a faithful servant should obey the Lord, acquitted by all of assuming anything arrogantly to himself, seeing that he is constrained to fear offending the Lord unless he does what he is commanded.

2. Know then that I have been admonished that, in offering the cup, the tradition of the Lord must be observed, and that nothing must be done by us but what the Lord first did on our behalf, as that the cup which is offered in remembrance of Him should be offered mingled with wine. For when Christ says, "I am the true

vine," the blood of Christ is assuredly not water, but wine; neither can His blood by which we are redeemed and quickened appear to be in the cup, when in the cup there is no wine whereby the blood of Christ is shown forth, which is declared by the sacrament and testimony of all the Scriptures.

3. For we find in Genesis also, in respect of the sacrament in Noe, this same thing was to them a precursor and figure of the Lord's passion; that he drank wine; that he was drunken; that he was made naked in his household; that he was lying down with his thighs naked and exposed; that the nakedness of the father was observed by his second son, and was told abroad, but was covered by two, the eldest and the youngest; and other matters which it is not necessary to follow out, since this is enough for us to embrace alone, that Noe, setting forth a type of the future truth, did not drink water, but wine, and thus expressed the figure of the passion of the Lord.

4. Also in the priest Melchizedek we see prefigured the sacrament of the sacrifice of the Lord, according to what divine Scripture testifies, and says, "And Melchizedek, king of Salem, brought forth bread and wine." Now he was a priest of the most high God, and blessed Abraham. And that Melchizedek bore a type of Christ, the Holy Spirit declares in the Psalms, saying from the person of the Father to the Son: "Before the morning star I begat Thee; Thou art a priest forever, after the order of Melchizedek;" which order is assuredly this coming from that sacrifice and thence descending; that Melchizedek was a priest of the most high God; that he offered wine and bread; that he blessed Abraham. For who is more a priest of the most high God than our Lord Jesus Christ, who offered a sacrifice to God the Father,

and offered that very same thing which Melchizedek had offered, that is, bread and wine, to wit, His body and blood? And with respect to Abraham, that blessing going before belonged to our people. For if Abraham believed in God, and it was accounted unto him for righteousness, assuredly whosoever believes in God and lives in faith is found righteous, and already is blessed in faithful Abraham, and is set forth as justified; as the blessed Apostle Paul proves, when he says, "Abraham believed God, and it was accounted to him for righteousness. Ye know, then, that they which are of faith, these are the children of Abraham. But the Scripture, foreseeing that God would justify the Gentiles through faith, pronounced before to Abraham that all nations should be blessed in him; therefore they who are of faith are blessed with faithful Abraham." Whence in the Gospel we find that "children of Abraham are raised from stones, that is, are gathered from the Gentiles." And when the Lord praised Zacchæus, He answered and said, "This day is salvation come to this house, forasmuch as he also is a son of Abraham." In Genesis, therefore, that the benediction, in respect of Abraham by Melchizedek the priest, might be duly celebrated, the figure of Christ's sacrifice precedes, namely, as ordained in bread and wine; which thing the Lord, completing and fulfilling, offered bread and the cup mixed with wine, and so He who is the fulness of truth fulfilled the truth of the image prefigured.

5. Moreover the Holy Spirit by Solomon shows before the type of the Lord's sacrifice, making mention of the immolated victim, and of the bread and wine, and, moreover, of the altar and of the apostles, and says, "Wisdom hath builded her house, she hath underlaid her seven pillars; she hath killed her victims; she hath

mingled her wine in the chalice; she hath also furnished her table: and she hath sent forth her servants, calling together with a lofty announcement to her cup, saying, Whoso is simple, let him turn to me; and to those that want understanding she hath said, Come, eat of my bread, and drink of the wine which I have mingled for you." He declares the wine mingled, that is, he foretells with prophetic voice the cup of the Lord mingled with water and wine, that it may appear that that was done in our Lord's passion which had been before predicted.

6. In the blessing of Judah also this same thing is signified, where there also is expressed a figure of Christ, that He should have praise and worship from his brethren; that He should press down the back of His enemies yielding and fleeing, with the hands with which He bore the cross and conquered death; and that He Himself is the Lion of the tribe of Judah, and should couch sleeping in His passion, and should rise up, and should Himself be the hope of the Gentiles. To which things divine Scripture adds, and says, "He shall wash His garment in wine, and His clothing in the blood of the grape." But when the blood of the grape is mentioned, what else is set forth than the wine of the cup of the blood of the Lord?

7. In Isaiah also the Holy Spirit testifies this same thing concerning the Lord's passion, saying, "Wherefore are Thy garments red, and Thy apparel as from the treading of the wine press full and well-trodden?" Can water make garments red? or is it water in the winepress, which is trodden by the feet, or pressed out by the press? Assuredly, therefore, mention is made of wine, that the Lord's blood may be understood, and that which was afterwards manifested in the cup of the Lord might be foretold by the prophets who announced it. The treading

also, and pressure of the wine-press, is repeatedly dwelt on; because just as the drinking of wine cannot be attained to unless the bunch of grapes be first trodden and pressed, so neither could we drink the blood of Christ unless Christ had first been trampled upon and pressed, and had first drunk the cup of which He should also give believers to drink.

8. But as often as water is named alone in the Holy Scriptures, baptism is referred to, as we see intimated in Isaiah: "Remember not," says he, "the former things, and consider not the things of old. Behold, I will do a new thing, which shall now spring forth; and ye shall know it. I will even make a way in the wilderness, and rivers in the dry place, to give drink to my elected people, my people whom I have purchased, that they might show forth my praise." There God foretold by the prophet, that among the nations, in places which previously had been dry, rivers should afterwards flow plenteously, and should provide water for the elected people of God, that is, for those who were made sons of God by the generation of baptism. Moreover, it is again predicted and foretold before, that the Jews, if they should thirst and seek after Christ, should drink with us, that is, should attain the grace of baptism. "If they shall thirst," he says, "He shall lead them through the deserts, shall bring forth water for them out of the rock; the rock shall be cloven, and the water shall flow, and my people shall drink;" which is fulfilled in the Gospel, when Christ, who is the Rock, is cloven by a stroke of the spear in His passion; who also, admonishing what was before announced by the prophet, cries and says, "If any man thirst, let him come and drink. He that believeth on me, as the Scripture saith, out of his belly shall flow rivers of living water." And that it might

be more evident that the Lord is speaking there, not of the cup, but of baptism, the Scripture adds, saying, "But this spoke He of the Spirit, which they that believe on Him should receive." For by baptism the Holy Spirit is received; and thus by those who are baptized, and have attained to the Holy Spirit, is attained the drinking of the Lord's cup. And let it disturb no one, that when the divine Scripture speaks of baptism, it says that we thirst and drink, since the Lord also in the Gospel says, "Blessed are they which do hunger and thirst after righteousness;" because what is received with a greedy and thirsting desire is drunk more fully and plentifully. As also, in another place, the Lord speaks to the Samaritan woman, saying, "Whosoever drinks of this water shall thirst again; but whosoever drinks of the water that I shall give him, shall not thirst for ever." By which is also signified the very baptism of saving water, which indeed is once received, and is not again repeated. But the cup of the Lord is always both thirsted for and drunk in the Church.

9. Nor is there need of very many arguments, dearest brother, to prove that baptism is always indicated by the appellation of water, and that thus we ought to understand it, since the Lord, when He came, manifested the truth of baptism and the cup in commanding that that faithful water, the water of life eternal, should be given to believers in baptism, but, teaching by the example of His own authority, that the cup should be mingled with a union of wine and water. For, taking the cup on the eve of His passion, He blessed it, and gave it to His disciples, saying, "Drink ye all of this; for this is my blood of the New Testament, which shall be shed for many, for the remission of sins. I say unto you, I will not drink henceforth of this fruit of the vine, until that day in which

I shall drink new wine with you in the kingdom of my Father." In which portion we find that the cup which the Lord offered was mixed, and that that was wine which He called His blood. Whence it appears that the blood of Christ is not offered if there be no wine in the cup, nor the Lord's sacrifice celebrated with a legitimate consecration unless our oblation and sacrifice respond to His passion. But how shall we drink the new wine of the fruit of the vine with Christ in the kingdom of His Father, if in the sacrifice of God the Father and of Christ we do not offer wine, nor mix the cup of the Lord by the Lord's own tradition?

10. Moreover, the blessed Apostle Paul, chosen and sent by the Lord, and appointed a preacher of the Gospel truth, lays down these very things in his epistle, saying, "The Lord Jesus, the same night in which He was betrayed, took bread; and when He had given thanks, He brake it, and said, This is my body, which shall be given for you: do this in remembrance of me. After the same manner also He took the cup, when he had supped, saying, This cup is the new testament in my blood: this do, as oft as ye drink it, in remembrance of me. For as often as ye eat this bread and drink this cup, ye shall show forth the Lord's death until He come." But if it is both enjoined by the Lord, and the same thing is confirmed and delivered by His apostle, that as often as we drink, we do in remembrance of the Lord the same thing which the Lord also did, we find that what was commanded is not observed by us, unless we also do what the Lord did; and that mixing the Lord's cup in like manner we do not depart from the divine teaching; but that we must not at all depart from the evangelical precepts, and that disciples ought also to observe and to do the same things which the

Master both taught and did. The blessed apostle in another place more earnestly and strongly teaches, saying, "I wonder that ye are so soon removed from Him that called you into grace, unto another gospel, which is not another; but there are some that trouble you, and would pervert the Gospel of Christ. But though we, or an angel from heaven, preach any otherwise than that which we have preached to you, let him be anathema. As we said before, so say I now again, If any man preaches any other gospel unto you than that ye have received, let him be anathema."

11. Since, then, neither the apostle himself nor an angel from heaven can preach or teach any otherwise than Christ has once taught and His apostles have announced, I wonder very much whence has originated this practice, that, contrary to evangelical and apostolical discipline, water is offered in some places in the Lord's cup, which water by itself cannot express the blood of Christ. The Holy Spirit also is not silent in the Psalms on the sacrament of this thing, when He makes mention of the Lord's cup, and says, "Thy inebriating cup, how excellent it is!" Now the cup which inebriates is assuredly mingled with wine, for water cannot inebriate anybody. And the cup of the Lord in such wise inebriates, as Noe also was intoxicated drinking wine, in Genesis. But because the intoxication of the Lord's cup and blood is not such as is the intoxication of the world's wine, since the Holy Spirit said in the Psalm, "Thy inebriating cup," He added, "how excellent it is," because doubtless the Lord's cup so inebriates them that drink, that it makes them sober; that it restores their minds to spiritual wisdom; that each one recovers from that flavor of the world to the understanding of God; and in the same way, that by that

common wine the mind is dissolved, and the soul relaxed, and all sadness is laid aside, so, when the blood of the Lord and the cup of salvation have been drunk, the memory of the old man is laid aside, and there arises an oblivion of the former worldly conversation, and the sorrowful and sad breast which before was oppressed by tormenting sins is eased by the joy of the divine mercy; because that only is able to rejoice him who drinks in the Church which, when it is drunk, retains the Lord's truth.

12. But how perverse and how contrary it is, that although the Lord at the marriage made wine of water, we should make water of wine, when even the sacrament of that thing ought to admonish and instruct us rather to offer wine in the sacrifices of the Lord. For because among the Jews there was a want of spiritual grace, wine also was wanting. For the vineyard of the Lord of hosts was the house of Israel; but Christ, when teaching and showing that the people of the Gentiles should succeed them, and that by the merit of faith we should subsequently attain to the place which the Jews had lost, of water made wine; that is, He showed that at the marriage of Christ and the Church, as the Jews failed, the people of the nations should rather flow together and assemble: for the divine Scripture in the Apocalypse declares that the waters signify the people, saying, "The waters which thou saw, upon which the whore sits, are peoples and multitudes, and nations of the Gentiles, and tongues," which we evidently see to be contained also in the sacrament of the cup.

13. For because Christ bore us all, in that He also bore our sins, we see that in the water is understood the people, but in the wine is showed the blood of Christ. But when the water is mingled in the cup with wine, the

people is made one with Christ, and the assembly of believers is associated and conjoined with Him on whom it believes; which association and conjunction of water and wine is so mingled in the Lord's cup, that that mixture cannot any more be separated. Whence, moreover, nothing can separate the Church—that is, the people established in the Church, faithfully and firmly persevering in that which they have believed—from Christ, in such a way as to prevent their undivided love from always abiding and adhering. Thus, therefore, in consecrating the cup of the Lord, water alone cannot be offered, even as wine alone cannot be offered. For if any one offer wine only, the blood of Christ is dissociated from us; but if the water be alone, the people are dissociated from Christ; but when both are mingled, and are joined with one another by a close union, there is completed a spiritual and heavenly sacrament. Thus the cup of the Lord is not indeed water alone, nor wine alone, unless each be mingled with the other; just as, on the other hand, the body of the Lord cannot be flour alone or water alone, unless both should be united and joined together and compacted in the mass of one bread; in which very sacrament our people are shown to be made one, so that in like manner as many grains, collected, and ground, and mixed together into one mass, make one bread; so in Christ, who is the heavenly bread, we may know that there is one body, with which our number is joined and united.

14. There is then no reason, dearest brother, for anyone to think that the custom of certain persons is to be followed, who have thought in time past that water alone should be offered in the cup of the Lord. For we must inquire whom they themselves have followed. For if in

the sacrifice which Christ offered none is to be followed but Christ, assuredly it behooves us to obey and do that which Christ did, and what He commanded to be done, since He Himself says in the Gospel, "If ye do whatsoever I command you, henceforth I call you not servants, but friends." And that Christ alone ought to be heard, the Father also testifies from heaven, saying, "This is my well-beloved Son, in whom I am well pleased; hear ye Him." Wherefore, if Christ alone must be heard, we ought not to give heed to what another before us may have thought was to be done, but what Christ, who is before all, first did. Neither is it becoming to follow the practice of man, but the truth of God; since God speaks by Isaiah the prophet, and says, "In vain do they worship me, teaching the commandments and doctrines of men." And again the Lord in the Gospel repeats this same saying, and says, "Ye reject the commandment of God, that ye may keep your own tradition." Moreover, in another place He establishes it, saying, "Whosoever shall break one of these least commandments, and shall teach men so, he shall be called the least in the kingdom of heaven." But if we may not break even the least of the Lord's commandments, how much rather is it forbidden to infringe such important ones, so great, so pertaining to the very sacrament of our Lord's passion and our own redemption, or to change it by human tradition into anything else than what was divinely appointed! For if Jesus Christ, our Lord and God, is Himself the chief priest of God the Father, and has first offered Himself a sacrifice to the Father, and has commanded this to be done in commemoration of Himself, certainly that priest truly discharges the office of Christ, who imitates that which Christ did; and he then offers a true and full sacrifice in the Church to God the Father, when he proceeds to offer it according to what he sees Christ Himself to have offered.

15. But the discipline of all religion and truth is overturned, unless what is spiritually prescribed be faithfully observed; unless indeed anyone should fear in the morning sacrifices, lest by the taste of wine he should be redolent of the blood of Christ. Therefore thus the brotherhood is beginning even to be kept back from the passion of Christ in persecutions, by learning in the offerings to be disturbed concerning His blood and His blood shedding. Moreover, however, the Lord says in the Gospel, "Whosoever shall be ashamed of me, of him shall the Son of man be ashamed." And the apostle also speaks, saying, "If I pleased men, I should not be the servant of Christ." But how can we shed our blood for Christ, who blush to drink the blood of Christ?

16. Does anyone perchance flatter himself with this notion, that although in the morning, water alone is seen to be offered, yet when we come to supper we offer the mingled cup? But when we sup, we cannot call the people together to our banquet, so as to celebrate the truth of the sacrament in the presence of all the brotherhood. But still it was not in the morning, but after supper, that the Lord offered the mingled cup. Ought we then to celebrate the Lord's cup after supper, that so by continual repetition of the Lord's supper we may offer the mingled cup? It behooved Christ to offer about the evening of the day, that the very hour of sacrifice might show the setting and the evening of the world; as it is written in Exodus, "And all the people of the synagogue of the children of Israel shall kill it in the evening." And again in the Psalms, "Let the lifting up of my hands be an evening

sacrifice." But we celebrate the resurrection of the Lord in the morning.

17. And because we make mention of His passion in all sacrifices (for the Lord's passion is the sacrifice which we offer), we ought to do nothing else than what He did. For Scripture says, "For as often as ye eat this bread and drink this cup, ye do show forth the Lord's death till He come." As often, therefore, as we offer the cup in commemoration of the Lord and of His passion, let us do what it is known the Lord did. And let this conclusion be reached, dearest brother: if from among our predecessors any have either by ignorance or simplicity not observed and kept this which the Lord by His example and teaching has instructed us to do, he may, by the mercy of the Lord, have pardon granted to his simplicity. But we cannot be pardoned who are now admonished and instructed by the Lord to offer the cup of the Lord mingled with wine according to what the Lord offered, and to direct letters to our colleagues also about this, so that the evangelical law and the Lord's tradition may be everywhere kept, and there be no departure from what Christ both taught and did.

18. To neglect these things any further, and to persevere in the former error, what is it else than to fall under the Lord's rebuke, who in the psalm reproved, and says, "What hast thou to do to declare my statutes, or that thou shouldest take my covenant into thy mouth, seeing thou hates instruction and casts my words behind thee? When thou saw a thief, thou consented with him, and hast been partaker with adulterers." For to declare the righteousness and the covenant of the Lord, and not to do the same that the Lord did, what else is it than to cast away His words and to despise the Lord's instruction, to

commit not earthly, but spiritual thefts and adulteries? While any one is stealing from evangelical truth the words and doings of our Lord, he is corrupting and adulterating the divine precepts, as it is written in Jeremiah. He says, "What is the chaff to the wheat? Therefore, behold, I am against the prophets, saith the Lord, who steal my words everyone from his neighbor, and cause my people to err by their lies and by their lightness." Also in the same prophet, in another place, He says, "She committed adultery with stocks and stones, and yet for all this she turned not unto me." That this theft and adultery may not fall unto us also, we ought to be anxiously careful, and fearfully and religiously to watch. For if we are priests of God and of Christ, I do not know any one whom we ought rather to follow than God and Christ, since He Himself emphatically says in the Gospel, "I am the light of the world; he that follows me shall not walk in darkness, but shall have the light of life." Lest therefore we should walk in darkness, we ought to follow Christ, and to observe his precepts, because He Himself told His apostles in another place, as He sent them forth, "All power is given unto me in heaven and earth. Go, therefore, and teach all nations, baptizing them in the name of the Father, and of the Son, and of the Holy Ghost: teaching them to observe all things whatsoever I have commanded you." Wherefore, if we wish to walk in the light of Christ, let us not depart from His precepts and monitions, giving thanks that, while He instructs for the future what we ought to do, He pardons for the past wherein we in our simplicity have erred. And because already His second coming draws near to us, His benign and liberal condescension is more and more illuminating our hearts with the light of truth.

19. Therefore it befits our religion, and our fear, and the place itself, and the office of our priesthood, dearest brother, in mixing and offering the cup of the Lord, to keep the truth of the Lord's tradition, and, on the warning of the Lord, to correct that which seems with some to have been erroneous; so that when He shall begin to come in His brightness and heavenly majesty, He may find that we keep what He admonished us; that we observe what He taught; that we do what He did. I bid you, dearest brother, ever heartily farewell.

Epistle LXIII.

To Epictetus and to the Congregation of Assuræ, Concerning Fortunatianus, Formerly Their Bishop.

Argument.—He Warns Epictetus and the Congregation of the Assuritans Not to Allow Fortunatianus, a Lapser, But Their Former Bishop, to Return to His Episcopate, as Well for Other Reasons as Because It Had Been Decreed that Lapsed Bishops Should Not Be Admitted to Their Former Rank.

1. Cyprian to Epictetus his brother, and to the people established at Assuræ, greeting. I was gravely and grievously disturbed, dearest brethren, at learning that Fortunatianus, formerly bishop among you, after the sad lapse of his fall, was now wishing to act as if he were sound and beginning to claim for himself the episcopate. Which thing distressed me; in the first place, on his own account, who, wretched man that he is, being either wholly blinded in the darkness of the devil, or deceived by the sacrilegious persuasion of certain persons; when he ought to be making atonement, and to give himself to the work of entreating the Lord night and day, by tears, and supplications, and prayers, dares still to claim to himself

the priesthood which he has betrayed, as if it were right, from the altars of the devil, to approach to the altar of God. Or as if he would not provoke a greater wrath and indignation of the Lord against himself in the day of judgment, who, not being able to be a guide to the brethren in faith and virtue, stands forth as a teacher in perfidy, in boldness, and in temerity; and he who has not taught the brethren to stand bravely in the battle, teaches those who are conquered and prostrate not even to ask for pardon; although the Lord says, "To them have ye poured a drink-offering, and to them have ye offered a meat-offering. Shall I not be angry for these things? saith the Lord." And in another place, "He that sacrifices to any god, save unto the Lord only, shall be destroyed." Moreover, the Lord again speaks, and says, "They have worshipped those whom their own fingers have made: and the mean man bows down, and the great man humbles himself: and I will not forgive them." In the Apocalypse also, we read the anger of the Lord threatening, and saying, "If any man worship the beast and his image, and receive his mark in his forehead or in his hand, the same shall drink of the wine of the wrath of God mixed in the cup of His anger; and he shall be tormented with fire and brimstone in the presence of the holy angels, and in the presence of the Lamb: and the smoke of their torments shall ascend up for ever and ever; neither shall they have rest day nor night, who worship the beast and his image."

2. Since, therefore, the Lord threatens these torments, these punishments in the day of judgment, to those who obey the devil and sacrifice to idols, how does he think that he can act as a priest of God who has obeyed and served the priests of the devil; or how does he think that his hand can be transferred to the sacrifice of God

and the prayer of the Lord which has been captive to sacrilege and to crime, when in the sacred Scriptures God forbids the priests to approach to sacrifice even if they have been in lighter guilt; and says in Leviticus: "The man in whom there shall be any blemish or stain shall not approach to offer gifts to God?" Also in Exodus: "And let the priests which come near to the Lord God sanctify themselves, lest perchance the Lord forsake them." And again: "And when they come near to minister at the altar of the Holy One, they shall not bring sin upon them, lest they die." Those, therefore, who have brought grievous sins upon themselves, that is, who, by sacrificing to idols, have offered sacrilegious sacrifices, cannot claim to themselves the priesthood of God, nor make any prayer for their brethren in His sight; since it is written in the Gospel, "God heareth not a sinner; but if any man be a worshipper of God, and doeth His will, him He heareth." Nevertheless the profound gloom of the falling darkness has so blinded the hearts of some, that they receive no light from the wholesome precepts, but, once turned away from the direct path of the true way, they are hurried headlong and suddenly by the night and error of their sins.

3. Nor is it wonderful if now those reject our counsels, or the Lord's precepts, who have denied the Lord. They desire gifts, and offerings, and gain, for which formerly they watched insatiably. They still long also for suppers and banquets, whose debauch they belched forth in the indigestion lately left to the day, most manifestly proving now that they did not before serve religion, but rather their belly and gain, with profane cupidity. Whence also we perceive and believe that this rebuke has come from God's searching out, that they might not continue to stand at the altar; and any further, as

unchaste persons, to have to do with modesty; as perfidious, to have to do with faith; as profane, with religion; as earthly, with things divine; as sacrilegious, with things sacred. That such persons may not return again to the profanation of the altar, and to the contagion of the brethren, we must keep watch with all our powers, and strive with all our strength, that, as far as in us lies, we may keep them back from this audacity of their wickedness, that they attempt not any longer to act in the character of priest; who, cast down to the lowest pit of death, have gone headlong with the weight of a greater destruction beyond the lapses of the laity.

4. But if, among these insane persons, their incurable madness shall continue, and, with the withdrawal of the Holy Spirit, the blindness which has begun shall remain in its deep night, our counsel will be to separate individual brethren from their deceitfulness; and, lest anyone should run into the toils of their error, to separate them from their contagion. Since neither can the oblation be consecrated where the Holy Spirit is not; nor can the Lord avail to any one by the prayers and supplications of one who himself has done despite to the Lord. But if Fortunatianus, either by the blindness induced by the devil forgetful of his crime, or become a minister and servant of the devil for deceiving the brotherhood, shall persevere in this his madness, do you, as far as in you lies, strive, and in this darkness of the rage of the devil, recall the minds of the brethren from error, that they may not easily consent to the madness of another; that they may not make themselves partakers in the crimes of abandoned men; but being sound, let them maintain the constant tenor of their salvation, and of the integrity preserved and guarded by them.

5. Let the lapsed, however, who acknowledge the greatness of their sin, not depart from entreating the Lord, nor forsake the Catholic Church, which has been appointed one and alone by the Lord; but, continuing in their atonements and entreating the Lord's mercy, let them knock at the door of the Church, that they may be received there where once they were, and may return to Christ from whom they have departed, and not listen to those who deceive them with a fallacious and deadly seduction; since it is written, "Let no man deceive you with vain words, for because of these things cometh the wrath of God upon the children of disobedience; be not ye therefore partakers with them." Therefore let no one associate himself with the contumacious, and those who do not fear God, and those who entirely with draw from the Church. But if anyone should be impatient of entreating the Lord who is offended, and should be unwilling to obey us, but should follow desperate and abandoned men, he must take the blame to himself when the day of judgment shall come. For how shall he be able in that day to entreat the Lord, who has both before this denied Christ, and now also the Church of Christ, and not obeying bishops sound and wholesome and living, has made himself an associate and a partaker with the dying? I bid you, dearest brethren and longed-for, ever heartily farewell.

Epistle LXIV.
To Rogatianus, Concerning the Deacon Who Contended Against the Bishop.
Argument.—Cyprian Warns the Bishop

Rogatianus to Restrain the Pride of the Deacon Who Had Provoked Him with His Insults, and to Compel Him to Repent of His Boldness; Taking Occasion to Repeat Once More Whatever He Has Said in the Previous Letter, About the Sacerdotal or Episcopal Power.

1. Cyprian to his brother Rogatianus, greeting. I and my colleagues who were present with me were deeply and grievously distressed, dearest brother, on reading your letter in which you complained of your deacon, that, forgetful of your priestly station, and unmindful of his own office and ministry, he had provoked you by his insults and injuries. And you indeed have acted worthily, and with your accustomed humility towards us, in rather complaining of him to us; although you have power, according to the vigor of the episcopate and the authority of your See, whereby you might be justified on him at once, assured that all we your colleagues would regard it as a matter of satisfaction, whatever you should do by your priestly power in respect of an insolent deacon, as you have in respect of men of this kind divine commands. Inasmuch as the Lord God says in Deuteronomy, "And the man that will do presumptuously, and will not hearken unto the priest or the judge, whoever he shall be in those days, that man shall die; and all the people, when they hear, shall fear, and shall no more do impiously." And that we may know that this voice of God came forth with His true and highest majesty to honour and avenge His priests; when three of the ministers—Korah, Dathan, and Abiram—dared to deal proudly, and to exalt their neck against Aaron the priest, and to equal themselves with the priest set over them; they were swallowed up and devoured by the opening of the earth, and so immediately suffered the penalty of their sacrilegious audacity. Nor

they alone, but also two hundred and fifty others, who were their companions in boldness, were consumed by a fire breaking forth from the Lord, that it might be proved that God's priests are avenged by Him who makes priests. In the book of Kings also, when Samuel the priest was despised by the Jewish people on account of his age, as you are now, the Lord in wrath exclaimed, and said, "They have not rejected thee, but they have rejected me." And that He might avenge this, He set over them Saul as a king, who afflicted them with grievous injuries, and trod on the people, and pressed down their pride with all insults and penalties, that the despised priest might be avenged by divine vengeance on a proud people.

2. Moreover also Solomon, established in the Holy Spirit, testifies and teaches what is the priestly authority and power, saying, "Fear the Lord with all thy soul, and reverence His priests;" and again, "Honour God with all thy soul, and honour His priests." Mindful of which precepts, the blessed Apostle Paul, according to what we read in the Acts of the Apostles, when it was said to him, "Reviles thou thus God's high priest?" answered and said, "I wist not, brethren, that he was the high priest; for it is written, Thou shalt not speak evil of the ruler of thy people." Moreover, our Lord Jesus Christ Himself, our King, and Judge, and God, even to the very day of His passion observed the honour to priests and high priests, although they observed neither the fear of God nor the acknowledgment of Christ. For when He had cleansed the leper, He said to him, "Go, show thyself to the priest, and offer the gift." With that humility which taught us also to be humble, He still called him a priest whom He knew to be sacrilegious; also under the very sting of His passion, when He had received a blow, and it was said to Him,

"Answers thou the high priest so?" He said nothing reproachfully against the person of the high priest, but rather maintained His own innocence saying, "If I have spoken evil, bear witness of the evil; but if well, why smites thou me?" All which things were therefore done by Him humbly and patiently, that we might have an example of humility and patience; for He taught that true priests were lawfully and fully to be honored, in showing Himself such as He was in respect of false priests.

3. But deacons ought to remember that the Lord chose apostles, that is, bishops and overseers; while apostles appointed for themselves deacons after the ascent of the Lord into heaven, as ministers of their episcopacy and of the Church. But if we may dare anything against God who makes bishops, deacons may also dare against us by whom they are made; and therefore it behooves the deacon of whom you write to repent of his audacity, and to acknowledge the honour of the priest, and to satisfy the bishop set over him with full humility. For these things are the beginnings of heretics, and the origins and endeavors of evilminded schismatics;—to please themselves, and with swelling haughtiness to despise him who is set over them. Thus they depart from the Church— thus a profane altar is set up outside—thus they rebel against the peace of Christ, and the appointment and the unity of God. But if, further, he shall harass and provoke you with his insults, you must exercise against him the power of your dignity, by either deposing him or excommunicating him. For if the Apostle Paul, writing to Timothy, said, "Let no man despise thy youth," how much rather must it be said by your colleagues to you, "Let no man despise thy age? And since you have written that one has associated himself with that same deacon of

yours, and is a partaker of his pride and boldness, you may either restrain or excommunicate him also, and any others that may appear of a like disposition, and act against God's priest. Unless, as we exhort and advise, they should rather perceive that they have sinned and make satisfaction and suffer us to keep our own purpose; for we rather ask and desire to overcome the reproaches and injuries of individuals by clemency and patience, than to punish them by our priestly power. I bid you, dearest brother, ever heartily farewell.

Epistle LXV.
To the Clergy and People Abiding at Furni, About Victor, Who Had Made the Presbyter Faustinus a Guardian.

Argument.—Since, Against the Decision of a Council of Bishops, Geminius Victor Had Named in His Will Geminius Faustinus the Presbyter as His Guardian or Curator, He Forbids that Offering Should Be Made for Him, or that the Sacrifice Should Be Celebrated for His Repose, Inferring by the Way, from the Example of the Levitical Tribe, that Clerics Ought Not to Mix Themselves Up in Secular Cares.

1. Cyprian to the presbyters, and deacons, and people abiding at Furni, greeting. I and my colleagues who were present with me were greatly disturbed, dearest brethren, as were also our fellow-presbyters who sate with us, when we were made aware that Geminius Victor, our brother, when departing this life, had named Geminius Faustinus the presbyter executor to his will, although long since it was decreed, in a council of the bishops, that no one should appoint any of the clergy and the ministers of God executor or guardian by his will, since every one

honored by the divine priesthood, and ordained in the clerical service, ought to serve only the altar and sacrifices, and to have leisure for prayers and supplications. For it is written: "No man that wars for God entangles himself with the affairs of this life, that he may please Him to whom he has pledged himself." As this is said of all men, how much rather ought those not to be bound by worldly anxieties and involvements, who, being busied with divine and spiritual things, are not able to withdraw from the Church, and to have leisure for earthly and secular doings! The form of which ordination and engagement the Levites formerly observed under the law, so that when the eleven tribes divided the land and shared the possessions, the Levitical tribe, which was left free for the temple and the altar, and for the divine ministries, received nothing from that portion of the division; but while others cultivated the soil, that portion only cultivated the favor of God, and received the tithes from the eleven tribes, for their food and maintenance, from the fruits which grew. All which was done by divine authority and arrangement, so that they who waited on divine services might in no respect be called away, nor be compelled to consider or to transact secular business. Which plan and rule is now maintained in respect of the clergy, that they who are promoted by clerical ordination in the Church of the Lord may be called off in no respect from the divine administration, nor be tied down by worldly anxieties and matters; but in the honour of the brethren who contribute, receiving as it were tenths of the fruits, they may not withdraw from the altars and sacrifices, but may serve day and night in heavenly and spiritual things.

  2. The bishops our predecessors religiously

considering this, and wholesomely providing for it, decided that no brother departing should name a cleric for executor or guardian; and if anyone should do this, no offering should be made for him, nor any sacrifice be celebrated for his repose. For he does not deserve to be named at the altar of God in the prayer of the priests, who has wished to call away the priests and ministers from the altar. And therefore, since Victor, contrary to the rule lately made in council by the priests, has dared to appoint Geminius Faustinus, a presbyter, his executor, it is not allowed that any offering be made by you for his repose, nor any prayer be made in the church in his name, that so the decree of the priests, religiously and needfully made, may be kept by us; and, at the same time, an example be given to the rest of the brethren, that no one should call away to secular anxieties the priests and ministers of God who are occupied with the service of His altar and Church. For care will probably be taken in time to come that this happen not with respect to the person of clerics anymore, if what has now been done has been punished. I bid you, dearest brethren, ever heartily farewell.

Epistle LXVI.
To Father Stephanus, Concerning Marcianus of Arles, Who Had Joined Himself to Novatian.
Argument.—As Marcianus, Bishop of Arles, When He Followed the Sect of Novatian, Had Seduced Many, and by His Schism Had Separated Himself from the Communion of the Rest of the Bishops, Cyprian Warns Stephanus, that He Should by Announcing the Excommunication of the Offender, Alike by Rome and Carthage, Enable the Church at Arles, to Elect Another in His Place; And that So Peace Might Be Granted, as Well

to the Lapsed as to Those Seduced by Him, Upon Their Repentance, and a Return to the Church Conceded to Them.

1. Cyprian to his brother Stephen, greeting. Faustinus our colleague, abiding at Lyons, has once and again written to me, dearest brother, informing me of those things which also I certainly know to have been told to you, as well by him as by others our fellow-bishops 368 established in the same province, that Marcianus, who abides at Arles, has associated himself with Novatian, and has departed from the unity of the Catholic Church, and from the agreement of our body and priesthood, holding that most extreme depravity of heretical presumption, that the comforts and aids of divine love and paternal tenderness are closed to the servants of God who repent, and mourn, and knock at the gate of the Church with tears, and groans, and grief; and that those who are wounded are not admitted for the soothing of their wounds, but that, forsaken without hope of peace and communion, they must be thrown to become the prey of wolves and the booty of the devil; which matter, dearest brother, it is our business to advise for and to aid in, since we who consider the divine clemency, and hold the balance in governing the Church, do thus exhibit the rebuke of vigor to sinners in such a way as that, nevertheless, we do not refuse the medicine of divine goodness and mercy in raising the lapsed and healing the wounded.

2. Wherefore it behooves you to write a very copious letter to our fellow-bishops appointed in Gaul, not to suffer any longer that Marcian, froward and haughty, and hostile to the divine mercy and to the salvation of the brotherhood, should insult our assembly,

because he does not yet seem to be excommunicated by us; in that he now for a long time boasts and announces that, adhering to Novatian, and following his frowardness, he has separated himself from our communion; although Novatian himself, whom he follows, has formerly been excommunicated, and judged an enemy to the Church; and when he sent ambassadors to us into Africa, asking to be received into our communion, he received back word from a council of several priests who were here present, that he himself had excluded himself, and could not by any of us be received into communion, as he had attempted to erect a profane altar, and to set up an adulterous throne, and to offer sacrilegious sacrifices opposed to the true priest; while the Bishop Cornelius was ordained in the Catholic Church by the judgment of God, and by the suffrages of the clergy and people. Therefore, if he were willing to return to a right mind, and to come to himself, he should repent and return to the Church as a suppliant. How vain it is, dearest brother, when Novatian has lately been repulsed and rejected, and excommunicated by God's priests throughout the whole world, for us still to suffer his flatterers now to jest with us, and to judge of the majesty and dignity of the Church!

3. Let letters be directed by you into the province and to the people abiding at Arles, by which, Marcian being excommunicated, another may be substituted in his place, and Christ's flock, which even to this day is contemned as scattered and wounded by him, may be gathered together. Let it suffice that many of our brethren have departed in these late years in those parts without peace; and certainly let the rest who remain be helped, who groan both day and night, and beseeching the divine and fatherly mercy, entreat the comfort of our succor. For,

for that reason, dearest brother, the body of priests is abundantly large, joined together by the bond of mutual concord, and the link of unity; so that if any one of our college should try to originate heresy, and to lacerate and lay waste Christ's flock, others may help, and as it were, as useful and merciful shepherds, gather together the Lord's sheep into the flock. For what if any harbor in the sea shall begin to be mischievous and dangerous to ships, by the breach of its defenses; do not the navigators direct their ships to other neighboring ports where there is a safe and practicable entrance, and a secure station? Or if, on the road, any inn should begin to be beset and occupied by robbers, so that whoever should enter would be caught by the attack of those who lie in wait there; do not the travelers, as soon as this its character is discovered, seek other houses of entertainment on the road, which shall be safer, where the lodging is trustworthy, and the inns safe for the travelers? And this ought now to be the case with us, dearest brother, that we should receive to us with ready and kindly humanity our brethren, who, tossed on the rocks of Marcian, are seeking the secure harbors of the Church; and that we afford such a place of entertainment for the travelers as is that in the Gospel, in which those who are wounded and maimed by robbers may be received and cherished, and protected by the host.

4. For what is a greater or a more worthy care of overseers, than to provide by diligent solicitude and wholesome medicine for cherishing and preserving the sheep? since the Lord speaks, and says, "The diseased have ye not strengthened, neither have ye healed that which was sick, neither have ye bound up that which was broken, neither have ye brought again that which was driven away, neither have ye sought that which was lost.

And my sheep were scattered because there is no shepherd; and they became meat to all the beasts of the field, and none did search or seek after them. Therefore thus saith the Lord, Behold, I am against the shepherds, and I will require my flock at their hands, and cause them to cease from feeding the flock; neither shall they feed them anymore: for I will deliver them from their mouth, and I will feed them with judgment." Since therefore the Lord thus threatens such shepherds by whom the Lord's sheep are neglected and perish, what else ought we to do, dearest brother, than to exhibit full diligence in gathering together and restoring the sheep of Christ, and to apply the medicine of paternal affection to cure the wounds of the lapsed, since the Lord also in the Gospel warns, and says, "They that be whole need not a physician, but they that are sick?" For although we are many shepherds, yet we feed one flock, and ought to collect and cherish all the sheep which Christ by His blood and passion sought for; nor ought we to suffer our suppliant and mourning brethren to be cruelly despised and trodden down by the haughty presumption of some, since it is written, "But the man that is proud and boastful shall bring nothing at all to perfection, who has enlarged his soul as hell." And the Lord, in His Gospel, blames and condemns men of that kind, saying, "Ye are they which justify yourselves before men, but God knows your hearts: for that which is highly esteemed among men is abomination in the sight of God." He says that those are execrable and detestable who please themselves, who, swelling and inflated, arrogantly assume anything to themselves. Since then Marcian has begun to be of these, and, allying himself with Novatian, has stood forth as the opponent of mercy and love, let him not pronounce sentence, but receive it; and let him not so act as if he himself were to judge of the college of priests, since he himself is judged by all the priests.

5. For the glorious honour of our predecessors, the blessed martyrs Cornelius and Lucius, must be maintained, whose memory as we hold in honour, much more ought you, dearest brother, to honour and cherish with your weight and authority, since you have become their vicar and successor. For they, full of the Spirit of God, and established in a glorious martyrdom, judged that peace should be granted to the lapsed, and that when penitence was undergone, the reward of peace and communion was not to be denied; and this they attested by their letters, and we all everywhere and entirely have judged the same thing. For there could not be among us a diverse feeling in whom there was one spirit; and therefore it is manifest that he does not hold the truth of the Holy Spirit with the rest, whom we observe to think differently. Intimate plainly to us who has been substituted at Arles in the place of Marcian, that we may know to whom to direct our brethren, and to whom we ought to write. I bid you, dearest brother, ever heartily farewell.

Epistle LXVII.
To the Clergy and People Abiding in Spain, Concerning Basilides and Martial.
Argument.—Basilides and Martial, Bishops, Having Lapsed and Become Contaminated by the Certificates of Idolatry, Cyprian with His Fellow-Bishops Praises the Clergy and People of Spain that They Had Substituted in Their Place by a Legitimate Election, Sabinus and Felix; Especially As, According to the Decision of Cornelius and His Colleagues, Lapsed

Bishops Might Indeed Be Received to Repentance, But Were Prohibited from the Priestly Honour. Moreover, He Alludes by the Way to Certain Matters About the Ancient Rite of Episcopal Election. The Context Indicates that This Was Written During the Episcopate of Stephen.

1. Cyprian, Cæcilius, Primus, Polycarp, Nicomedes, Lucilianus, Successus, Sedatus, Fortunatus, Januarius, Secundinus, Pomponius, Honoratus, Victor, Aurelius, Sattius, Petrus, another Januarius, Saturninus, another Aurelius, Venantius, Quietus, Rogatianus, Tenax, Felix, Faustinus, Quintus, another Saturninus, Lucius, Vincentius, Libosus, Geminius, Marcellus, Iambus, Adelphius, Victoricus, and Paulus, to Felix the presbyter, and to the peoples abiding at Legio and Asturica, also to Lælius the deacon, and the people abiding at Emerita, brethren in the Lord, greeting. When we had come together, dearly beloved brethren, we read your letters, which according to the integrity of your faith and your fear of God you wrote to us by Felix and Sabinus our fellow-bishops, signifying that Basilides and Martial, being stained with the certificates of idolatry, and bound with the consciousness of wicked crimes, ought not to hold the episcopate and administer the priesthood of God; and you desired an answer to be written to you again concerning these things, and your solicitude, no less just than needful, to be relieved either by the comfort or by the help of our judgment. Nevertheless to this your desire not so much our counsels as the divine precepts reply, in which it is long since bidden by the voice of Heaven and prescribed by the law of God, who and what sort of persons ought to serve the altar and to celebrate the divine sacrifices. For in Exodus God speaks to Moses, and warns him, saying, "Let the priests which come near to the Lord

God sanctify themselves, lest the Lord forsake them." And again: "And when they come near to the altar of the Holy One to minister they shall not bring sin upon them, lest they die." Also in Leviticus the Lord commands and says, "Whosoever hath any spot or blemish upon him, shall not approach to offer gifts to God."

2. Since these things are announced and are made plain to us, it is necessary that our obedience should wait upon the divine precepts; nor in matters of this kind can human indulgence accept any man's person, or yield anything to anyone, when the divine prescription has interfered, and establishes a law. For we ought not to be forgetful what the Lord spoke to the Jews by Isaiah the prophet, rebuking, and indignant that they had despised the divine precepts and followed human doctrines. "This people," he says, honors me with their lips, but their heart is widely removed from me; but in vain do they worship me, teaching the doctrines and commandments of men." This also the Lord repeats in the Gospel, and says, "Ye reject the commandment of God, that ye may establish your own tradition." Having which things before our eyes, and solicitously and religiously considering them, we ought in the ordinations of priests to choose none but unstained and upright ministers, who, holily and worthily offering sacrifices to God, may be heard in the prayers which they make for the safety of the Lord's people, since it is written, "God heareth not a sinner; but if any man be a worshipper of God, and doeth His will, him He heareth." On which account it is fitting, that with full diligence and sincere investigation those should be chosen for God's priesthood whom it is manifest God will hear.

3. Nor let the people flatter themselves that they can be free from the contagion of sin, while

communicating with a priest who is a sinner, and yielding their consent to the unjust and unlawful episcopacy of their overseer, when the divine reproof by Hosea the prophet threatens, and says, "Their sacrifices shall be as the bread of mourning; all that eat thereof shall be polluted;" teaching manifestly and showing that all are absolutely bound to the sin who have been contaminated by the sacrifice of a profane and unrighteous priest. Which, moreover, we find to be manifested also in Numbers, when Korah, and Dathan, and Abiram claimed for themselves the power of sacrificing in opposition to Aaron the priest. There also the Lord commanded by Moses that the people should be separated from them, lest, being associated with the wicked, themselves also should be bound closely in the same wickedness. "Separate yourselves," said He, "from the tents of these wicked and hardened men, and touch not those things which belong to them, lest ye perish together in their sins." On which account a people obedient to the Lord's precepts, and fearing God, ought to separate themselves from a sinful prelate, and not to associate themselves with the sacrifices of a sacrilegious priest, especially since they themselves have the power either of choosing worthy priests, or of rejecting unworthy ones.

4. Which very thing, too, we observe to come from divine authority, that the priest should be chosen in the presence of the people under the eyes of all, and should be approved worthy and suitable by public judgment and testimony; as in the book of Numbers the Lord commanded Moses, saying, "Take Aaron thy brother, and Eleazar his son, and place them in the mount, in the presence of all the assembly, and strip Aaron of his garments, and put them upon Eleazar his son; and let

Aaron die there, and be added to his people." God commands a priest to be appointed in the presence of all the assembly; that is, He instructs and shows that the ordination of priests ought not to be solemnized except with the knowledge of the people standing near, that in the presence of the people either the crimes of the wicked may be disclosed, or the merits of the good may be declared, and the ordination, which shall have been examined by the suffrage and judgment of all, may be just and legitimate. And this is subsequently observed, according to divine instruction, in the Acts of the Apostles, when Peter speaks to the people of ordaining an apostle in the place of Judas. "Peter," it says, "stood up in the midst of the disciples, and the multitude were in one place." Neither do we observe that this was regarded by the apostles only in the ordinations of bishops and priests, but also in those of deacons, of which matter itself also it is written in their Acts: "And they twelve called together," it says, "the whole congregation of the disciples, and said to them;" which was done so diligently and carefully, with the calling together of the whole of the people, surely for this reason, that no unworthy person might creep into the ministry of the altar, or to the office of a priest. For that unworthy persons are sometimes ordained, not according to the will of God, but according to human presumption, and that those things which do not come of a legitimate and righteous ordination are displeasing to God, God Himself manifests by Hosea the prophet, saying, "They have set up for themselves a king, but not by me."

5. For which reason you must diligently observe and keep the practice delivered from divine tradition and apostolic observance, which is also maintained among us,

and almost throughout all the provinces; that for the proper celebration of ordinations all the neighboring bishops of the same province should assemble with that people for which a prelate is ordained. And the bishop should be chosen in the presence of the people, who have most fully known the life of each one and have looked into the doings of each one as respects his habitual conduct. And this also, we see, was done by you in the ordination of our colleague Sabinus; so that, by the suffrage of the whole brotherhood, and by the sentence of the bishops who had assembled in their presence, and who had written letters to you concerning him, the episcopate was conferred upon him, and hands were imposed on him in the place of Basilides. Neither can it rescind an ordination rightly perfected, that Basilides, after the detection of his crimes, and the baring of his conscience even by his own confession, went to Rome and deceived Stephen our colleague, placed at a distance, and ignorant of what had been done, and of the truth, to canvass that he might be replaced unjustly in the episcopate from which he had been righteously deposed. The result of this is, that the sins of Basilides are not so much abolished as enhanced, inasmuch as to his former sins he has also added the crime of deceit and circumvention. For he is not so much to be blamed who has been through heedlessness surprised by fraud, as he is to be execrated who has fraudulently taken him by surprise. But if Basilides could deceive men, he cannot deceive God, since it is written, "God is not mocked." But neither can deceit advantage Martialis, in such a way as that he who also is involved in great crimes should hold his bishopric, since the apostle also warns, and says, "A bishop must be blameless, as the steward of God."

6. Wherefore, since as ye have written, dearly beloved brethren, and as Felix and Sabinus our colleagues affirm, and as another Felix of Caesar Augusta, a maintainer of the faith and a defender of the truth, signifies in his letter, Basilides and Martialis have been contaminated by the abominable certificate of idolatry; and Basilides, moreover, besides the stain of the certificate, when he was prostrate in sickness, blasphemed against God, and confessed that he blasphemed; and because of the wound to his own conscience, voluntarily laying down his episcopate, turned himself to repentance, entreating God, and considering himself sufficiently happy if it might be permitted him to communicate even as a layman: Martialis also, besides the long frequenting of the disgraceful and filthy banquets of the Gentiles in their college, and placing his sons in the same college, after the manner of foreign nations, among profane sepulchers, and burying them together with strangers, has also affirmed, by acts which are publicly taken before a ducenarian procurator, that he had yielded himself to idolatry, and had denied Christ; and as there are many other and grave crimes in which Basilides and Martialis are held to be implicated; such persons attempt to claim for themselves the episcopate in vain; since it is evident that men of that kind may neither rule over the Church of Christ, nor ought to offer sacrifices to God, especially since Cornelius also, our colleague, a peaceable and righteous priest, and moreover honored by the condescension of the Lord with martyrdom, has long ago decreed with us, and with all the bishops appointed throughout the whole world, that men of this sort might indeed be admitted to repentance, but were prohibited from the ordination of the clergy, and from the priestly

honour.

7. Nor let it disturb you, dearest brethren, if with some, in these last times, either an uncertain faith is wavering, or a fear of God without religion is vacillating, or a peaceable concord does not continue. These things have been foretold as about to happen in the end of the world; and it was predicted by the voice of the Lord, and by the testimony of the apostles, that now that the world is failing, and the Antichrist is drawing near, everything good shall fail, but evil and adverse things shall prosper.

8. Yet although, in these last times, evangelic rigour has not so failed in the Church of God, nor the strength of Christian virtue or faith so languished, that there is not left a portion of the priests which in no respect gives way under these ruins of things and wrecks of faith; but, bold and steadfast, they maintain the honour of the divine majesty and the priestly dignity, with full observance of fear. We remember and keep in view that, although others succumbed and yielded, Mattathias boldly vindicated God's law; that Elias, when the Jews gave way and departed from the divine religion, stood and nobly contended; that Daniel, deterred neither by the loneliness of a foreign country nor by the harassment of continual persecution, frequently and gloriously suffered martyrdoms; also that the three youths, subdued neither by their tender years nor by threats, stood up faithfully against the Babylonian fires, and conquered the victor king even in their very captivity itself. Let the number either of prevaricators or of traitors see to it, who have now begun to rise in the Church against the Church, and to corrupt as well the faith as the truth. Among very many there still remains a sincere mind and a substantial religion, and a spirit devoted to nothing but the Lord and

its God. Nor does the perfidy of others press down the Christian faith into ruin, but rather stimulates and exalts it to glory, according to what the blessed Apostle Paul exhorts, and says: "For what if some of these have fallen from their faith: hath their unbelief made the faith of God of none effect? God forbid. For God is true, but every man a liar." But if every man is a liar, and God only true, what else ought we, the servants, and especially the priests, of God, to do, than forsake human errors and lies, and continue in the truth of God, keeping the Lord's precepts?

9. Wherefore, although there have been found some among our colleagues, dearest brethren, who think that the godly discipline may be neglected, and who rashly hold communion with Basilides and Martialis, such a thing as this ought not to trouble our faith, since the Holy Spirit threatens such in the Psalms, saying, "But thou hates instruction, and casted my words behind thee: when thou saw a thief, thou consented unto him, and hast been partaker with adulterers." He shows that they become sharers and partakers of other men's sins who are associated with the delinquents. And besides, Paul the apostle writes, and says the same thing: "Whisperers, backbiters, haters of God, injurious, proud, boasters of themselves, inventors of evil things, who, although they knew the judgment of God, did not understand that they which commit such things are worthy of death, not only they which commit those things, but they also which consent unto those who do these things." Since they, says he, who do such things are worthy of death, he makes manifest and proves that not only they are worthy of death, and come into punishment who do evil things, but also those who consent unto those who do such things—

who, while they are mingled in unlawful communion with the evil and sinners, and the unrepenting, are polluted by the contact of the guilty, and, being joined in the fault, are thus not separated in its penalty. For which reason we not only approve, but applaud, dearly beloved brethren, the religious solicitude of your integrity and faith, and exhort you as much as we can by our letters, not to mingle in sacrilegious communion with profane and polluted priests but maintain the sound and sincere constancy of your faith with religious fear. I bid you, dearest brethren, ever heartily farewell.

Epistle LXVIII.
To Florentius Pupianus, on Calumniators.
Argument.—Cyprian Clears Himself in the Eyes of Florentius Pupianus from Various Crimes of Which He is Accused by Him; And Argues the Lightness of His Mind, in that He Has So Hastily Trusted Calumniators.

1. Cyprian, who is also called Thascius, to Florentius, who is also Pupianus, his brother, greeting. I had believed, brother, that you were now at length turned to repentance for having either rashly heard or believed in time past things so wicked, so disgraceful, so execrable even among Gentiles, concerning me. But even now in your letter I perceive that you are still the same as you were before—that you believe the same things concerning me, and that you persist in what you did believe, and, lest by chance the dignity of your eminence and your martyrdom should be stained by communion with me, that you are inquiring carefully into my character; and after God the Judge who makes priests, that you wish to judge—I will not say of me, for what am I?—but of the judgment of God and of Christ. This is not to believe in

God—this is to stand forth as a rebel against Christ and His Gospel; so that although He says, "Are not two sparrows sold for a farthing? and neither of them falls to the ground without the will of my Father," and His majesty and truth prove that even things of little consequence are not done without the consciousness and permission of God, you think that God's priests are ordained in the Church without His knowledge. For to believe that they who are ordained are unworthy and unchaste, what else is it than to believe that his priests are not appointed in the Church by God, nor through God?

2. Think you that my testimony of myself is better than that of God? when the Lord Himself teaches, and says that testimony is not true, if any one himself appears as a witness concerning himself, for the reason that everyone would assuredly favor himself. Nor would anyone put forward mischievous and adverse things against himself, but there may be a simple confidence of truth if, in what was announced of us, another is the announcer and witness. "If," He says, "I bear witness of myself, my testimony is not true; but there is another who bears witness of me." But if the Lord Himself, who will by and by judge all things, was unwilling to be believed on His own testimony, but preferred to be approved by the judgment and testimony of God the Father, how much more does it behoove His servants to observe this, who are not only approved by, but even glory in the judgment and testimony of God! But with you the fabrication of hostile and malignant men has prevailed against the divine decree, and against our conscience resting upon the strength of its faith, as if among lapsed and profane persons placed outside the Church, from whose breasts the Holy Spirit has departed, there could be anything else

than a depraved mind and a deceitful tongue, and venomous hatred, and sacrilegious lies, which whosoever believes, must of necessity be found with them when the day of judgment shall come.

3. But with respect to what you have said, that priests should be lowly, because both the Lord and His apostles were lowly; both all the brethren and Gentiles also well know and love my humility; and you also knew and loved it while you were still in the Church, and were in communion with me. But which of us is far from humility: I, who daily serve the brethren, and kindly receive with good-will and gladness every one that comes to the Church; or you, who appoint yourself bishop of a bishop, and judge of a judge, given for the time by God? Although the Lord God says in Deuteronomy, "And the man that will do presumptuously, and will not hearken unto the priests or unto the judge who shall be in those days, even that man shall die; and all the people, when they hear, shall fear, and do no more presumptuously." And again He speaks to Samuel, and says, "They have not despised thee, but they have despised me." And moreover the Lord, in the Gospel, when it was said to Him, "Answers thou the high priest so?" guarding the priestly dignity, and teaching that it ought to be maintained, would say nothing against the high priest, but only clearing His own innocence, answered, saying, "If I have spoken evil, bear witness of the evil; but if well, why smites thou me?" The blessed apostle also, when it was said to him, "Reviles thou God's high priest?" spoke nothing reproachfully against the priest, when he might have lifted up himself boldly against those who had crucified the Lord, and who had already sacrificed God and Christ, and the temple and the priesthood; but even

although in false and degraded priests, considering still the mere empty shadow of the priestly name, he said, "I wist not, brethren, that he was the high priest; for it is written, Thou shalt not speak evil of the ruler of thy people."

4. Unless perchance I was a priest to you before the persecution, when you held communion with me, and ceased to be a priest after the persecution! For the persecution, when it came, lifted you to the highest sublimity of martyrdom. But it depressed me with the burden of proscription, since it was publicly declared, "If anyone holds or possesses any of the property of Cæcilius Cyprian, bishop of the Christians;" so that even they who did not believe in God appointing a bishop, could still believe in the devil proscribing a bishop. Nor do I boast of these things, but with grief I bring them forward, since you constitute yourself a judge of God and of Christ, who says to the apostles, and thereby to all chief rulers, who by vicarious ordination succeed to the apostles: "He that heareth you, heareth me; and he that heareth me, heareth Him that sent me; and he that despises you, despises me, and Him that sent me."

5. For from this have arisen, and still arise, schisms and heresies, in that the bishop who is one and rules over the Church is contemned by the haughty presumption of some persons; and the man who is honored by God's condescension, is judged unworthy by men. For what swelling of pride is this, what arrogance of soul, what inflation of mind, to call prelates and priests to one's own recognition, and unless I may be declared clear in your sight and absolved by your judgment, behold now for six years the brotherhood has neither had a bishop, nor the people a prelate, nor the flock a pastor, nor the Church

a governor, nor Christ a representative, nor God a priest! Pupianus must come to the rescue, and give judgment, and declare the decision of God and Christ accepted, that so great a number of the faithful who have been summoned away, under my rule, may not appear to have departed without hope of salvation and of peace; that the new crowd of believers may not be considered to have failed of attaining any grace of baptism and the Holy Spirit by my ministry; that the peace conferred upon so many lapsed and penitent persons, and the communion vouchsafed by my examination, may not be abrogated by the authority of your judgment. Condescend for once, and deign to pronounce concerning us, and to establish our episcopate by the authority of your recognition, that God and His Christ may thank you, in that by your means a representative and ruler has been restored as well to their altar as to their people.

6. Bees have a king, and cattle a leader, and they keep faith to him. Robbers obey their chief with an obedience full of humility. How much more simple and better than you are the brute cattle and dumb animals, and robbers, although bloody, and raging among swords and weapons! The chief among them is acknowledged and feared, whom no divine judgment has appointed, but on whom an abandoned faction and a guilty band have agreed.

7. You say, indeed, that the scruple into which you have fallen ought to be taken from your mind. You have fallen into it, but it was by your irreligious credulity. You have fallen into it, but it was by your own sacrilegious disposition and will in easily hearkening to unchaste, to impious, to unspeakable things against your brother, against a priest, and in willingly believing them in

defending other men's falsehoods, as if they were your own and your private property; and in not remembering that it is written, "Hedge thine ears with thorns, and hearken not to a wicked tongue;" and again: "A wicked doer giveth heed to the tongue of the unjust; but a righteous man regards not lying lips." Wherefore have not the martyrs fallen into this scruple, full of the Holy Ghost, and already by their passion near to the presence of God and of His Christ; martyrs who, from their dungeon, directed letters to Cyprian the bishop, acknowledging the priest of God, and bearing witness to him? Wherefore have not so many bishops, my colleagues, fallen into this scruple, who either, when they departed from the midst of us, were proscribed, or being taken were cast into prison and were in chains; or who, sent away into exile, have gone by an illustrious road to the Lord; or who in some places, condemned to death, have received heavenly crowns from the glorification of the Lord? Wherefore have not they fallen into this scruple, from among that people of ours which is with us, and is by God's condescension committed to us—so many confessors who have been put to the question and tortured, and glorious by the memory of illustrious wounds and scars; so many chaste virgins, so many praiseworthy widows; finally, all the churches throughout the whole world who are associated with us in the bond of unity? Unless all these, who are in communion with me, as you have written, are polluted with the pollution of my lips, and have lost the hope of eternal life by the contagion of my communion. Pupianus alone, sound, inviolate, holy, modest, who would not associate himself with us, shall dwell alone in paradise and in the kingdom of heaven.

8. You have written also, that on my account the

Church has now a portion of herself in a state of dispersion, although the whole people of the Church are collected, and united, and joined to itself in an undivided concord: they alone have remained without, who even, if they had been within, would have had to be cast out. Nor does the Lord, the protector of His people, and their guardian, suffer the wheat to be snatched from His floor; but the chaff alone can be separated from the Church, since also the apostle says, "For what if some of them have departed from the faith? shall their unbelief make the faith of God of none effect? God forbid; for God is true, but every man a liar." And the Lord also in the Gospel, when disciples forsook Him as He spoke, turning to the twelve, said, "Will ye also go away?" then Peter answered Him, "Lord, to whom shall we go? Thou hast the word of eternal life; and we believe, and are sure, that Thou art the Son of the living God." Peter speaks there, on whom the Church was to be built, teaching and showing in the name of the Church, that although a rebellious and arrogant multitude of those who will not hear and obey may depart, yet the Church does not depart from Christ; and they are the Church who are a people united to the priest, and the flock which adheres to its pastor. Whence you ought to know that the bishop is in the Church, and the Church in the bishop; and if anyone be not with the bishop, that he is not in the Church, and that those flatter themselves in vain who creep in, not having peace with God's priests, and think that they communicate secretly with some; while the Church, which is Catholic and one, is not cut nor divided, but is indeed connected and bound together by the cement of priests who cohere with one another.

9. Wherefore, brother, if you consider God's

majesty who ordains priests, if you will for once have respect to Christ, who by His decree and word, and by His presence, both rules prelates themselves, and rules the Church by prelates; if you will trust, in respect of the innocence of bishops, not human hatred, but the divine judgment; if you will begin even a late repentance for your temerity, and pride, and insolence; if you will most abundantly make satisfaction to God and His Christ whom I serve, and to whom with pure and unstained lips I ceaselessly offer sacrifices, not only in peace, but in persecution; we may have some ground for communion with you, even although there still remain among us respect and fear for the divine censure; so that first I should consult my Lord whether He would permit peace to be granted to you, and you to be received to the communion of His Church by His own showing and admonition.

10. For I remember what has already been manifested to me, nay, what has been prescribed by the authority of our Lord and God to an obedient and fearing servant; and among other things which He condescended to show and to reveal, He also added this: "Whoso therefore does not believe Christ, who makes the priest, shall hereafter begin to believe Him who avenges the priest." Although I know that to some men dreams seem ridiculous and visions foolish, yet assuredly it is to such as would rather believe in opposition to the priest, than believe the priest. But it is no wonder, since his brethren said of Joseph, "Behold, this dreamer cometh; come now therefore, let us slay him." And afterwards the dreamer attained to what he had dreamed; and his slayers and sellers were put to confusion, so that they, who at first did not believe the words, afterwards believed the deeds. But

of those things that you have done, either in persecution or in peace, it is foolish for me to pretend to judge you, since you rather appoint yourself a judge over us. These things, of the pure conscience of my mind, and of my confidence in my Lord and my God, I have written at length. You have my letter, and I yours. In the day of judgment, before the tribunal of Christ, both will be read.

Epistle LXIX.
To Januarius and Other Numidian Bishops, on Baptizing Heretics.

Argument.—The Argument of This Letter and the Next is Found in a Subsequent Epistle to Stephen; "That What Heretics Use is Not Baptism; And that None Among Them Can Receive Benefit by the Grace of Christ, Who Oppose Christ; Has Been Lately Carefully Expressed in a Letter Which Was Written on that Subject to Quintus, Our Colleague, Established in Mauritania; As Also in a Letter Which Our Colleagues Previously Wrote to the Bishops Presiding in Numidia; Of Both of Which Letters I Have Subjoined Copies."

1. Cyprian, Liberalis, Caldonius, Junius, Primus, Cæcilius, Polycarp, Nicomedes, Felix, Marrutius, Successus, Lucianus, Honoratus, Fortunatus, Victor, Donatus, Lucius, Herculanus, Pomponius, Demetrius, Quintus, Saturninus, Januarius, Marcus, another Saturninus, another Donatus, Rogatianus, Sedatus, Tertullus, Hortensianus, still another Saturninus, Sattius, to their brethren Januarius, Saturninus, Maximus, Victor, another Victor, Cassius, Proculus, Modianus, Cittinus, Gargilius, Eutycianus, another Gargilius, another Saturninus, Nemesianus, Nampulus, Antonianus, Rogatianus, Honoratus, greeting. When we were together

in council, dearest brethren, we read your letter which you wrote to us concerning those who seem to be baptized by heretics and schismatics, (asking) whether, when they come to the Catholic Church, which is one, they ought to be baptized. On which matter, although you yourselves hold thereupon the truth and certainty of the Catholic rule, yet since you have thought that of our mutual love we ought to be consulted, we put forward our opinion, not as a new one, but we join with you in equal agreement, in an opinion long since decreed by our predecessors, and observed by us,—judging, namely, and holding it for certain that no one can be baptized abroad outside the Church, since there is one baptism appointed in the holy Church. And it is written in the words of the Lord, "They have forsaken me, the fountain of living waters, and hewed them out broken cisterns, which can hold no water." And again, sacred Scripture warns, and says, "Keep thee from the strange water, and drink not from a fountain of strange water." It is required, then, that the water should first be cleansed and sanctified by the priest, that it may wash away by its baptism the sins of the man who is baptized; because the Lord says by Ezekiel the prophet: "Then will I sprinkle clean water upon you, and ye shall be cleansed from all your filthiness; and from all your idols will I cleanse you: a new heart also will I give you, and a new spirit will I put within you." But how can he cleanse and sanctify the water who is himself unclean, and in whom the Holy Spirit is not? since the Lord says in the book of Numbers, "And whatsoever the unclean person touches shall be unclean." Or how can he who baptizes give to another remission of sins who himself, being outside the Church, cannot put away his own sins?

2. But, moreover, the very interrogation which is

put in baptism is a witness of the truth. For when we say, "Dost thou believe in eternal life and remission of sins through the holy Church?" we mean that remission of sins is not granted except in the Church, and that among heretics, where there is no Church, sins cannot be put away. Therefore they who assert that heretics can baptize, must either change the interrogation or maintain the truth; unless indeed they attribute a church also to those who, they contend, have baptism. It is also necessary that he should be anointed who is baptized; so that, having received the chrism, that is, the anointing, he may be anointed of God, and have in him the grace of Christ. Further, it is the Eucharist whence the baptized are anointed with the oil sanctified on the altar. But he cannot sanctify the creature of oil, who has neither an altar nor a church; whence also there can be no spiritual anointing among heretics, since it is manifest that the oil cannot be sanctified nor the Eucharist celebrated at all among them. But we ought to know and remember that it is written, "Let not the oil of a sinner anoint my head," which the Holy Spirit before forewarned in the Psalms, lest anyone going out of the way and wandering from the path of truth should be anointed by heretics and adversaries of Christ. Besides, what prayer can a priest who is impious and a sinner offer for a baptized person? since it is written, "God heareth not a sinner; but if any man be a worshipper of God, and doeth His will, him He heareth." Who, moreover, can give what he himself has not? or how can he discharge spiritual functions who himself has lost the Holy Spirit? And therefore he must be baptized and renewed who comes untrained to the Church, that he may be sanctified within by those who are holy, since it is written, "Be ye holy, for I am holy, saith the Lord." So that he who has been seduced into error, and baptized outside of the Church, should lay aside even this very thing in the true and ecclesiastical baptism, viz., that he a man coming to God, while he seeks for a priest, fell by the deceit of error upon a profane one.

3. But it is to approve the baptism of heretics and schismatics, to admit that they have truly baptized. For therein a part cannot be void, and part be valid. If one could baptize, he could also give the Holy Spirit. But if he cannot give the Holy Spirit, because he that is appointed without is not endowed with the Holy Spirit, he cannot baptize those who come; since both baptism is one and the Holy Spirit is one, and the Church founded by Christ the Lord upon Peter, by a source and principle of unity, is one also. Hence it results, that since with them all things are futile and false, nothing of that which they have done ought to be approved by us. For what can be ratified and established by God which is done by them whom the Lord calls His enemies and adversaries? setting forth in His Gospel, "He that is not with me is against me; and he that gathered not with me, scattered." And the blessed Apostle John also, keeping the commandments and precepts of the Lord, has laid it down in his epistle, and said, "Ye have heard that antichrist shall come: even now there are many Antichrists; whereby we know that it is the last time. They went out from us, but they were not of us; for if they had been of us, no doubt they would have continued with us." Whence we also ought to gather and consider whether they who are the Lord's adversaries, and are called antichrists, can give the grace of Christ. Wherefore we who are with the Lord, and maintain the unity of the Lord, and according to His condescension ad☐minister His priesthood in the Church, ought to repudiate and

reject and regard as profane whatever His adversaries and the antichrists do; and to those who, coming out of error and wickedness, acknowledge the true faith of the one Church, we should give the truth both of unity and faith, by means of all the sacraments of divine grace. We bid you, dearest brethren, ever heartily farewell.

>Epistle LXX.
>To Quintus, Concerning the Baptism of Heretics.

Argument.—An Answer is Given to Quintus a Bishop in Mauritania, Who Has Asked Advice Concerning the Baptism of Heretics.

1. Cyprian to Quintus his brother, greeting. Lucian, our co-presbyter, has reported to me, dearest brother, that you have wished me to declare to you what I think concerning those who seem to have been baptized by heretics and schismatics; of which matter, that you may know what several of us fellow-bishops, with the brother presbyters who were present, lately determined in council, I have sent you a copy of the same epistle. For I know not by what presumption some of our colleagues are led to think that they who have been dipped by heretics ought not to be baptized when they come to us, for the reason that they say that there is one baptism which indeed is therefore one, because the Church is one, and there cannot be any baptism out of the Church. For since there cannot be two baptisms, if heretics truly baptize, they themselves have this baptism. And he who of his own authority grants this advantage to them yields and consents to them, that the enemy and adversary of Christ should seem to have the power of washing, and purifying, and sanctifying a man. But we say that those who come thence are not re-baptized among us but are

baptized. For indeed they do not receive anything there, where there is nothing; but they come to us, that here they may receive where there is both grace and all truth, because both grace and truth are one. But again some of our colleagues would rather give honour to heretics than agree with us; and while by the assertion of one baptism they are unwilling to baptize those that come, they thus either themselves make two baptisms in saying that there is a baptism among heretics; or certainly, which is a matter of more importance, they strive to set before and prefer the sordid and profane washing of heretics to the true and only and legitimate baptism of the Catholic Church, not considering that it is written, "He who is baptized by one dead, what availed his washing?" Now it is manifest that they who are not in the Church of Christ are reckoned among the dead; and another cannot be made alive by him who himself is not alive, since there is one Church which, having attained the grace of eternal life, both lives forever and quickens the people of God.

2. And they say that in this matter they follow ancient custom; although among the ancients these were as yet the first beginnings of heresy and schisms, so that those were involved in them who departed from the Church, having first been baptized therein; and these, therefore, when they returned to the Church and repented, it was not necessary to baptize. Which also we observe in the present day, that it is sufficient to lay hands for repentance upon those who are known to have been baptized in the Church, and have gone over from us to the heretics, if, subsequently acknowledging their sin and putting away their error, they return to the truth and to their parent; so that, because it had been a sheep, the Shepherd may receive into His fold the estranged and

vagrant sheep. But if he who comes from the heretics has not previously been baptized in the Church, but comes as a stranger and entirely profane, he must be baptized, that he may become a sheep, because in the holy Church is the one water which makes sheep. And therefore, because there can be nothing common to falsehood and truth, to darkness and light, to death and immortality, to Antichrist and Christ, we ought by all means to maintain the unity of the Catholic Church, and not to give way to the enemies of faith and truth in any respect.

3. Neither must we prescribe this from custom but overcome opposite custom by reason. For neither did Peter, whom first the Lord chose, and upon whom He built His Church, when Paul disputed with him afterwards about circumcision, claim anything to himself insolently, nor arrogantly assume anything; so as to say that he held the primacy, and that he ought rather to be obeyed by novices and those lately come. Nor did he despise Paul because he had previously been a persecutor of the Church, but admitted the counsel of truth, and easily yielded to the lawful reason which Paul asserted, furnishing thus an illustration to us both of concord and of patience, that we should not obstinately love our own opinions, but should rather adopt as our own those which at any time are usefully and wholesomely suggested by our brethren and colleagues, if they be true and lawful. Paul, moreover, looking forward to this, and consulting faithfully for concord and peace, has laid down in his epistle this rule: "Moreover, let the prophets speak two or three, and let the rest judge. But if anything be revealed to another that sits by, let the first hold his peace." In which place he has taught and shown that many things are revealed to individuals for the better, and that each one

ought not obstinately to contend for that which he had once imbibed and held; but if anything has appeared better and more useful, he should gladly embrace it. For we are not overcome when better things are presented to us, but we are instructed, especially in those matters which pertain to the unity of the Church and the truth of our hope and faith; so that we, priests of God and prelates of His Church, by His condescension, should know that remission of sins cannot be given save in the Church, nor can the adversaries of Christ claim to themselves anything belonging to His grace.

4. Which thing, indeed, Agrippinus also, a man of worthy memory, with his other fellow-bishops, who at that time governed the Lord's Church in the province of Africa and Numidia, decreed, and by the well-weighed examination of the common council established: whose opinion, as being both religious and lawful and salutary, and in harmony with the Catholic faith and Church, we also have followed. And that you may know what kind of letters we have written on this subject, I have transmitted for our mutual love a copy of them, as well for your own information as for that of our fellow-bishops who are in those parts. I bid you, dearest brother, ever heartily farewell.

Epistle LXXI.
To Stephen, Concerning a Council.
Argument.—Cyprian with His Colleagues in a Certain Council Tells Stephen, the Roman Bishop, that It Had Been Decreed by Them, Both that Those Who Returned from Heresy into the Church Should Be Baptized, and that Bishops or Priests Coming from the Heretics Should Be Received on No Other Condition,

Than that They Should Communicate as Lay People. a.d. 255.

1. Cyprian and others, to Stephen their brother, greeting. We have thought it necessary for the arranging of certain matters, dearest brother, and for their investigation by the examination of a common council, to gather together and to hold a council, at which many priests were assembled at once; at which, moreover, many things were brought forward and transacted. But the subject in regard to which we had chiefly to write to you, and to confer with your gravity and wisdom, is one that more especially pertains both to the priestly authority and to the unity, as well as the dignity, of the Catholic Church, arising as these do from the ordination of the divine appointment; to wit, that those who have been dipped abroad outside the Church, and have been stained among heretics and schismatics with the taint of profane water, when they come to us and to the Church which is one, ought to be baptized, for the reason that it is a small matter to "lay hands on them that they may receive the Holy Ghost," unless they receive also the baptism of the Church. For then finally can they be fully sanctified, and be the sons of God, if they be born of each sacrament; since it is written, "Except a man be born again of water, and of the Spirit, he cannot enter into the kingdom of God." For we find also, in the Acts of the Apostles, that this is maintained by the apostles, and kept in the truth of the saving faith, so that when, in the house of Cornelius the centurion, the Holy Ghost had descended upon the Gentiles who were there, fervent in the warmth of their faith, and believing in the Lord with their whole heart; and when, filled with the Spirit, they blessed God in divers tongues, still none the less the blessed Apostle

Peter, mindful of the divine precept and the Gospel, commanded that those same men should be baptized who had already been filled with the Holy Spirit, that nothing might seem to be neglected to the observance by the apostolic instruction in all things of the law of the divine precept and Gospel. But that that is not baptism which the heretics use; and that none of those who oppose Christ can profit by the grace of Christ; has lately been set forth with care in the letter which was written on that subject to Quintus, our colleague, established in Mauritania; as also in a letter which our colleagues previously wrote to our fellow-bishops presiding in Numidia, of both which letters I have subjoined copies.

2. We add, however, and connect with what we have said, dearest brother, with common consent and authority, that if, again, any presbyters or deacons, who either have been before ordained in the Catholic Church, and have subsequently stood forth as traitors and rebels against the Church, or who have been promoted among the heretics by a profane ordination by the hands of false bishops and antichrists contrary to the appointment of Christ, and have attempted to offer, in opposition to the one and divine altar, false and sacrilegious sacrifices without, that these also be received when they return, on this condition, that they communicate as laymen, and hold it to be enough that they should be received to peace, after having stood forth as enemies of peace; and that they ought not, on returning, to retain those arms of ordination and honour with which they rebelled against us. For it behooves priests and ministers, who wait upon the altar and sacrifices, to be sound and stainless; since the Lord God speaks in Leviticus, and says, "No man that hath a stain or a blemish shall come nigh to offer gifts to the

Lord." Moreover, in Exodus, He prescribes this same thing, and says, "And let the priests which come near to the Lord God sanctify themselves, lest the Lord forsake them." And again: "And when they come near to minister at the altar of the holy place, they shall not bear iniquity upon them, lest they die." But what can be greater iniquity, or what stain can be more odious, than to have stood in opposition to Christ; than to have scattered His Church, which He purchased and founded with His blood; than, unmindful of evangelical peace and love, to have fought with the madness of hostile discord against the unanimous and accordant people of God? Such as these, although they themselves return to the Church, still cannot restore and recall with them those who, seduced by them, and forestalled by death without, have perished outside the Church without communion and peace; whose souls in the day of judgment shall be required at the hands of those who have stood forth as the authors and leaders of their ruin. And therefore to such, when they return, it is sufficient that pardon should be granted; since perfidy ought certainly not to receive promotion in the household of faith. For what do we reserve for the good and innocent, and those who do not depart from the Church, if we honour those who have departed from us, and stood in opposition to the Church?

3. We have brought these things, dearest brother, to your knowledge, for the sake of our mutual honour and sincere affection; believing that, according to the truth of your religion and faith, those things which are no less religious than true will be approved by you. But we know that some will not lay aside what they have once imbibed, and do not easily change their purpose; but, keeping fast the bond of peace and concord among their colleagues,

retain certain things peculiar to themselves, which have once been adopted among them. In which behalf we neither do violence to, nor impose a law upon, anyone, since each prelate has in the administration of the Church the exercise of his will free, as he shall give an account of his conduct to the Lord. We bid you, dearest brother, ever heartily farewell.

 Epistle LXXII.
 To Jubaianus, Concerning the Baptism of Heretics.
 Argument.—Cyprian Refutes a Letter Enclosed to Him by Jubaianus, and with the Greatest Care Collects Whatever He Thinks Will Avail for the Defense of His Cause. Moreover, He Sends Jubaianus a Copy of the Letter to the Numidians and to Quintus, and Probably the Decrees of the Last Synod.
 1. Cyprian to Jubaianus his brother, greeting. You have written to me, dearest brother, wishing that the impression of my mind should be signified to you, as to what I think concerning the baptism of heretics; who, placed without, and established outside the Church, arrogate to themselves a matter neither within their right nor their power. This baptism we cannot consider as valid or legitimate, since it is manifestly unlawful among them; and since we have already expressed in our letters what we thought on this matter, I have, as a compendious method, sent you a copy of the same letters, what we decided in council when very many of us were present, and what, moreover, I subsequently wrote back to Quintus, our colleague, when he asked about the same thing. And now also, when we had met together, bishops as well of the province of Africa as of Numidia, to the

number of seventy-one, we established this same matter once more by our judgment, deciding that there is one baptism which is appointed in the Catholic Church; and that by this those are not re-baptized, but baptized by us, who at any time come from the adulterous and unhallowed water to be washed and sanctified by the truth of the saving water.

2. Nor does what you have described in your letters disturb us, dearest brother, that the Novatians re-baptize those whom they entice from us, since it does not in any wise matter to us what the enemies of the Church do, so long as we ourselves hold a regard for our power, and the steadfastness of reason and truth. For Novatian, after the manner of apes—which, although they are not men, yet imitate human doings—wishes to claim to himself the authority and truth of the Catholic Church, while he himself is not in the Church; nay, moreover, has stood forth hitherto as a rebel and enemy against the Church. For, knowing that there is one baptism, he arrogates to himself this one, so that he may say that the Church is with him, and make us heretics. But we who hold the head and root of the one Church know, and trust for certain, that nothing is lawful there outside the Church, and that the baptism which is one is among us, where he himself also was formerly baptized, when he maintained both the wisdom and truth of the divine unity. But if Novatian thinks that those who have been baptized in the Church are to be re-baptized outside—without the Church—he ought to begin by himself, that he might first be re-baptized with an extraneous and heretical baptism, since he thinks that after the Church, yea, and contrary to the Church, people are to be baptized without. But what sort of a thing is this, that, because Novatian dares to do

this thing, we are to think that we must not do it! What then? Because Novatian also usurps the honour of the priestly throne, ought we therefore to renounce our throne? Or because Novatian endeavors wrongfully to set up an altar and to offer sacrifices, does it behoove us to cease from our altar and sacrifices, lest we should appear to be celebrating the same or like things with him? Utterly vain and foolish is it, that because Novatian arrogates to himself outside the Church the image of the truth, we should forsake the truth of the Church.

3. But among us it is no new or sudden thing for us to judge that those are to be baptized who come to the Church from among the heretics, since it is now many years and a long time ago, that, under Agrippinus—a man of worthy memory—very many bishops assembling together have decided this; and thenceforward until the present day, so many thousands of heretics in our provinces have been converted to the Church, and have neither despised nor delayed, nay, they have both reasonably and gladly embraced, the opportunity to attain the grace of the life-giving laver and of saving baptism. For it is not difficult for a teacher to insinuate true and lawful things into his mind, who, having condemned heretical pravity, and discovered the truth of the Church, comes for this purpose, that he may learn, and learns for the purpose that he may live. We ought not to increase the stolidity of heretics by the patronage of our consent, when they gladly and readily obey the truth.

4. Certainly, since I found in the letter the copy of which you transmitted to me, that it was written, "That it should not be asked who baptized, since he who is baptized might receive remission of sins according to what he believed," I thought that this topic was not to be

passed by, especially since I observed in the same epistle that mention was also made of Marcion, saying that "even those that came from him did not need to be baptized, because they seemed to have been already baptized in the name of Jesus Christ." Therefore we ought to consider their faith who believe without, whether in respect of the same faith they can obtain any grace. For if we and heretics have one faith, we may also have one grace. If the Patripassians, Anthropians, Valentinians, Apelletians, Ophites, Marcionites, and other pests, and swords, and poisons of heretics for subverting the truth, confess the same Father, the same Son, the same Holy Ghost, the same Church with us, they may also have one baptism if they have also one faith.

5. And lest it should be wearisome to go through all the heresies, and to enumerate either the follies or the madness of each of them, because it is no pleasure to speak of that which one either dreads or is ashamed to know, let us examine in the meantime about Marcion alone, the mention of whom has been made in the letter transmitted by you to us, whether the ground of his baptism can be made good. For the Lord after His resurrection, sending His disciples, instructed and taught them in what manner they ought to baptize, saying, "All power is given unto me in heaven and in earth. Go ye, therefore, and teach all nations, baptizing them in the name of the Father, and of the Son, and of the Holy Ghost." He suggests the Trinity, in whose sacrament the nations were to be baptized. Does Marcion then maintain the Trinity? Does he then assert the same Father, the Creator, as we do? Does he know the same Son, Christ born of the Virgin Mary, who as the Word was made flesh, who bare our sins, who conquered death by dying,

who by Himself first of all originated the resurrection of the flesh, and showed to His disciples that He had risen in the same flesh? Widely different is the faith with Marcion, and, moreover, with the other heretics; nay, with them there is nothing but perfidy, and blasphemy, and contention, which is hostile to holiness and truth. How then can one who is baptized among them seem to have obtained remission of sins, and the grace of the divine mercy, by his faith, when he has not the truth of the faith itself? For if, as some suppose, one could receive anything abroad out of the Church according to his faith, certainly he has received what he believed; but if he believes what is false, he could not receive what is true; but rather he has received things adulterous and profane, according to what he believed.

6. This matter of profane and adulterous baptism Jeremiah the prophet plainly rebukes, saying, "Why do they who afflict me prevail? My wound is hard; whence shall I be healed? while it has indeed become unto me as deceitful water which has no faithfulness." The Holy Spirit makes mention by the prophet of deceitful water which has no faithfulness. What is this deceitful and faithless water? Certainly that which falsely assumes the resemblance of baptism and frustrates the grace of faith by a shadowy presence. But if, according to a perverted faith, one could be baptized without, and obtain remission of sins, according to the same faith he could also attain the Holy Spirit; and there is no need that hands should be laid on him when he comes, that he might obtain the Holy Ghost, and be sealed. Either he could obtain both privileges without by his faith, or he who has been without has received neither.

7. But it is manifest where and by whom remission

of sins can be given; to wit, that which is given in baptism. For first of all the Lord gave that power to Peter, upon whom He built the Church, and whence He appointed and showed the source of unity—the power, namely, that whatsoever he loosed on earth should be loosed in heaven. And after the resurrection, also, He speaks to the apostles, saying, "As the Father hath sent me, even so I send you. And when He had said this, He breathed on them, and saith, unto them, Receive ye the Holy Ghost: whosesoever sins ye remit, they are remitted unto them; and whosesoever sins ye retain, they are retained." Whence we perceive that only they who are set over the Church and established in the Gospel law, and in the ordinance of the Lord, are allowed to baptize and to give remission of sins; but that without, nothing can either be bound or loosed, where there is none who can either bind or loose anything.

8. Nor do we propose this, dearest brother, without the authority of divine Scripture, when we say that all things are arranged by divine direction by a certain law and by special ordinance, and that none can usurp to himself, in opposition to the bishops and priests, anything which is not of his own right and power. For Korah, Dathan, and Abiram endeavored to usurp, in opposition to Moses and Aaron the priest, the power of sacrificing; and they did not do without punishment what they unlawfully dared. The sons of Aaron also, who placed strange fire upon the altar, were at once consumed in the sight of an angry Lord; which punishment remains to those who introduce strange water by a false baptism, that the divine vengeance may avenge and chastise when heretics do that in opposition to the Church, which the Church alone is allowed to do.

9. But in respect of the assertion of some concerning those who had been baptized in Samaria, that when the Apostles Peter and John came, only hands were imposed on them, that they might receive the Holy Ghost, yet that they were not re-baptized; we see that that place does not, dearest brother, touch the present case. For they who had believed in Samaria had believed with a true faith; and within, in the Church which is one, and to which alone it is granted to bestow the grace of baptism and to remit sins, had been baptized by Philip the deacon, whom the same apostles had sent. And therefore, because they had obtained a legitimate and ecclesiastical baptism, there was no need that they should be baptized any more, but only that which was needed was performed by Peter and John; viz., that prayer being made for them, and hands being imposed, the Holy Spirit should be invoked and poured out upon them, which now too is done among us, so that they who are baptized in the Church are brought to the prelates of the Church, and by our prayers and by the imposition of hands obtain the Holy Spirit, and are perfected with the Lord's seal.

10. There is no ground, therefore, dearest brother, for thinking that we should give way to heretics so far as to contemplate the betrayal to them of that baptism, which is only granted to the one and only Church. It is a good soldier's duty to defend the camp of his general against rebels and enemies. It is the duty of an illustrious leader to keep the standards entrusted to him. It is written, "The Lord thy God is a jealous God." We who have received the Spirit of God ought to have a jealousy for the divine faith; with such a jealousy as that wherewith Phineas both pleased God and justly allayed His wrath when He was angry, and the people were perishing. Why do we receive

as allowed an adulterous and alien church, a foe to the divine unity, when we know only one Christ and His one Church? The Church, setting forth the likeness of paradise, includes within her walls fruit-bearing trees, whereof that which does not bring forth good fruit is cut off and is cast into the fire. These trees she waters with four rivers, that is, with the four Gospels, wherewith, by a celestial inundation, she bestows the grace of saving baptism. Can anyone water from the Church's fountains who is not within the Church? Can one impart those wholesome and saving draughts of paradise to anyone if he is perverted, and of himself condemned, and banished outside the fountains of paradise, and has dried up and failed with the dryness of an eternal thirst?

11. The Lord cries aloud, that "whosoever thirsts should come and drink of the rivers of living water that flowed out of His bosom." Whither is he to come who thirsts? Shall he come to the heretics, where there is no fountain and river of living water at all; or to the Church which is one, and is founded upon one who has received the keys of it by the Lord's voice? It is she who holds and possesses alone all the power of her spouse and Lord. In her we preside; for her honour and unity we fight; her grace, as well as her glory, we defend with faithful devotedness. We by the divine permission water the thirsting people of God; we guard the boundaries of the living fountains. If, therefore, we hold the right of our possession, if we acknowledge the sacrament of unity, wherefore are we esteemed prevaricators against truth? Wherefore are we judged betrayers of unity? The faithful, and saving, and holy water of the Church cannot be corrupted and adulterated, as the Church herself also is uncorrupted, and chaste, and modest. If heretics are

devoted to the Church and established in the Church, they may use both her baptism and her other saving benefits. But if they are not in the Church, nay more, if they act against the Church, how can they baptize with the Church's baptism?

12. For it is no small and insignificant matter, which is conceded to heretics, when their baptism is recognized by us; since thence springs the whole origin of faith and the saving access to the hope of life eternal, and the divine condescension for purifying and quickening the servants of God. For if anyone could be baptized among heretics, certainly he could also obtain remission of sins. If he attained remission of sins, he was also sanctified. If he was sanctified, he also was made the temple of God. I ask, of what God? If of the Creator; he could not be, because he has not believed in Him. If of Christ; he could not become His temple, since he denies that Christ is God. If of the Holy Spirit; since the three are one, how can the Holy Spirit be at peace with him who is the enemy either of the Son or of the Father?

13. Hence it is in vain that some who are overcome by reason oppose to us custom, as if custom were greater than truth; or as if that were not to be sought after in spiritual matters which has been revealed as the better by the Holy Spirit. For one who errs by simplicity may be pardoned, as the blessed Apostle Paul says of himself, "I who at first was a blasphemer, and a persecutor, and injurious; yet obtained mercy, because I did it ignorantly." But after inspiration and revelation made to him, he who intelligently and knowingly perseveres in that course in which he had erred, sins without pardon for his ignorance. For he resists with a certain presumption and obstinacy, when he is overcome

by reason. Nor let anyone say, "We follow that which we have received from the apostles," when the apostles only delivered one Church, and one baptism, which is not ordained except in the same Church. And we cannot find that anyone, when he had been baptized by heretics, was received by the apostles in the same baptism, and communicated in such a way as that the apostles should appear to have approved the baptism of heretics.

14. For as to what some say, as if it tended to favor heretics, that the Apostle Paul declared, "Only every way, whether in pretense or in truth, let Christ be preached," we find that this also can avail nothing to their benefit who support and applaud heretics. For Paul, in his epistle, was not speaking of heretics, nor of their baptism, so that anything can be shown to have been alleged which pertained to this matter. He was speaking of brethren, whether as walking disorderly and against the discipline of the Church, or as keeping the truth of the Gospel with the fear of God. And he said that certain of them spoke the word of God with constancy and courage, but some acted in envy and dissension; that some maintained towards him a benevolent love, but that some indulged a malevolent spirit of dissension; but yet that he bore all patiently, so long only as, whether in truth or in pretense, the name of Christ which Paul preached might come to the knowledge of many; and the sowing of the word, which as yet had been new and irregular, might increase through the preaching of the speakers. Besides, it is one thing for those who are within the Church to speak concerning the name of Christ; it is another for those who are without, and act in opposition to the Church, to baptize in the name of Christ. Wherefore, let not those who favor heretics put forward what Paul spoke

concerning brethren, but let them show if he thought anything was to be conceded to the heretic, or if he approved of their faith or baptism, or if he appointed that perfidious and blasphemous men could receive remission of their sins outside the Church.

15. But if we consider what the apostles thought about heretics, we shall find that they, in all their epistles, execrated and detested the sacrilegious wickedness of heretics. For when they say that "their word creeps as a canker," how is such a word as that able to give remission of sins, which creeps like a canker to the ears of the hearers? And when they say that there can be no fellowship between righteousness and unrighteousness, no communion between light and darkness,2865 how can either darkness illuminate, or unrighteousness justify? And when they say that "they are not of God, but are of the spirit of Antichrist," how can they transact spiritual and divine matters, who are the enemies of God, and whose hearts the spirit of Antichrist has possessed? Wherefore, if, laying aside the errors of human dispute, we return with a sincere and religious faith to the evangelical authority and to the apostolical tradition, we shall perceive that they may do nothing towards conferring the ecclesiastical and saving grace, who, scattering and attacking the Church of Christ, are called adversaries by Christ Himself, but by His apostles, Antichrists.

16. Again, there is no ground for any one, for the circumvention of Christian truth, opposing to us the name of Christ, and saying, "All who are baptized everywhere, and in any manner, in the name of Jesus Christ, have obtained the grace of baptism,"—when Christ Himself speaks, and says, "Not everyone that saith unto me, Lord,

Lord, shall enter into the kingdom of heaven." And again, He forewarns and instructs, that no one should be easily deceived by false prophets and false Christs in His name. "Many," He says, "shall come in my name, saying, I am Christ, and shall deceive many." And afterwards He added: "But take ye heed; behold, I have foretold you all things." Whence it appears that all things are not at once to be received and assumed which are boasted of in the name of Christ, but only those things which are done in the truth of Christ.

17. For whereas in the Gospels, and in the epistles of the apostles, the name of Christ is alleged for the remission of sins; it is not in such a way as that the Son alone, without the Father, or against the Father, can be of advantage to anybody; but that it might be shown to the Jews, who boasted as to their having the Father, that the Father would profit them nothing, unless they believed on the Son whom He had sent. For they who know God the Father the Creator, ought also to know Christ the Son, lest they should flatter and applaud themselves about the Father alone, without the acknowledgment of His Son, who also said, "No man cometh to the Father but by me." But He, the same, sets forth, that it is the knowledge of the two which saves, when He says, "And this is life eternal, that they might know Thee, the only true God, and Jesus Christ, whom thou hast sent." Since, therefore, from the preaching and testimony of Christ Himself, the Father who sent must be first known, then afterwards Christ, who was sent, and there cannot be a hope of salvation except by knowing the two together; how, when God the Father is not known, nay, is even blasphemed, can they who among the heretics are said to be baptized in the name of Christ, be judged to have obtained the

remission of sins? For the case of the Jews under the apostles was one, but the condition of the Gentiles is another. The former, because they had already gained the most ancient baptism of the law and Moses, were to be baptized also in the name of Jesus Christ, in conformity with what Peter tells them in the Acts of the Apostles, saying, "Repent, and be baptized every one of you in the name of the Lord Jesus Christ, for the remission of sins, and ye shall receive the gift of the Holy Ghost. For this promise is unto you, and to your children, and to all that are afar off, even as many as the Lord our God shall call." Peter makes mention of Jesus Christ, not as though the Father should be omitted, but that the Son also might be joined to the Father.

18. Finally, when, after the resurrection, the apostles are sent by the Lord to the heathens, they are bidden to baptize the Gentiles "in the name of the Father, and of the Son, and of the Holy Ghost." How, then, do some say, that a Gentile baptized without, outside the Church, yea, and in opposition to the Church, so that it be only in the name of Jesus Christ, everywhere, and in whatever manner, can obtain remission of sin, when Christ Himself commands the heathen to be baptized in the full and united Trinity? Unless while one who denies Christ is denied by Christ, he who denies His Father whom Christ Himself confessed is not denied; and he who blasphemes against Him whom Christ called His Lord and His God, is rewarded by Christ, and obtains remission of sins, and the sanctification of baptism! But by what power can he who denies God the Creator, the Father of Christ, obtain, in baptism, the remission of sins, since Christ received that very power by which we are baptized and sanctified, from the same Father, whom He called

"greater" than Himself, by whom He desired to be glorified, whose will He fulfilled even unto the obedience of drinking the cup, and of undergoing death? What else is it then, than to become a partaker with blaspheming heretics, to wish to maintain and assert, that one who blasphemes and gravely sins against the Father and the Lord and God of Christ, can receive remission of sins in the name of Christ? What, moreover, is that, and of what kind is it, that he who denies the Son of God has not the Father, and he who denies the Father should be thought to have the Son, although the Son Himself testifies, and says, "No man can come unto me except it were given unto him of my Father?" So that it is evident, that no remission of sins can be received in baptism from the Son, which it is not plain that the Father has granted. Especially, since He further repeats, and says, "Every plant which my heavenly Father hath not planted shall be rooted up."

19. But if Christ's disciples are unwilling to learn from Christ what veneration and honour is due to the name of the Father, still let them learn from earthly and secular examples, and know that Christ has declared, not without the strongest rebuke, "The children of this world are wiser in their generation than the children of light." In this world of ours, if anyone have offered an insult to the father of any; if in injury and frowardness he have wounded his reputation and his honour by a malevolent tongue, the son is indignant, and wrathful, and with what means he can, strives to avenge his injured father's wrong. Think you that Christ grants impunity to the impious and profane, and the blasphemers of His Father, and that He puts away their sins in baptism, who it is evident, when baptized, still heap up evil words on the

person of the Father, and sin with the unceasing wickedness of a blaspheming tongue? Can a Christian, can a servant of God, either conceive this in his mind, or believe it in faith, or put it forward in discourse? And what will become of the precepts of the divine law, which say, "Honour thy father and thy mother?" If the name of father, which in man is commanded to be honored, is violated with impunity in God, what will become of what Christ Himself lays down in the Gospel, and says, "He that curses father or mother, let him die the death;" if He who bids that those who curse their parents after the flesh should be punished and slain, Himself quickens those who revile their heavenly and spiritual Father, and are hostile to the Church, their Mother? An execrable and detestable thing is actually asserted by some, that He who threatens the man who blasphemes against the Holy Spirit, that he shall be guilty of eternal sin, Himself condescends to sanctify those who blaspheme against God the Father with saving baptism. And now, those who think that they must communicate with such as come to the Church without baptism, do not consider that they are becoming partakers with other men's, yea, with eternal sins, when they admit without baptism those who cannot, except in baptism, put off the sins of their blasphemies.

20. Besides, how vain and perverse a thing it is, that when the heretics themselves, having repudiated and forsaken either the error or the wickedness in which they had previously been, acknowledge the truth of the Church, we should mutilate the rights and sacrament of that same truth, and say to those who come to us and repent, that they had obtained remission of sins when they confess that they have sinned, and are for that reason come to seek the pardon of the Church! Wherefore,

dearest brother, we ought both firmly to maintain the faith and truth of the Catholic Church, and to teach, and by all the evangelical and apostolical precepts to set forth, the plan of the divine dispensation and unity.

21. Can the power of baptism be greater or of more avail than confession, than suffering, when one confesses Christ before men and is baptized in his own blood? And yet even this baptism does not benefit a heretic, although he has confessed Christ, and been put to death outside the Church, unless the patrons and advocates of heretics declare that the heretics who are slain in a false confession of Christ are martyrs, and assign to them the glory and the crown of martyrdom contrary to the testimony of the apostle, who says that it will profit them nothing although they were burnt and slain. But if not even the baptism of a public confession and blood can profit a heretic to salvation, because there is no salvation out of the Church, how much less shall it be of advantage to him, if in a hiding-place and a cave of robbers, stained with the contagion of adulterous water, he has not only not put off his old sins, but rather heaped up still newer and greater ones! Wherefore baptism cannot be common to us and to heretics, to whom neither God the Father, nor Christ the Son, nor the Holy Ghost, nor the faith, nor the Church itself, is common. And therefore it behooves those to be baptized who come from heresy to the Church, that so they who are prepared, in the lawful, and true, and only baptism of the holy Church, by divine regeneration, for the kingdom of God, may be born of both sacraments, because it is written, "Except a man be born of water and of the Spirit, he cannot enter into the kingdom of God."

22. On which place some, as if by human

reasoning they were able to make void the truth of the Gospel declaration, object to us the case of catechumens; asking if any one of these, before he is baptized in the Church, should be apprehended and slain on confession of the name, whether he would lose the hope of salvation and the reward of confession, because he had not previously been born again of water? Let men of this kind, who are aiders and favorers of heretics, know therefore, first, that those catechumens hold the sound faith and truth of the Church, and advance from the divine camp to do battle with the devil, with a full and sincere acknowledgment of God the Father, and of Christ, and of the Holy Ghost; then, that they certainly are not deprived of the sacrament of baptism who are baptized with the most glorious and greatest baptism of blood, concerning which the Lord also said, that He had "another baptism to be baptized with." But the same Lord declares in the Gospel, that those who are baptized in their own blood, and sanctified by suffering, are perfected, and obtain the grace of the divine promise, when He speaks to the thief believing and confessing in His very passion and promises that he should be with Himself in paradise. Wherefore we who are set over the faith and truth ought not to deceive and mislead those who come to the faith and truth, and repent, and beg that their sins should be remitted to them; but to instruct them when corrected by us and reformed for the kingdom of heaven by celestial discipline.

23. But someone says, "What, then, shall become of those who in past times, coming from heresy to the Church, were received without baptism?" The Lord is able by His mercy to give indulgence, and not to separate from the gifts of His Church those who by simplicity were

admitted into the Church, and in the Church have fallen asleep. Nevertheless it does not follow that, because there was error at one time, there must always be error; since it is more fitting for wise and God-fearing men, gladly and without delay to obey the truth when laid open and perceived, than pertinaciously and obstinately to struggle against brethren and fellow-priests on behalf of heretics.

24. Nor let anyone think that, because baptism is proposed to them, heretics will be kept back from coming to the Church, as if offended at the name of a second baptism; nay, but on this very account they are rather driven to the necessity of coming by the testimony of truth shown and proved to them. For if they shall see that it is determined and decreed by our judgment and sentence, that the baptism wherewith they are there baptized is considered just and legitimate, they will think that they are justly and legitimately in possession of the Church also, and the other gifts of the Church; nor will there be any reason for their coming to us, when, as they have baptism, they seem also to have the rest. But further, when they know that there is no baptism without, and that no remission of sins can be given outside the Church, they more eagerly and readily hasten to us, and implore the gifts and benefits of the Church our Mother, assured that they can in no wise attain to the true promise of divine grace unless they first come to the truth of the Church. Nor will heretics refuse to be baptized among us with the lawful and true baptism of the Church, when they shall have learnt from us that they also were baptized by Paul, who already had been baptized with the baptism of John, as we read in the Acts of the Apostles.

25. And now by certain of us the baptism of heretics is asserted to occupy the (like) ground, and, as if

by a certain dislike of re-baptizing, it is counted unlawful to baptize after God's enemies. And this, although we find that they were baptized whom John had baptized: John, esteemed the greatest among the prophets; John, filled with divine grace even in his mother's womb; who was sustained with the spirit and power of Elias; who was not an adversary of the Lord, but His precursor and announcer; who not only foretold our Lord in words, but even showed Him to the eyes; who baptized Christ Himself by whom others are baptized. But if on that account a heretic could obtain the right of baptism, because he first baptized, then baptism will not belong to the person that has it, but to the person that seizes it. And since baptism and the Church can by no means be separated from one another, and 386 divided, he who has first been able to lay hold on baptism has equally also laid hold on the Church; and you begin to appear to him as a heretic, when you being anticipated, have begun to be last, and by yielding and giving way have relinquished the right which you had received. But how dangerous it is in divine matters, that anyone should depart from his right and power, Holy Scripture declares when, in Genesis, Esau thence lost his birthright, nor was able afterwards to regain that which he had once given up.

26. These things, dearest brother, I have briefly written to you, according to my abilities, prescribing to none, and prejudging none, so as to prevent any one of the bishops doing what he thinks well, and having the free exercise of his judgment. We, as far as in us lies, do not contend on behalf of heretics with our colleagues and fellow-bishops, with whom we maintain a divine concord and the peace of the Lord; especially since the apostle says, "If any man, however, is thought to be contentious,

we have no such custom, neither the Church of God." Charity of spirit, the honour of our college, the bond of faith, and priestly concord, are maintained by us with patience and gentleness. For this reason, moreover, we have with the best of our poor abilities, with the permission and inspiration of the Lord, written a treatise on the "Benefit of Patience," which for the sake of our mutual love we have transmitted to you. I bid you, dearest brother, ever heartily farewell.

 Epistle LXXIII.
To Pompey, Against the Epistle of Stephen About the Baptism of Heretics.
 Argument.—The Purport of This Epistle is Given in St. Augustine's "Contra Donatistas," Lib. V. Cap. 23. He Says There: "Cyprian, Moreover, Writes to Pompey on the Same Subject, When He Plainly Signifies that Stephen, Who, as We Learn, Was Then a Bishop of the Roman Church, Not Only Did Not Agree with Him on Those Points, But Even Had Written and Charged in Opposition to Him."
 1. Cyprian to his brother Pompeius, greeting. Although I have fully comprised what is to be said concerning the baptism of heretics in the letters of which I sent you copies, dearest brother, yet, since you have desired that what Stephen our brother replied to my letters should be brought to your knowledge, I have sent you a copy of his reply; on the reading of which, you will more and more observe his error in endeavoring to maintain the cause of heretics against Christians, and against the Church of God. For among other matters, which were either haughtily assumed, or were not pertaining to the matter, or contradictory to his own view, which he

unskillfully and without foresight wrote, he moreover added this saying: "If any one, therefore, come to you from any heresy whatever, let nothing be innovated (or done) which has not been handed down, to wit, that hands be imposed on him for repentance; since the heretics themselves, in their own proper character, do not baptize such as come to them from one another, but only admit them to communion."

2. He forbade one coming from any heresy to be baptized in the Church; that is, he judged the baptism of all heretics to be just and lawful. And although special heresies have special baptisms and different sins, he, holding communion with the baptism of all, gathered up the sins of all, heaped together into his own bosom. And he charged that nothing should be innovated except what had been handed down; as if he were an innovator, who, holding the unity, claims for the one Church one baptism; and not manifestly he who, forgetful of unity, adopts the lies and the contagions of a profane washing. Let nothing be innovated, says he, nothing maintained, except what has been handed down. Whence is that tradition? Whether does it descend from the authority of the Lord and of the Gospel, or does it come from the commands and the epistles of the apostles? For that those things which are written must be done, God witnesses and admonishes, saying to Joshua the son of Nun: "The book of this law shall not depart out of thy mouth; but thou shalt meditate in it day and night, that thou mayest observe to do according to all that is written therein." Also the Lord, sending His apostles, commands that the nations should be baptized, and taught to observe all things which He commanded. If, therefore, it is either prescribed in the Gospel, or contained in the epistles or

Acts of the Apostles, that those who come from any heresy should not be baptized, but only hands laid upon them to repentance, let this divine and holy tradition be observed. But if everywhere heretics are called nothing else than adversaries and antichrists, if they are pronounced to be people to be avoided, and to be perverted and condemned of their own selves, wherefore is it that they should not be thought worthy of being condemned by us, since it is evident from the apostolic testimony that they are of their own selves condemned? So that no one ought to defame the apostles as if they had approved of the baptisms of heretics, or had communicated with them without the Church's baptism, when they, the apostles, wrote such things of the heretics. And this, too, while as yet the more terrible plagues of heresy had not broken forth; while Marcion of Pontus had not yet emerged from Pontus, whose master Cerdon came to Rome,—while Hyginus was still bishop, who was the ninth bishop in that city,—whom Marcion followed, and with greater impudence adding other enhancements to his crime, and more daringly set himself to blaspheme against God the Father, the Creator, and armed with sacrilegious arms the heretical madness that rebelled against the Church with greater wickedness and determination.

3. But if it is evident that subsequently heresies became more numerous and worse; and if, in time past, it was never at all prescribed nor written that only hands should be laid upon a heretic for repentance, and that so he might be communicated with; and if there is only one baptism, which is with us, and is within, and is granted of the divine condescension to the Church alone, what obstinacy is that, or what presumption, to prefer human tradition to divine ordinance, and not to observe that God

is indignant and angry as often as human tradition relaxes and passes by the divine precepts, as He cries out, and says by Isaiah the prophet, "This people honors me with their lips, but their heart is far from me. But in vain do they worship me, teaching the doctrines and commandments of men." Also the Lord in the Gospel, similarly, rebuking and reproving, utters and says, "Ye reject the commandment of God, that ye may keep your own tradition." Mindful of which precept, the blessed Apostle Paul himself also warns and instructs, saying, "If any man teach otherwise, and consent not to the wholesome words of our Lord Jesus Christ, and to His doctrine, he is proud, knowing nothing: from such withdraw thyself."

4. Certainly an excellent and lawful tradition is set before us by the teaching of our brother Stephen, which may afford us suitable authority! For in the same place of his epistle he has added and continued: "Since those who are specially heretics do not baptize those who come to them from one another, but only receive them to communion." To this point of evil has the Church of God and spouse of Christ been developed, that she follows the examples of heretics; that for the purpose of celebrating the celestial sacraments, light should borrow her discipline from darkness, and Christians should do that which antichrists do. But what is that blindness of soul, what is that degradation of faith, to refuse to recognize the unity which comes from God the Father, and from the tradition of Jesus Christ the Lord and our God! For if the Church is not with heretics, therefore, because it is one, and cannot be divided; and if thus the Holy Spirit is not there, because He is one, and cannot be among profane persons, and those who are without; certainly also

baptism, which consists in the same unity, cannot be among heretics, because it can neither be separated from the Church nor from the Holy Spirit.

5. Or if they attribute the effect of baptism to the majesty of the name, so that they who are baptized anywhere and anyhow, in the name of Jesus Christ, are judged to be renewed and sanctified; wherefore, in the name of the same Christ, are not hands laid upon the baptized persons among them, for the reception of the Holy Spirit? Why does not the same majesty of the same name avail in the imposition of hands, which, they contend, availed in the sanctification of baptism? For if anyone born out of the Church can become God's temple, why cannot the Holy Spirit also be poured out upon the temple? For he who has been sanctified, his sins being put away in baptism, and has been spiritually reformed into a new man, has become fitted for receiving the Holy Spirit; since the apostle says, "As many of you as have been baptized into Christ have put on Christ." He who, having been baptized among the heretics, is able to put on Christ, may much more receive the Holy Spirit whom Christ sent. Otherwise He who is sent will be greater than Him who sends; so that one baptized without may begin indeed to put on Christ, but not to be able to receive 388 the Holy Spirit, as if Christ could either be put on without the Spirit, or the Spirit be separated from Christ. Moreover, it is silly to say, that although the second birth is spiritual, by which we are born in Christ through the laver of regeneration, one may be born spiritually among the heretics, where they say that the Spirit is not. For water alone is not able to cleanse away sins, and to sanctify a man, unless he have also the Holy Spirit. Wherefore it is necessary that they should grant the Holy Spirit to be

there, where they say that baptism is; or else there is no baptism where the Holy Spirit is not, because there cannot be baptism without the Spirit.

6. But what a thing it is, to assert and contend that they who are not born in the Church can be the sons of God! For the blessed apostle sets forth and proves that baptism is that wherein the old man dies, and the new man is born, saying, "He saved us by the washing of regeneration." But if regeneration is in the washing, that is, in baptism, how can heresy, which is not the spouse of Christ, generate sons to God by Christ? For it is the Church alone which, conjoined and united with Christ, spiritually bears sons; as the same apostle again says, "Christ loved the Church, and gave Himself for it, that He might sanctify it, cleansing it with the washing of water." If then, she is the beloved and spouse who alone is sanctified by Christ, and alone is cleansed by His washing, it is manifest that heresy, which is not the spouse of Christ, nor can be cleansed nor sanctified by His washing, cannot bear sons to God.

7. But further, one is not born by the imposition of hands when he receives the Holy Ghost, but in baptism, that so, being already born, he may receive the Holy Spirit, even as it happened in the first man Adam. For first God formed him, and then breathed into his nostrils the breath of life. For the Spirit cannot be received, unless he who receives first have an existence. But as the birth of Christians is in baptism, while the generation and sanctification of baptism are with the spouse of Christ alone, who is able spiritually to conceive and to bear sons to God, where and of whom and to whom is he born, who is not a son of the Church, so as that he should have God as his Father, before he has had the Church for his

Mother? But as no heresy at all, and equally no schism, being without, can have the sanctification of saving baptism, why has the bitter obstinacy of our brother Stephen broken forth to such an extent, as to contend that sons are born to God from the baptism of Marcion; moreover, of Valentinus and Apelles, and of others who blaspheme against God the Father; and to say that remission of sins is granted in the name of Jesus Christ where blasphemy is uttered against the Father and against Christ the Lord God?

8. In which place, dearest brother, we must consider, for the sake of the faith and the religion of the sacerdotal office which we discharge, whether the account can be satisfactory in the day of judgment for a priest of God, who maintains, and approves, and acquiesces in the baptism of blasphemers, when the Lord threatens, and says, "And now, O ye priests, this commandment is for you: if ye will not hear, and if ye will not lay it to heart to give glory unto my name, saith the Lord Almighty, I will even send a curse upon you, and I will curse your blessings." Does he give glory to God, who communicates with the baptism of Marcion? Does he give glory to God, who judges that remission of sins is granted among those who blaspheme against God? Does he give glory to God, who affirms that sons are born to God without, of an adulterer and a harlot? Does he give glory to God, who does not hold the unity and truth that arise from the divine law, but maintains heresies against the Church? Does he give glory to God, who, a friend of heretics and an enemy to Christians, thinks that the priests of God, who support the truth of Christ and the unity of the Church, are to be excommunicated? If glory is thus given to God, if the fear and the discipline of God is thus

preserved by His worshippers and His priests, let us cast away our arms; let us give ourselves up to captivity; let us deliver to the devil the ordination of the Gospel, the appointment of Christ, the majesty of God; let the sacraments of the divine warfare be loosed; let the standards of the heavenly camp be betrayed; and let the Church succumb and yield to heretics, light to darkness, faith to perfidy, hope to despair, reason to error, immortality to death, love to hatred, truth to falsehood, Christ to Antichrist! Deservedly thus do heresies and schisms arise day by day, more frequently and more fruitfully grow up, and with serpents' locks shoot forth and cast out against the Church of God with greater force the poison of their venom; whilst, by the advocacy of some, both authority and support are afforded them; whilst their baptism is defended, whilst faith, whilst truth, is betrayed; whilst that which is done without against the Church is defended within in the very Church itself.

9. But if there be among us, most beloved brother, the fear of God, if the maintenance of the faith prevail, if we keep the precepts of Christ, if we guard the incorrupt and inviolate sanctity of His spouse, if the words of the Lord abide in our thoughts and hearts, when he says, "Thinks thou, when the Son of man cometh, shall He find faith on the earth?" then, because we are God's faithful soldiers, who war for the faith and sincere religion of God, let us keep the camp entrusted to us by God with faithful valor. Nor ought custom, which had crept in among some, to prevent the truth from prevailing and conquering; for custom without truth is the antiquity of error. On which account, let us forsake the error and follow the truth, knowing that in Esdras also the truth conquers, as it is written: "Truth endures and grows

strong to eternity, and lives and prevails for ever and ever. With her there is no accepting of persons or distinctions; but what is just she does: nor in her judgments is there unrighteousness, but the strength, and the kingdom, and the majesty, and the power of all ages. Blessed be the Lord God of truth!" This truth Christ showed to us in His Gospel, and said, "I am the truth." Wherefore, if we are in Christ, and have Christ in us, if we abide in the truth, and the truth abides in us, let us keep fast those things which are true.

10. But it happens, by a love of presumption and of obstinacy, that one would rather maintain his own evil and false position, than agree in the right and true which belongs to another. Looking forward to which, the blessed Apostle Paul writes to Timothy, and warns him that a bishop must not be "litigious, nor contentious, but gentle and teachable." Now he is teachable who is meek and gentle to the patience of learning. For it behooves a bishop not only to teach, but also to learn; because he also teaches better who daily increases and advances by learning better; which very thing, moreover, the same Apostle Paul teaches, when he admonishes, "that if anything better be revealed to one sitting by, the first should hold his peace." But there is a brief way for religious and simple minds, both to put away error, and to find and to elicit truth. For if we return to the head and source of divine tradition, human error ceases; and having seen the reason of the heavenly sacraments, whatever lay hid in obscurity under the gloom and cloud of darkness, is opened into the light of the truth. If a channel supplying water, which formerly flowed plentifully and freely, suddenly fail, do we not go to the fountain, that there the reason of the failure may be ascertained, whether from the

drying up of the springs the water has failed at the fountainhead, or whether, flowing thence free and full, it has failed in the midst of its course; that so, if it has been caused by the fault of an interrupted or leaky channel, that the constant stream does not flow uninterruptedly and continuously, then the channel being repaired and strengthened, the water collected may be supplied for the use and drink of the city, with the same fertility and plenty with which it issues from the spring? And this it behooves the priests of God to do now, if they would keep the divine precepts, that if in any respect the truth have wavered and vacillated, we should return to our original and Lord, and to the evangelical and apostolical tradition; and thence may arise the ground of our action, whence has taken rise both our order and our origin.

11. For it has been delivered to us, that there is one God, and one Christ, and one hope, and one faith, and one Church, and one baptism ordained only in the one Church, from which unity whosoever will depart must needs be found with heretics; and while he upholds them against the Church, he impugns the sacrament of the divine tradition. The sacrament of which unity we see expressed also in the Canticles, in the person of Christ, who says, "A garden enclosed is my sister, my spouse, a fountain sealed, a well of living water, a garden with the fruit of apples." But if His Church is a garden enclosed, and a fountain sealed, how can he who is not in the Church enter into the same garden, or drink from its fountain? Moreover, Peter himself, showing and vindicating the unity, has commanded and warned us that we cannot be saved, except by the one only baptism of one Church. "In the ark," says he, "of Noah, few, that is, eight souls, were saved by water, as also baptism shall in

like manner save you." In how short and spiritual a summary has he set forth the sacrament of unity! For as, in that baptism of the world in which its ancient iniquity was purged away, he who was not in the ark of Noah could not be saved by water, so neither can he appear to be saved by baptism who has not been baptized in the Church which is established in the unity of the Lord according to the sacrament of the one ark.

12. Therefore, dearest brother, having explored and seen the truth; it is observed and held by us, that all who are converted from any heresy whatever to the Church must be baptized by the only and lawful baptism of the Church, with the exception of those who had previously been baptized in the Church, and so had passed over to the heretics. For it behooves these, when they return, having repented, to be received by the imposition of hands only, and to be restored by the shepherd to the sheep-fold whence they had strayed. I bid you, dearest brother, ever heartily farewell.

Epistle LXXIV.
Firmilian, Bishop of Cæsarea in Cappadocia, to Cyprian, Against the Letter of Stephen. a.d. 256.

Argument.—The Argument of This Letter is Exactly the Same as that of the Previous One, But Written with a Little More Vehemence and Acerbity Than Becomes a Bishop, Chiefly for the Reason, as May Be Suspected, that Stephen Had Also Written Another Letter to Firmilianus, Helenus, and Other Bishops of Those Parts.

1. Firmilianus to Cyprian, his brother in the Lord, greeting. We have received by Rogatian, our beloved deacon, the letter sent by you which you wrote to us,

well-beloved brother; and we gave the greatest thanks to the Lord, because it has happened that we who are separated from one another in body are thus united in spirit, as if we were not only occupying one country, but inhabiting together one and the self-same house. Which also it is becoming for us to say, because, indeed, the spiritual house of God is one. "For it shall come to pass in the last days," saith the prophet, "that the mountain of the Lord shall be manifest, and the house of God above the tops of the mountains." Those that come together into this house are united with gladness, according to what is asked from the Lord in the psalm, to dwell in the house of the Lord all the days of one's life. Whence in another place also it is made manifest that among the saints there is great and desirous love for assembling together. "Behold," he says, "how good and how pleasant a thing it is for brethren to dwell together in unity!"

2. For unity and peace and concord afford the greatest pleasure not only to men who believe and know the truth, but also to heavenly angels themselves, to whom the divine word says it is a joy when one sinner repents and returns to the bond of unity. But assuredly this would not be said of the angels, who have their conversation in heaven, unless they themselves also were united to us, who rejoice at our unity; even as, on the other hand, they are assuredly saddened when they see the diverse minds and the divided wills of some, as if not only they do not together invoke one and the same God, but as if, separated and divided from one another, they can neither have a common conversation nor discourse. Except that we may in this matter give thanks to Stephen, that it has now happened through his unkindness that we receive the proof of your faith and wisdom. But although

we have received the favor of this benefit on account of Stephen, certainly Stephen has not done anything deserving of kindness and thanks. For neither can Judas be thought worthy by his perfidy and treachery wherewith he wickedly dealt concerning the Savior, as though he had been the cause of such great advantages, that through him the world and the people of the Gentiles were delivered by the Lord's passion.

3. But let these things which were done by Stephen be passed by for the present, lest, while we remember his audacity and pride, we bring a more lasting sadness on ourselves from the things that he has wickedly done. And knowing, concerning you, that you have settled this matter, concerning which there is now a question, according to the rule of truth and the wisdom of Christ; we have exulted with great joy, and have given God thanks that we have found in brethren placed at such a distance such a unanimity of faith and truth with us. For the grace of God is mighty to associate and join together in the bond of charity and unity even those things which seem to be divided by a considerable space of earth, according to the way in which of old also the divine power associated in the bond of unanimity Ezekiel and Daniel, though later in their age, and separated from them by a long space of time, to Job and Noah, who were among the first; so that although they were separated by long periods, yet by divine inspiration they felt the same truths. And this also we now observe in you, that you who are separated from us by the most extensive regions, approve yourselves to be, nevertheless, joined with us in mind and spirit. All which arises from the divine unity. For even as the Lord who dwells in us is one and the same, He everywhere joins and couples His own people in

the bond of unity, whence their sound has gone out into the whole earth, who are sent by the Lord swiftly running in the spirit of unity; as, on the other hand, it is of no advantage that some are very near and joined together bodily, if in spirit and mind they differ, since souls cannot at all be united which divide themselves from God's unity. "For, lo," it says, "they that are far from Thee shall perish." But such shall undergo the judgment of God according to their desert, as depart from His words who prays to the Father for unity, and says, "Father, grant that, as Thou and I are one, so they also may be one in us."

4. But we receive those things which you have written as if they were our own; nor do we read them cursorily, but by frequent repetition have committed them to memory. Nor does it hinder saving usefulness, either to repeat the same things for the confirmation of the truth, or, moreover, to add some things for the sake of accumulating proof. But if anything has been added by us, it is not added as if there had been too little said by you; but since the divine discourse surpasses human nature, and the soul cannot conceive or grasp the whole and perfect word, therefore also the number of prophets is so great, that the divine wisdom in its multiplicity may be distributed through many. Whence also he who first speaks in prophecy is bidden to be silent if a revelation be made to a second. For which reason it happens of necessity among us, that year by year we, the elders and prelates, assemble together to arrange those matters which are committed to our care, so that if any things are more serious they may be directed by the common counsel. Moreover, we do this that some remedy may be sought for by repentance for lapsed brethren, and for those wounded by the devil after the saving laver, not as though

they obtained remission of sins from us, but that by our means they may be converted to the understanding of their sins, and may be compelled to give fuller satisfaction to the Lord.

5. But since that messenger sent by you was in haste to return to you, and the winter season was pressing, we replied what we could to your letter. And indeed, as respects what Stephen has said, as though the apostles forbade those who come from heresy to be baptized, and delivered this also to be observed by their successors, you have replied most abundantly, that no one is so foolish as to believe that the apostles delivered this, when it is even well known that these heresies themselves, execrable and detestable as they are, arose subsequently; when even Marcion the disciple of Cerdo is found to have introduced his sacrilegious tradition against God long after the apostles, and after long lapse of time from them. Apelles, also consenting to his blasphemy, added many other new and more important matters hostile to faith and truth. But also the time of Valentinus and Basilides is manifest, that they too, after the apostles, and after a long period, rebelled against the Church of God with their wicked lies. It is plain that the other heretics, also, afterwards introduced their evil sects and perverse inventions, even as everyone was led by error; all of whom, it is evident, were self-condemned, and have declared against themselves an inevitable sentence before the day of judgment; and he who confirms the baptism of these, what else does he do but adjudge himself with them, and condemn himself, making himself a partaker with such?

6. But that they who are at Rome do not observe those things in all cases which are handed down from the beginning, and vainly pretend the authority of the

apostles; any one may know also from the fact, that concerning the celebration of Easter, and concerning many other sacraments of divine matters, he may see that there are some diversities among them, and that all things are not observed among them alike, which are observed at Jerusalem, just as in very many other provinces also many things are varied because of the difference of the places and names. And yet on this account there is no departure at all from the peace and unity of the Catholic Church, such as Stephen has now dared to make; breaking the peace against you, which his predecessors have always kept with you in mutual love and honour, even herein defaming Peter and Paul the blessed apostles, as if the very men delivered this who in their epistles execrated heretics, and warned us to avoid them. Whence it appears that this tradition is of men which maintains heretics, and asserts that they have baptism, which belongs to the Church alone.

7. But, moreover, you have well answered that part where Stephen said in his letter that heretics themselves also are of one mind in respect of baptism; and that they do not baptize such as come to them from one another, but only communicate with them; as if we also ought to do this. In which place, although you have already proved that it is sufficiently ridiculous for anyone to follow those that are in error, yet we add this moreover, over and above, that it is not wonderful for heretics to act thus, who, although in some lesser matters they differ, yet in that which is greatest they hold one and the same agreement to blaspheme the Creator, figuring for themselves certain dreams and phantasms of an unknown God. Assuredly it is but natural that these should agree in having a baptism which is unreal, in the same way as they

agree in repudiating the truth of the divinity. Of whom, since it is tedious to reply to their several statements, either wicked or foolish, it is sufficient shortly to say in sum, that they who do not hold the true Lord the Father cannot hold the truth either of the Son or of the Holy Spirit; according to which also they who are called Cataphrygians, and endeavor to claim to themselves new prophecies, can have neither the Father, nor the Son, nor the Holy Spirit, of whom, if we ask what Christ they announce, they will reply that they preach Him who sent the Spirit that speaks by Montanus and Prisca. And in these, when we observe that there has been not the spirit of truth, but of error, we know that they who maintain their false prophesying against the faith of Christ cannot have Christ. Moreover, all other heretics, if they have separated themselves from the Church of God, can have nothing of power or of grace, since all power and grace are established in the Church where the elders preside, who possess the power both of baptizing, and of imposition of hands, and of ordaining. For as a heretic may not lawfully ordain nor lay on hands, so neither may he baptize, nor do anything holily or spiritually, since he is an alien from spiritual and deifying sanctity. All which we some time back confirmed in Iconium, which is a place in Phrygia, when we were assembled together with those who had gathered from Galatia and Cilicia, and other neighboring countries, as to be held and firmly vindicated against heretics, when there was some doubt in certain minds concerning that matter.

8. And as Stephen and those who agree with him contend that putting away of sins and second birth may result from the baptism of heretics, among whom they themselves confess that the Holy Spirit is not; let them

consider and understand that spiritual birth cannot be without the Spirit; in conformity with which also the blessed Apostle Paul baptized anew with a spiritual baptism those who had already been baptized by John before the Holy Spirit had been sent by the Lord, and so laid hands on them that they might receive the Holy Ghost. But what kind of a thing is it, that when we see that Paul, after John's baptism, baptized his disciples again, we are hesitating to baptize those who come to the Church from heresy after their unhallowed and profane dipping. Unless, perchance, Paul was inferior to the bishops of these times, so that these indeed can by imposition of hands alone give the Holy Spirit to those heretics who come (to the Church), while Paul was not fitted to give the Holy Spirit by imposition of hands to those who had been baptized by John, unless he had first baptized them also with the baptism of the Church.

9. That, moreover, is absurd, that they do not think it is to be inquired who was the person that baptized, for the reason that he who has been baptized may have obtained grace by the invocation of the Trinity, of the names of the Father, and of the Son, and of the Holy Ghost. Then this will be the wisdom which Paul writes is in those who are perfected. But who in the Church is perfect and wise who can either defend or believe this, that this bare invocation of names is sufficient to the remission of sins and the sanctification of baptism; since these things are only then of advantage, when both he who baptizes has the Holy Spirit, and the baptism itself also is not ordained without the Spirit? But, say they, he who in any manner whatever is baptized without, may obtain the grace of baptism by his disposition and faith, which doubtless is ridiculous in itself, as if either a

wicked disposition could attract to itself from heaven the sanctification of the righteous, or a false faith the truth of believers. But that not all who call on the name of Christ are heard, and that their invocation cannot obtain any grace, the Lord Himself manifests, saying, "Many shall come in my name, saying, I am Christ, and shall deceive many." Because there is no difference between a false prophet and a heretic. For as the former deceives in the name of God or Christ, so the latter deceives in the sacrament of baptism. Both strive by falsehood to deceive men's wills.

10. But I wish to relate to you some facts concerning a circumstance which occurred among us, pertaining to this very matter. About two-and-twenty years ago, in the times after the Emperor Alexander, there happened in these parts many struggles and difficulties, either in general to all men, or privately to Christians. Moreover, there were many and frequent earthquakes, so that many places were overthrown throughout Cappadocia and Pontus; even certain cities, dragged into the abyss, were swallowed up by the opening of the gaping earth. So that from this also a severe persecution arose against us of the Christian name; and this after the long peace of the previous age arose suddenly, and with its unusual evils was made more terrible for the disturbance of our people. Serenianus was then governor in our province, a bitter and terrible persecutor. But the faithful being set in this state of disturbance, and fleeing hither and thither for fear of the persecution, and leaving their country and passing over into other regions—for there was an opportunity of passing over, for the reason that that persecution was not over the whole world, but was local—there arose among us on a sudden a certain woman, who in a state of ecstasy

announced herself as a prophetess, and acted as if filled with the Holy Ghost. And she was so moved by the impetus of the principal demons, that for a long time she made anxious and deceived the brotherhood, accomplishing certain wonderful and portentous things, and promised that she would cause the earth to be shaken. Not that the power of the demon was so great that he could prevail to shake the earth, or to disturb the elements; but that sometimes a wicked spirit, prescient, and perceiving that there will be an earthquake, pretends that he will do what he sees will happen. By these lies and boastings he had so subdued the minds of individuals, that they obeyed him and followed whithersoever he commanded and led. He would also make that woman walk in the keen winter with bare feet over frozen snow, and not to be troubled or hurt in any degree by that walking. Moreover, she would say that she was hurrying to Judea and to Jerusalem, feigning as if she had come thence. Here also she deceived one of the presbyters, a countryman, and another, a deacon, so that they had intercourse with that same woman, which was shortly afterwards detected. For on a sudden there appeared unto her one of the exorcists, a man approved and always of good conversation in respect of religious discipline; who, stimulated by the exhortation also of very many brethren who were themselves strong and praiseworthy in the faith, raised himself up against that wicked spirit to overcome it; which moreover, by its subtle fallacy, had predicted this a little while before, that a certain adverse and unbelieving tempter would come. Yet that exorcist, inspired by God's grace, bravely resisted, and showed that that which was before thought holy, was indeed a most wicked spirit. But that woman, who previously by wiles and deceitfulness of the demon was attempting many things for the deceiving of the faithful, among other things by which she had deceived many, also had frequently dared this; to pretend that with an invocation not to be contemned she sanctified bread and celebrated the Eucharist, and to offer sacrifice to the Lord, not without the sacrament of the accustomed utterance; and also to baptize many, making use of the usual and lawful words of interrogation, that nothing might seem to be different from the ecclesiastical rule.

11. What, then, shall we say about the baptism of this woman, by which a most wicked demon baptized through means of a woman? Do Stephen and they who agree with him approve of this also especially when neither the symbol of the Trinity nor the legitimate and ecclesiastical interrogatory were wanting to her? Can it be believed that either remission of sins was given, or the regeneration of the saving laver duly completed, when all things, although after the image of truth, yet were done by a demon? Unless, perchance, they who defend the baptism of heretics contend that the demon also conferred the grace of baptism in the name of the Father, and of the Son, and of the Holy Spirit. Among them, no doubt, there is the same error—it is the very deceitfulness of devils, since among them the Holy Spirit is not at all.

12. Moreover, what is the meaning of that which Stephen would assert, that the presence and holiness of Christ is with those who are baptized among heretics? For if the apostle does not speak falsely when he says, "As many of you as are baptized into Christ, have put on Christ," certainly he who has been baptized among them into Christ, has put on Christ. But if he has put on Christ, he might also receive the Holy Ghost, who was sent by

Christ, and hands are vainly laid upon him who comes to us for the reception of the Spirit; unless, perhaps, he has not put on the Spirit from Christ, so that Christ indeed may be with heretics, but the Holy Spirit not be with them.

13. But let us briefly run through the other matters also, which were spoken of by you abundantly and most fully, especially as Rogatianus, our well-beloved deacon, is hurrying to you. For it follows that they must be asked by us, when they defend heretics, whether their baptism is carnal or spiritual. For if it is carnal, they differ in no respect from the baptism of the Jews, which they use in such a manner that in it, as if in a common and vulgar laver, only external filth is washed away. But if it is spiritual, how can baptism be spiritual among those among whom there is no Holy Spirit? And thus the water wherewith they are washed is to them only a carnal washing, not a sacrament of baptism.

14. But if the baptism of heretics can have the regeneration of the second birth, those who are baptized among them must be counted not heretics, but children of God. For the second birth, which occurs in baptism, begets sons of God. But if the spouse of Christ is one, which is the Catholic Church, it is she herself who alone bears sons of God. For there are not many spouses of Christ, since the apostle says, "I have espoused you, that I may present you as a chaste virgin to Christ;" and, "Hearken, O daughter, and consider, and incline thine ear; forget also thine own people, for the King hath greatly desired thy beauty;" and, "Come with me, my spouse, from Lebanon; thou shalt come, and shalt pass over from the source of thy faith;" and, "I am come into my garden, my sister, my spouse." We see that one person is

everywhere set forward, because also the spouse is one. But the synagogue of heretics is not one with us, because the spouse is not an adulteress and a harlot. Whence also she cannot bear children of God; unless, as appears to Stephen, heresy indeed brings them forth and exposes them, while the Church takes them up when exposed, and nourishes those for her own whom she has not born, although she cannot be the mother of strange children. And therefore Christ our Lord, setting forth that His spouse is one, and declaring the sacrament of His unity, says, "He that is not with me is against me, and he that gathered not with me scattered." For if Christ is with us, but the heretics are not with us, certainly the heretics are in opposition to Christ; and if we gather with Christ, but the heretics do not gather with us, doubtless they scatter.

15. But neither must we pass over what has been necessarily remarked by you, that the Church, according to the Song of Songs, is a garden enclosed, and a fountain sealed, a paradise with the fruit of apples. They who have never entered into this garden, and have not seen the paradise planted by God the Creator, how shall they be able to afford to another the living water of the saving lava from the fountain which is enclosed within, and sealed with a divine seal? And as the ark of Noah was nothing else than the sacrament of the Church of Christ, which then, when all without were perishing, kept those only safe who were within the ark, we are manifestly instructed to look to the unity of the Church. Even as also the Apostle Peter laid down, saying, "Thus also shall baptism in like manner make you safe;" showing that as they who were not in the ark with Noah not only were not purged and saved by water, but at once perished in that deluge; so now also, whoever are not in the Church with

Christ will perish outside, unless they are converted by penitence to the only and saving lava of the Church.

16. But what is the greatness of his error, and what the depth of his blindness, who says that remission of sins can be granted in the synagogues of heretics, and does not abide on the foundation of the one Church which was once based by Christ upon the rock, may be perceived from this, that Christ said to Peter alone, "Whatsoever thou shalt bind on earth shall be bound in heaven, and whatsoever thou shalt loose on earth shall be loosed in heaven." And again, in the Gospel, when Christ breathed on the apostles alone, saying, "Receive ye the Holy Ghost: whose soever sins ye remit they are remitted unto them, and whose soever sins ye retain they are retained." Therefore the power of remitting sins was given to the apostles, and to the churches which they, sent by Christ, established, and to the bishops who succeeded to them by vicarious ordination. But the enemies of the one Catholic Church in which we are, and the adversaries of us who have succeeded the apostles, asserting for themselves, in opposition to us, unlawful priesthoods, and setting up profane altars, what else are they than Korah, Dathan, and Abiram, profane with a like wickedness, and about to suffer the same punishments which they did, as well as those who agree with them, just as their partners and abettors perished with a like death to theirs?

17. And in this respect I am justly indignant at this so open and manifest folly of Stephen, that he who so boasts of the place of his episcopate, and contends that he holds the succession from Peter, on whom the foundations of the Church were laid, should introduce many other rocks and establish new buildings of many churches; maintaining that there is baptism in them by his authority.

For they who are baptized, doubtless, fill up the number of the Church. But he who approves their baptism maintains, of those baptized, that the Church is also with them. Nor does he understand that the truth of the Christian Rock is overshadowed, and in some measure abolished, by him when he thus betrays and deserts unity. The apostle acknowledges that the Jews, although blinded by ignorance, and bound by the grossest wickedness, have yet a zeal for God. Stephen, who announces that he holds by succession the throne of Peter, is stirred with no zeal against heretics, when he concedes to them, not a moderate, but the very greatest power of grace: so far as to say and assert that, by the sacrament of baptism, the filth of the old man is washed away by them, that they pardon the former mortal sins, that they make sons of God by heavenly regeneration, and renew to eternal life by the sanctification of the divine laver. He who concedes and gives up to heretics in this way the great and heavenly gifts of the Church, what else does he do but communicate with them for whom he maintains and claims so much grace? And now he hesitates in vain to consent to them, and to be a partaker with them in other matters also, to meet together with them, and equally with them to mingle their prayers, and appoint a common altar and sacrifice.

18. But, says he, "the name of Christ is of great advantage to faith and the sanctification of baptism; so that whosoever is anywhere so-ever baptized in the name of Christ, immediately obtains the grace of Christ:" although this position may be briefly met and answered, that if baptism without in the name of Christ availed for the cleansing of man; in the name of the same Christ, the imposition of hands might avail also for the reception of

the Holy Spirit; and the other things also which are done among heretics will begin to seem just and lawful when they are done in the name of Christ; as you have maintained in your letter that the name of Christ could be of no avail except in the Church alone, to which alone Christ has conceded the power of heavenly grace.

19. But with respect to the refutation of custom which they seem to oppose to the truth, who is so foolish as to prefer custom to truth, or when he sees the light, not to forsake the darkness?—unless most ancient custom in any respect avail the Jews, upon the advent of Christ, that is, the Truth, in remaining in their old usage, and forsaking the new way of truth. And this indeed you Africans are able to say against Stephen, that when you knew the truth you forsook the error of custom. But we join custom to truth, and to the Romans' custom we oppose custom, but the custom of truth; holding from the beginning that which was delivered by Christ and the apostles. Nor do we remember that this at any time began among us, since it has always been observed here, that we knew none but one Church of God, and accounted no baptism holy except that of the holy Church. Certainly, since some doubted about the baptism of those who, although they receive the new prophets, yet appear to recognize the same Father and Son with us; very many of us meeting together in Iconium very carefully examined the matter, and we decided that every baptism was altogether to be rejected which is arranged for without the Church.

20. But to what they allege and say on behalf of the heretics, that the apostle said, "Whether in pretense or in truth, Christ is preached," it is idle for us to reply; when it is manifest that the apostle, in his epistle wherein he

said this, made mention neither of heretics nor of baptism of heretics, but spoke of brethren only, whether as perfidiously speaking in agreement with himself, or as persevering in sincere faith; nor is it needful to discuss this in a long argument, but it is sufficient to read the epistle itself, and to gather from the apostle himself what the apostle said.

21. What then, say they, will become of those who, coming from the heretics, have been received without the baptism of the Church? If they have departed this life, they are reckoned in the number of those who have been catechumens indeed among us, but have died before they were baptized,—no trifling advantage of truth and faith, to which they had attained by forsaking error, although, being prevented by death, they had not gained the consummation of grace. But they who still abide in life should be baptized with the baptism of the Church, that they may obtain remission of sins, lest by the presumption of others they remain in their old error and die without the completion of grace. But what a crime is theirs on the one hand who receive, or on the other, theirs who are received, that their foulness not being washed away by the laver of the Church, nor their sins put away, communion being rashly seized, they touch the body and blood of the Lord, although it is written, "Whosoever shall eat the bread or drink the cup of the Lord unworthily, shall be guilty of the body and blood of the Lord!"

22. We have judged that those also whom they, who had formerly been bishops in the Catholic Church, and afterwards had assumed to themselves the power of clerical ordination, had baptized, are to be regarded as not baptized. And this is observed among us, that whosoever

dipped by them come to us are baptized among us as strangers and having obtained nothing, with the only and true baptism of the Catholic Church and obtain the regeneration of the laver of life. And yet there is a great difference between him who unwillingly and constrained by the necessity of persecution has given way, and him who with a profane will boldly rebels against the Church, or with impious voice blasphemes against the Father and God of Christ and the Creator of the whole world. And Stephen is not ashamed to assert and to say that remission of sins can be granted by those who are themselves set fast in all kinds of sins, as if in the house of death there could be the laver of salvation.

23. What, then, is to be made of what is written, "Abstain from strange water, and drink not from a strange fountain," if, leaving the sealed fountain of the Church, you take up strange water for your own, and pollute the Church with unhallowed fountains? For when you communicate with the baptism of heretics, what else do you do than drink from their slough and mud; and while you yourself are purged with the Church's sanctification, you become befouled with the contact of the filth of others? And do you not fear the judgment of God when you are giving testimony to heretics in opposition to the Church, although it is written, "A false witness shall not be unpunished?" But indeed you are worse than all heretics. For when many, as soon as their error is known, come over to you from them that they may receive the true light of the Church, you assist the errors of those who come, and, obscuring the light of ecclesiastical truth, you heap up the darkness of the heretical night; and although they confess that they are in sins, and have no grace, and therefore come to the Church, you take away from them

remission of sins, which is given in baptism, by saying that they are already baptized and have obtained the grace of the Church outside the Church, and you do not perceive that their souls will be required at your hands when the day of judgment shall come, for having denied to the thirsting the drink of the Church, and having been the occasion of death to those that were desirous of living. And, after all this, you are indignant!

24. Consider with what want of judgment you dare to blame those who strive for the truth against falsehood. For who ought more justly to be indignant against the other?—whether he who supports God's enemies, or he who, in opposition to him who supports God's enemies, unites with us on behalf of the truth of the Church?—except that it is plain that the ignorant are also excited and angry, because by the want of counsel and discourse they are easily turned to wrath; so that of none more than of you does divine Scripture say, "A wrathful man stirs up strifes, and a furious man heaps up sins." For what strife and dissensions have you stirred up throughout the churches of the whole world! Moreover, how great sin have you heaped up for yourself, when you cut yourself off from so many flocks! For it is yourself that you have cut off. Do not deceive yourself, since he is really the schismatic who has made himself an apostate from the communion of ecclesiastical unity. For while you think that all may be excommunicated by you, you have excommunicated yourself alone from all; and not even the precepts of an apostle have been able to mold you to the rule of truth and peace, although he warned, and said, "I therefore, the prisoner of the Lord, beseech you that ye walk worthy of the vocation wherewith ye are called, with all lowliness and meekness, with long-suffering,

forbearing one another in love; endeavoring to keep the unity of the Spirit in the bond of peace. There is one body and one Spirit, even as ye are called in one hope of your calling; one Lord, one faith, one baptism; one God and Father of all, who is above all, and through all, and in us all."

25. How carefully has Stephen fulfilled these salutary commands and warnings of the apostle, keeping in the first-place lowliness of mind and meekness! For what is more lowly or meek than to have disagreed with so many bishops throughout the whole world, breaking peace with each one of them in various kinds of discord: at one time with the eastern churches, as we are sure you know; at another time with you who are in the south, from whom he received bishops as messengers sufficiently patiently and meekly not to receive them even to the speech of an ordinary conference; and even more, so mindful of love and charity as to command the entire fraternity, that no one should receive them into his house, so that not only peace and communion, but also a shelter and entertainment, were denied to them when they came! This is to have kept the unity of the Spirit in the bond of peace, to cut himself off from the unity of love, and to make himself a stranger in all respects from his brethren, and to rebel against the sacrament and the faith with the madness of contumacious discord! With such a man can there be one Spirit and one body, in whom perchance there is not even one mind, so slippery, and shifting, and uncertain is it?

26. But as far as he is concerned, let us leave him; let us rather deal with that concerning which there is the greatest question. They who contend that persons baptized among the heretics ought to be received as if

they had obtained the grace of lawful baptism, say that baptism is one and the same to them and to us, and differs in no respect. But what says the Apostle Paul? "One Lord, one faith, one baptism, one God." If the baptism of heretics be one and the same with ours, without doubt their faith also is one; but if our faith is one, assuredly also we have one Lord: if there is one Lord, it follows that we say that He is one. But if this unity which cannot be separated and divided at all, is itself also among heretics, why do we contend anymore? Why do we call them heretics and not Christians? Moreover, since we and heretics have not one God, nor one Lord, nor one Church, nor one faith, nor even one Spirit, nor one body, it is manifest that neither can baptism be common to us with heretics, since between us there is nothing at all in common. And yet Stephen is not ashamed to afford patronage to such in opposition to the Church, and for the sake of maintaining heretics to divide the brotherhood and in addition, to call Cyprian "a false Christ and a false apostle, and a deceitful worker." And he, conscious that all these characters are in himself, has been in advance of you, by falsely objecting to another those things which he himself ought deservedly to hear. We all bid you, for all our sakes, with all the bishops who are in Africa, and all the clergy, and all the brotherhood, farewell; that, constantly of one mind, and thinking the same thing, we may find you united with us even though afar off.

Epistle LXXV.
To Magnus, on Baptizing the Novatians, and Those Who Obtain Grace on a Sick-Bed.
Argument.—The Former Part of This Letter is of the Same Tenor with Those that Pre☐cede, Except that

He Inculcates Concerning the Novatians What He Had in Substance Said Concerning All Heretics; Moreover, Insinuating by the Way that the Legitimate Succession of Cornelius at Rome is Known, as the Church May Be Known. In the Second Part (Which Hitherto, as the Title Sufficiently Indicates, Has Been Wrongly Published as a Separate Letter) He Teaches that that is a True Baptism Wherein One is Baptized by Sprinkling on a Sick-Bed, as Well as by Immersion in the Church.

1. Cyprian to Magnus his son, greeting. With your usual religious diligence, you have consulted my poor intelligence, dearest son, as to whether, among other heretics, they also who come from Novatian ought, after his profane washing, to be baptized, and sanctified in the Catholic Church, with the lawful, and true, and only baptism of the Church. Respecting which matter, as much as the capacity of my faith and the sanctity and truth of the divine Scriptures suggest, I answer that no heretics and schismatics at all have any power or right. For which reason Novatian neither ought to be nor can be expected, inasmuch as he also is without the Church and acting in opposition to the peace and love of Christ, from being counted among adversaries and antichrists. For our Lord Jesus Christ, when He testified in His Gospel that those who were not with Him were His adversaries, did not point out any species of heresy, but showed that all whatsoever who were not with Him, and who, not gathering with Him, were scattering His flock, were His adversaries; saying, "He that is not with me is against me, and he that gathered not with me scattered." Moreover, the blessed Apostle John himself distinguished no heresy or schism, neither did he set down any as specially separated; but he called all who had gone out from the

Church, and who acted in opposition to the Church, antichrists, saying, "Ye have heard that Antichrist cometh, and even now are come many antichrists; wherefore we know that this is the last time. They went out from us, but they were not of us; for if they had been of us, they would have continued with us." Whence it appears, that all are adversaries of the Lord and antichrists, who are known to have departed from charity and from the unity of the Catholic Church. In addition, moreover, the Lord establishes it in His Gospel, and says, "But if he neglect to hear the Church, let him be unto thee as a heathen man and a publican." Now if they who despise the Church are counted heathens and publicans, much more certainly is it necessary that rebels and enemies, who forge false altars, and lawless priesthoods, and sacrilegious sacrifices, and corrupted names, should be counted among heathens and publicans; since they who sin less, and are only despisers of the Church, are by the Lord's sentence judged to be heathens and publicans.

2. But that the Church is one, the Holy Spirit declares in the Song of Songs, saying, in the person of Christ, "My dove, my undefiled, is one; she is the only one of her mother, she is the choice one of her that bare her." Concerning which also He says again, "A garden enclosed is my sister, my spouse; a spring sealed up, a well of living water." But if the spouse of Christ, which is the Church, is a garden enclosed; a thing that is closed up cannot lie open to strangers and profane persons. And if it is a fountain sealed, he who, being placed without has no access to the spring, can neither drink thence nor be sealed. And the well also of living water, if it is one and the same within, he who is placed without cannot be quickened and sanctified from that water of which it is

only granted to those who are within to make any use, or to drink. Peter also, showing this, set forth that the Church is one, and that only they who are in the Church can be baptized; and said, "In the ark of Noah, few, that is, eight souls, were saved by water; the like figure where-unto even baptism shall save you;" proving and attesting that the one ark of Noah was a type of the one Church. If then, in that baptism of the world thus expiated and purified, he who was not in the ark of Noah could be saved by water, he who is not in the Church to which alone baptism is granted, can also now be quickened by baptism. Moreover, too, the Apostle Paul, more openly and clearly still manifesting this same thing, writes to the Ephesians, and says, "Christ loved the Church, and gave Himself for it, that He might sanctify and cleanse it with the washing of water." But if the Church is one which is loved by Christ, and is alone cleansed by His washing, how can he who is not in the Church be either loved by Christ, or washed and cleansed by His washing?

3. Wherefore, since the Church alone has the living water, and the power of baptizing and cleansing man, he who says that anyone can be baptized and sanctified by Novatian must first show and teach that Novatian is in the Church or presides over the Church. For the Church is one, and as she is one, cannot be both within and without. For if she is with Novatian, she was not with Cornelius. But if she was with Cornelius, who succeeded the bishop Fabian by lawful ordination, and whom, beside the honour of the priesthood, the Lord glorified also with martyrdom, Novatian is not in the Church; nor can he be reckoned as a bishop, who, succeeding to no one, and despising the evangelical and apostolic tradition, sprang from himself. For he who has

not been ordained in the Church can neither have nor hold to the Church in any way.

4. For the faith of the sacred Scripture sets forth that the Church is not without, nor can be separated nor divided against itself, but maintains the unity of an inseparable and undivided house; since it is written of the sacrament of the Passover, and of the lamb, which Lamb designated Christ: "In one house shall it be eaten: ye shall not carry forth the flesh abroad out of the house." Which also we see expressed concerning Rahab, who herself also bore a type of the Church, who received the command which said, "Thou shalt bring thy father, and thy mother, and thy brethren, and all thy father's household unto thee into thine house; and whosoever shall go out of the doors of thine house into the street, his blood shall be upon him." In which mystery is declared, that they who will live, and escape from the destruction of the world, must be gathered together into one house alone, that is, into the Church; but whosoever of those thus collected together shall go out abroad, that is, if any one, although he may have obtained grace in the Church, shall depart and go out of the Church, that his blood shall be upon him; that is, that he himself must charge it upon himself that he perishes; which the Apostle Paul explains, teaching and enjoining that a heretic must be avoided, as perverse, and a sinner, and as condemned of himself. For that man will be guilty of his own ruin, who, not being cast out by the bishop, but of his own accord deserting from the Church is by heretical presumption condemned of himself.

5. And therefore the Lord, suggesting to us a unity that comes from divine authority, lays it down, saying, "I and my Father are one." To which unity reducing His Church, He says again, "And there shall be one flock,

and one shepherd." But if the flock is one, how can he be numbered among the flock who is not in the number of the flock? Or how can he be esteemed a pastor, who,—while the true shepherd remains and presides over the Church of God by successive ordination,—succeeding to no one, and beginning from himself, becomes a stranger and a profane person, an enemy of the Lord's peace and of the divine unity, not dwelling in the house of God, that is, in the Church of God, in which none dwell except they are of one heart and one mind, since the Holy Spirit speaks in the Psalms, and says, "It is God who makes men to dwell of one mind in a house."

6. Besides even the Lord's sacrifices themselves declare that Christian unanimity is linked together with itself by a firm and inseparable charity. For when the Lord calls bread, which is combined by the union of many grains, His body, He indicates our people whom He bore as being united; and when He calls the wine, which is pressed from many grapes and clusters and collected together, His blood, He also signifies our flock linked together by the mingling of a united multitude. If Novatian is united to this bread of the Lord, if he also is mingled with this cup of Christ, he may also seem to be able to have the grace of the one baptism of the Church, if it be manifest that he holds the unity of the Church. In fine, how inseparable is the sacrament of unity, and how hopeless are they, and what excessive ruin they earn for themselves from the indignation of God, who make a schism, and, forsaking their bishop, appoint another false bishop for themselves without,—Holy Scripture declares in the books of Kings; where ten tribes were divided from the tribe of Judah and Benjamin, and, forsaking their king, appointed for themselves another one without. It says,

"And the Lord was very angry with all the seed of Israel, and removed them away, and delivered them into the hand of spoilers, until He had cast them out of His sight; for Israel was scattered from the house of David, and they made themselves a king, Jeroboam the son of Nebat." It says that the Lord was very angry, and gave them up to perdition, because they were scattered from unity, and had made another king for themselves. And so great was the indignation of the Lord against those who had made the schism, that even when the man of God was sent to Jeroboam, to charge upon him his sins, and predict the future vengeance, he was forbidden to eat bread or to drink water with them. And when he did not observe this, and took meat against the command of God, he was immediately smitten by the majesty of the divine judgment, so that returning thence he was slain on the way by the jaws of a lion which attacked him. And dares any one to say that the saving water of baptism and heavenly grace can be in common with schismatics, with whom neither earthly food nor worldly drink ought to be in common? Moreover, the Lord satisfies us in His Gospel, and shows forth a still greater light of intelligence, that the same persons who had then divided themselves from the tribe of Judah and Benjamin, and forsaking Jerusalem had seceded to Samaria, should be reckon among profane persons and Gentiles. For when first He sent His disciples on the ministry of salvation, He bade them, saying, "Go not into the way of the Gentiles, and into any city of the Samaritans enter ye not." Sending first to the Jews, He commands the Gentiles as yet to be passed over; but by adding that even the city of the Samaritans was to be omitted, where there were schismatics, He shows that schismatics were to be put on the same level as Gentiles.

7. But if any one objects, by way of saying that Novatian holds the same law which the Catholic Church holds, baptizes with the same symbol with which we baptize, knows the same God and Father, the same Christ the Son, the same Holy Spirit, and that for this reason he may claim the power of baptizing, namely, that he seems not to differ from us in the baptismal interrogatory; let any one that thinks that this may be objected, know first of all, that there is not one law of the Creed, nor the same interrogatory common to us and to schismatics. For when they say, "Dost thou believe the remission of sins and life eternal through the holy Church?" they lie in their interrogatory, since they have not the Church. Then, besides, with their own voice they themselves confess that remission of sins cannot be given except by the holy Church; and not having this, they show that sins cannot be remitted among them.

8. But that they are said to have the same God the Father as we, to know the same Christ the Son, the same Holy Spirit, can be of no avail to such as these. For even Korah, Dathan, and Abiram knew the same God as did the priest Aaron and Moses. Living under the same law and religion, they invoke the one and true God, who was to be invoked and worshipped; yet, because they transgressed the ministry of their office in opposition to Aaron the priest, who had received the legitimate priesthood by the condescension of God and the ordination of the Lord, and claimed to themselves the power of sacrificing, divinely stricken, they immediately suffered punishment for their unlawful endeavors; and sacrifices offered irreligiously and lawlessly, contrary to the right of divine appointment, could not be accepted, nor profit them. Even those very

censers in which incense had been lawlessly offered, lest they should any more be used by the priests, but that they might rather exhibit a memorial of the divine vengeance and indignation for the correction of their successors, being by the command of the Lord melted and purged by fire, were beaten out into flexible plates, and fastened to the altars, according to what the Holy Scripture says, "to be," it says, "a memorial to the children of Israel, that no stranger which is not of the seed of Aaron come near to offer incense before the Lord, that he be not as Korah." And yet those men had not made a schism, nor had gone out abroad, and in opposition to God's priests rebelled shamelessly and with hostility; but this these men are now doing who divide the Church, and, as rebels against the peace and unity of Christ, attempt to establish a throne for themselves, and to assume the primacy, and to claim the right of baptizing and of offering. How can they complete what they do, or obtain anything by lawless endeavors from God, seeing that they are endeavoring against God what is not lawful to them? Wherefore they who patronize Novatian or other schismatics of that kind, contend in vain that anyone can be baptized and sanctified with a saving baptism among them, when it is plain that he who baptizes has not the power of baptizing.

9. And, moreover, that it may be better understood what is the divine judgment against audacity of the like kind, we find that in such wickedness, not only the leaders and originators, but also the partakers, are destined to punishment, unless they have separated themselves from the communion of the wicked; as the Lord by Moses commands, and says, "Separate yourselves from the tents of these most hardened men, and touch nothing of theirs, lest ye be consumed in their sins." And what the Lord had

threatened by Moses He fulfilled, that whosoever had not separated himself from Korah, and Dathan, and Abiram, immediately suffered punishment for his impious communion. By which example is shown and proved, that all will be liable to guilt as well as its punishment, who with irreligious boldness mingle themselves with schismatics in opposition to prelates and priests; even as also by the prophet Osea the Holy Spirit witnesses, and says, "Their sacrifices shall be unto them as the bread of mourning; all that thereof shall be polluted;" teaching, doubtless, and showing that all are absolutely joined with the leaders in punishment, who have been contaminated by their crime.

10. What, then, can be their deserving in the sight of God, on whom punishment are divinely denounced? or how can such persons justify and sanctify the baptized, who, being enemies of the priests, strive to usurp things foreign and lawless, and by no right conceded to them? And yet we do not wonder that, in accordance with their wickedness, they do contend for them. For it is necessary that each one of them should maintain what they do; nor when vanquished will they easily yield, although they know that what they do is not lawful. That is to be wondered at, yea, rather to be indignant and aggrieved at, that Christians should support antichrists; and that prevaricators of the faith, and betrayers of the Church, should stand within in the Church itself. And these, although otherwise obstinate and unteachable, yet still at least confess this—that all, whether heretics or schismatics, are without the Holy Ghost, and therefore can indeed baptize, but cannot confer the Holy Spirit; and at this very point they are held fast by us, inasmuch as we show that those who have not the Holy Ghost are not able

to baptize at all.

11. For since in baptism everyone has his own sins remitted, the Lord proves and declares in His Gospel that sins can only be put away by those who have the Holy Spirit. For after His resurrection, sending forth His disciples, He speaks to them, and says, "As the Father hath sent me, even so send I you. And when He had said this, He breathed on them, and said to them, Receive ye the Holy Ghost. Whose soever sins ye remit, they shall be remitted unto them; and whose soever sins ye retain, they shall be retained." In which place He shows that he alone can baptize and give remission of sins who has the Holy Spirit. Moreover, John, who was to baptize Christ our Lord Himself, previously received the Holy Ghost while he was yet in his mother's womb, that it might be certain and manifest that none can baptize save those who have the Holy Spirit. Therefore those who patronize heretics or schismatics must answer us whether they have or have not the Holy Ghost. If they have, why are hands imposed on those who are baptized among them when they come to us, that they may receive the Holy Ghost, since He must surely have been received there, where if He was He could be given? But if heretics and schismatics baptized without have not the Holy Spirit, and therefore hands are imposed on them among us, that here may be received what there neither is nor can be given; it is plain, also, that remission of sins cannot be given by those who, it is certain, have not the Holy Spirit. And therefore, in order that, according to the divine arrangement and the evangelical truth, they may be able to obtain remission of sins, and to be sanctified, and to become temples of God, they must all absolutely be baptized with the baptism of the Church who come from adversaries and antichrists to

the Church of Christ.

12. You have asked also, dearest son, what I thought of those who obtain God's grace in sickness and weakness, whether they are to be accounted legitimate Christians, for that they are not to be washed, but sprinkled, with the saving water. In this point, my diffidence and modesty prejudges none, so as to prevent any from feeling what he thinks right, and from doing what he feels to be right. As far as my poor understanding conceives it, I think that the divine benefits can in no respect be mutilated and weakened; nor can anything less occur in that case, where, with full and entire faith both of the giver and receiver, is accepted what is drawn from the divine gifts. For in the sacrament of salvation the contagion of sins is not in such wise washed away, as the filth of the skin and of the body is washed away in the carnal and ordinary washing, as that there should be need of saltpeter and other appliances also, and a bath and a basin wherewith this vile body must be washed and purified. Otherwise is the breast of the believer washed; otherwise is the mind of man purified by the merit of faith. In the sacraments of salvation, when necessity compels, and God bestows His mercy, the divine methods confer the whole benefit on believers; nor ought it to trouble any one that sick people seem to be sprinkled or effused, when they obtain the Lord's grace, when Holy Scripture speaks by the mouth of the prophet Ezekiel, and says, "Then will I sprinkle clean water upon you, and ye shall be clean: from all your filthiness and from all your idols will I cleanse you. And I will give you a new heart, and a new spirit will I put within you." Also in Numbers: "And the man that shall be unclean until the evening shall be purified on the third day, and on the seventh day shall

be clean: but if he shall not be purified on the third day, on the seventh day he shall not be clean. And that soul shall be cut off from Israel: because the water of sprinkling hath not been sprinkled upon him." And again: "And the Lord spoke unto Moses saying, Take the Levites from among the children of Israel, and cleanse them. And thus shalt thou do unto them, to cleanse them: thou shalt sprinkle them with the water of purification." And again: "The water of sprinkling is a purification." Whence it appears that the sprinkling also of water prevails equally with the washing of salvation; and that when this is done in the Church, where the faith both of receiver and giver is sound, all things hold and may be consummated and perfected by the majesty of the Lord and by the truth of faith.

  13. But, moreover, in respect of some calling those who have obtained the peace of Christ by the saving water and by legitimate faith, not Christians, but Clinics, I do not find whence they take up this name, unless perhaps, having read more, and of a more recondite kind, they have taken these Clinics from Hippocrates or Soranus. For I, who know of a Clinic in the Gospel, know that to that paralytic and infirm man, who lay on his bed during the long course of his life, his infirmity presented no obstacle to his attainment in the fullest degree of heavenly strength. Nor was he only raised from his bed by the divine indulgence, but he also took up his bed itself with his restored and increased strength. And therefore, as far as it is allowed me by faith to conceive and to think, this is my opinion, that anyone should be esteemed a legitimate Christian, who by the law and right of faith shall have obtained the grace of God in the Church. Or if anyone think that those have gained nothing by having

only been sprinkled with the saving water, but that they are still empty and void, let them not be deceived, so as if they escape the evil of their sickness, and get well, they should seek to be baptized. But if they cannot be baptized who have already been sanctified by ecclesiastical baptism, why are they offended in respect of their faith and the mercy of the Lord? Or have they obtained indeed the divine favor, but in a shorter and more limited measure of the divine gift and of the Holy Spirit, so as indeed to be esteemed Christians, but yet not to be counted equal with others?

14. Nay, verily, the Holy Spirit is not given by measure, but is poured out altogether on the believer. For if the day rises alike to all, and if the sun is diffused with like and equal light overall, how much more does Christ, who is the true sun and the true day, bestow in His Church the light of eternal life with the like equality! Of which equality we see the sacrament celebrated in Exodus, when the manna flowed down from heaven, and, prefiguring the things to come, showed forth the nourishment of the heavenly bread and the food of the coming Christ. For there, without distinction either of sex or of age, an omer was collected equally by each one. Whence it appeared that the mercy of Christ, and the heavenly grace that would subsequently follow, was equally divided among all; without difference of sex, without distinction of years, without accepting of persons, upon all the people of God the gift of spiritual grace was shed. Assuredly the same spiritual grace which is equally received in baptism by believers, is subsequently either increased or diminished in our conversation and conduct; as in the Gospel the Lord's seed is equally sown, but, according to the variety of the soil, some is wasted, and

some is increased into a large variety of plenty, with an exuberant fruit of either thirty or sixty or a hundred fold. But, once more, when each was called to receive a penny, wherefore should what is distributed equally by God be diminished by human interpretation?

15. But if anyone is moved by this, that some of those who are baptized in sickness are still tempted by unclean spirits, let him know that the obstinate wickedness of the devil prevails even up to the saving water, but that in baptism it loses all the poison of his wickedness. An instance of this we see in the king Pharaoh, who, having struggled long, and delayed in his perfidy, could resist and prevail until he came to the water; but when he had come thither, he was both conquered and destroyed. And that that sea was a sacrament of baptism, the blessed Apostle Paul declares, saying, "Brethren, I would not have you ignorant how that all our fathers were under the cloud, and all passed through the sea, and were all baptized unto Moses in the cloud and in the sea;" and he added, saying, "Now all these things were our examples." And this also is done in the present day, in that the devil is scourged, and burned, and tortured by exorcists, by the human voice, and by divine power; and although he often says that he is going out, and will leave the men of God, yet in that which he says he deceives, and puts in practice what was before done by Pharaoh with the same obstinate and fraudulent deceit. When, however, they come to the water of salvation and to the sanctification of baptism, we ought to know and to trust that there the devil is beaten down, and the man, dedicated to God, is set free by the divine mercy. For as scorpions and serpents, which prevail on the dry ground, when cast into water, cannot prevail nor retain

their venom; so also the wicked spirits, which are called scorpions and serpents, and yet are trodden under foot by us, by the power given by the Lord, cannot remain any longer in the body of a man in whom, baptized and sanctified, the Holy Spirit is beginning to dwell.

16. This, finally, in very fact also we experience, that those who are baptized by urgent necessity in sickness, and obtain grace, are free from the unclean spirit wherewith they were previously moved, and live in the Church in praise and honour, and day by day make more and more advance in the increase of heavenly grace by the growth of their faith. And, on the other hand, some of those who are baptized in health, if subsequently they begin to sin, are shaken by the return of the unclean spirit, so that it is manifest that the devil is driven out in baptism by the faith of the believer, and returns if the faith afterwards shall fail. Unless, indeed, it seems just to some, that they who, outside the Church among adversaries and antichrists, are polluted with profane water, should be judged to be baptized; while they who are baptized in the Church are thought to have attained less of divine mercy and grace; and so great consideration be had for heretics, that they who come from heresy are not interrogated whether they are washed or sprinkled, whether they be clinics or peripatetics; but among us the sound truth of faith is disparaged, and in ecclesiastical baptism its majesty and sanctity suffer derogation.

17. I have replied, dearest son, to your letter, so far as my poor ability prevailed; and I have shown, as far as I could, what I think; prescribing to no one, so as to prevent any prelate from determining what he thinks right, as he shall give an account of his own doings to the Lord, according to what the blessed Apostle Paul in his Epistle

to the Romans writes and says: "Every one of us shall give account for himself: let us not therefore judge one another." I bid you, dearest son, ever heartily farewell.

Epistle LXXVI.
Cyprian to Nemesianus and Other Martyrs in the Mines.

Argument.—He Extols with Wonderful Commendations the Martyrs in the Mines, Opposing, in a Beautiful Antithesis, to the Tortures of Each, the Consolations of Each.

1. Cyprian to Nemesianus, Felix, Lucius, another Felix, Litteus, Polianus, Victor, Jader, and Dativus, his fellow-bishops, also to his fellow-presbyters and deacons, and the rest of the brethren in the mines, martyrs of God the Father Almighty, and of Jesus Christ our Lord, and of God our preserver, everlasting greeting. Your glory, indeed, would demand, most blessed and beloved brethren, that I myself should come to see and to embrace you, if the limits of the place appointed me did not restrain me, banished as I am for the sake of the confession of the Name. But in what way I can, I bring myself into your presence; and even though it is not permitted me to come to you in body and in movement, yet in love and in spirit I come expressing my mind in my letter, in which mind I joyfully exult in those virtues and praises of yours, counting myself a partaker with you, although not in bodily suffering, yet in community of love. Could I be silent and restrain my voice in stillness, when I am made aware of so many and such glorious things concerning my dearest friends, things with which the divine condescension has honored you, so that part of you have already gone before by the consummation of

their martyrdom to receive from their Lord the crown of their deserts? Part still abide in the dungeons of the prison, or in the mines and in chains, exhibiting by the very delays of their punishments, greater examples for the strengthening and arming of the brethren, advancing by the tediousness of their tortures to more ample titles of merit, to receive as many payments in heavenly rewards, as days are now counted in their punishments. I do not marvel, most brave and blessed brethren, that these things have happened to you in consideration of the desert of your religion and your faith; that the Lord should thus have lifted you to the lofty height of glory by the honour of His glorification, seeing that you have always flourished in His Church, guarding the tenor of the faith, keeping firmly the Lord's commands; in simplicity, innocence; in charity, concord; modesty in humility, diligence in administration, watchfulness in helping those that suffer, mercy in cherishing the poor, constancy in defending the truth, judgment in severity of discipline. And that nothing should be wanting to the example of good deeds in you, even now, in the confession of your voice and the suffering of your body, you provoke the minds of your brethren to divine martyrdom, by exhibiting yourselves as leaders of virtue, that while the flock follows its pastors, and imitates what it sees to be done by those set over it, it may be crowned with the like merits of obedience by the Lord.

2. But that, being first severely beaten with clubs, and ill-used, you have begun by sufferings of that kind, the glorious firstlings of your confession, is not a matter to be execrated by us. For a Christian body is not very greatly terrified at clubs, seeing all its hope is in the Wood. The servant of Christ acknowledges the sacrament

of his salvation: redeemed by wood to life eternal, he is advanced by wood to the crown. But what wonder if, as golden and silver vessels, you have been committed to the mine that is the home of gold and silver, except that now the nature of the mines is changed, and the places which previously had been accustomed to yield gold and silver have begun to receive them? Moreover, they have put fetters on your feet, and have bound your blessed limbs, and the temples of God with disgraceful chains, as if the spirit also could be bound with the body, or your gold could be stained by the contact of iron. To men who are dedicated to God, and attesting their faith with religious courage, such things are ornaments, not chains; nor do they bind the feet of the Christians for infamy but glorify them for a crown. Oh feet blessedly bound, which are loosed, not by the smith but by the Lord! Oh feet blessedly bound, which are guided to paradise in the way of salvation! Oh feet bound for the present time in the world, that they may be always free with the Lord! Oh feet, lingering for a while among the fetters and crossbars, but to run quickly to Christ on a glorious road! Let cruelty, either envious or malignant, hold you here in its bonds and chains as long as it will, from this earth and from these sufferings you shall speedily come to the kingdom of heaven. The body is not cherished in the mines with couch and cushions, but it is cherished with the refreshment and solace of Christ. The frame wearied with labors lies prostrate on the ground, but it is no penalty to lie down with Christ. Your limbs unbathed, are foul and disfigured with filth and dirt; but within they are spiritually cleansed, although without the flesh is defiled.
 There the bread is scarce; but man lives not by bread alone, but by the word of God. Shivering, you want

clothing; but he who puts on Christ is both abundantly clothed and adorned. The hair of your half-shorn head seems repulsive; but since Christ is the head of the man, anything whatever must needs become that head which is illustrious on account of Christ's name. All that deformity, detestable and foul to Gentiles, with what splendor shall it be recompensed! This temporal and brief suffering, how shall it be exchanged for the reward of a bright and eternal honour, when, according to the word of the blessed apostle, "the Lord shall change the body of our humiliation, that it may be fashioned like to the body of His brightness!"

3. But there cannot be felt any loss of either religion or faith, most beloved brethren, in the fact that now there is given no opportunity there to God's priests for offering and celebrating the divine sacrifices; yea, you celebrate and offer a sacrifice to God equally precious and glorious, and that will greatly profit you for the retribution of heavenly rewards, since the sacred Scripture speaks, saying, "The sacrifice of God is a broken spirit; a contrite and humbled heart God doth not despise." You offer this sacrifice to God; you celebrate this sacrifice without intermission day and night, being made victims to God, and exhibiting yourselves as holy and unspotted offerings, as the apostle exhorts and says, "I beseech you therefore, brethren, by the mercies of God, that ye present your bodies a living sacrifice, holy, acceptable unto God. And be not conformed to this world; but be ye transformed by the renewing of your mind, that ye may prove what is that good, and acceptable, and perfect will of God."

4. For this it is which especially pleases God; it is this wherein our works with greater deserts are successful in earning God's good-will; this it is which alone the

obedience of our faith and devotion can render to the Lord for His great and saving benefits, as the Holy Spirit declares and witnesses in the Psalms: "What shall I render," says He, "to the Lord for all His benefits towards me? I will take the cup of salvation, and I will call upon the name of the Lord. Precious in the sight of the Lord is the death of His saints." Who would not gladly and readily receive the cup of salvation? Who would not with joy and gladness desire that in which he himself also may render somewhat unto His Lord? Who would not bravely and unfalteringly receive a death precious in the sight of the Lord, to please His eyes, who, looking down from above upon us who are placed in the conflict for His name, approves the willing, assists the struggling, crowns the conquering with the recompense of patience, goodness, and affection, rewarding in us whatever He Himself has bestowed, and honoring what He has accomplished?

 5. For that it is His doing that we conquer, and that we attain by the subduing of the adversary to the palm of the greatest contest, the Lord declares and teaches in His Gospel, saying, "But when they deliver you up, take no thought how or what ye shall speak; for it shall be given you in that same hour what ye shall speak. For it is not ye that speak, but the Spirit of your Father which speaks in you." And again: "Settle it therefore in your hearts, not to meditate before what ye shall answer; for I will give you a mouth and wisdom, which your adversaries shall not be able to resist." In which, indeed, is both the great confidence of believers, and the gravest fault of the faithless, that they do not trust Him who promises to give His help to those who confess Him, and do not on the other hand fear Him who threatens eternal punishment to

those who deny Him.

6. All which things, most brave and faithful soldiers of Christ, you have suggested to your brethren, fulfilling in deeds what ye have previously taught in words, hereafter to be greatest in the kingdom of heaven, as the Lord promises and says, "Whosoever shall do and teach so, shall be called the greatest in the kingdom of heaven." Moreover, a manifold portion of the people, following your example, have confessed alike with you, and alike have been crowned, associated with you in the bond of the strongest charity, and separated from their prelates neither by the prison nor by the mines; in the number of whom neither are there wanting virgins in whom the hundred-fold are added to the fruit of sixty-fold, and whom a double glory has advanced to the heavenly crown. In boys also a courage greater than their age has surpassed their years in the praise of their confession, so that every sex and every age should adorn the blessed flock of your martyrdom.

7. What now must be the vigor, beloved brethren, of your victorious consciousness, what the loftiness of your mind, what exultation in feeling, what triumph in your breast, that every one of you stands near to the promised reward of God, are secure from the judgment of God, walk in the mines with a body captive indeed, but with a heart reigning, that you know Christ is present with you, rejoicing in the endurance of His servants, who are ascending by His footsteps and in His paths to the eternal kingdoms! You daily expect with joy the saving day of your departure; and already about to withdraw from the world, you are hastening to the rewards of martyrdom, and to the divine homes, to behold after this darkness of the world the purest light, and to receive a glory greater

than all sufferings and conflicts, as the apostle witnesses, and says, "The sufferings of this present time are not worthy to be compared with the glory that shall be revealed in us." And because now your word is more effectual in prayers, and supplication is more quick to obtain what is sought for in afflictions, seek more eagerly, and ask that the divine condescension would consummate the confession of all of us; that from this darkness and these snares of the world God would set us also free with you, sound and glorious; that we who here are united in the bond of charity and peace, and have stood together against the wrongs of heretics and the oppressions of the heathens, may rejoice together in the heavenly kingdom. I bid you, most blessed and most beloved brethren, ever farewell in the Lord, and always and everywhere remember me.

Epistle LXXVII.
The Reply of Nemesianus, Dativus, Felix, and Victor, to Cyprian.
Argument.—This Epistle and the Two Following Contain Nothing Else Than Replies to the Foregoing, Inasmuch as They Contain The Thanksgiving as Well for the Comfort Conveyed by the Letter as for the Assistance Sent Therewith. But from the Fact that Three Distinct Letters are Sent in Reply to the Single One of Cyprian's, We are to Gather that the Bishops Who Wrote Them Were Placed in Different Departments of the Mines.

1. Nemesianus, Dativus, Felix, and Victor, to their brother Cyprian, in the Lord eternal salvation. You speak, dearly beloved Cyprian, in your letters always with deep meaning, as suits the condition of the time, by the assiduous reading of which letters both the wicked are

corrected and men of good faith are confirmed. For while you do not cease in your writings to lay bare the hidden mysteries, you thus make us to grow in faith, and men from the world to draw near to belief. For by whatever good things you have introduced in your many books, unconsciously you have described yourself to us. For you are greater than all men in discourse, in speech more eloquent, in counsel wiser, in patience more simple, in works more abundant, in abstinence more holy, in obedience more humble, and in good deeds more innocent. And you yourself know, beloved, that our eager wish was that we might see you, our teacher and our lover, attain to the crown of a great confession.

2. For, in the proceedings before the proconsul, as a good and true teacher you first have pronounced that which we your disciples, following you, ought to say before the president. And, as a sounding trumpet, you have stirred up God's soldiers, furnished with heavenly arms, to the close encounter; and fighting in the first rank, you have slain the devil with a spiritual sword: you have also ordered the troops of the brethren, on the one hand and on the other, with your words, so that snares were on all sides laid for the enemy, and the severed sinews of the very carcasses of the public foe were trodden under foot. Believe us, dearest, that your innocent spirit is not far from the hundred-fold reward, seeing that it has feared neither the first onsets of the world, nor shrunk from going into exile, nor hesitated to leave the city, nor dreaded to dwell in a desert place; and since it furnished many with an example of confession, itself first spoke the martyr-witness. For it provoked others to acts of martyrdom by its own example; and not only began to be a companion of the martyrs already departing from the

world, but also linked a heavenly friendship with those who should be so.

3. Therefore they who were condemned with us give you before God the greatest thanks, beloved Cyprian, that in your letter you have refreshed their suffering breasts; have healed their limbs wounded with clubs; have loosened their feet bound with fetters; have smoothed the hair of their half-shorn head; have illuminated the darkness of the dungeon; have brought down the mountains of the mine to a smooth surface; have even placed fragrant flowers to their nostrils, and have shut out the foul odor of the smoke. Moreover, your continued gifts, and those of our beloved Quirinus, which you sent to be distributed by Herennianus the sub-deacon, and Lucian, and Maximus, and Amantius the acolytes, provided a supply of whatever had been wanting for the necessities of their bodies. Let us, then, be in our prayers helpers of one another: and let us ask, as you have bidden us, that we may have God and Christ and the angels as supporters in all our actions. We bid you, lord and brother, ever heartily farewell, and have us in mind. Greet all who are with you. All ours who are with us love you, and greet you, and desire to see you.

Epistle LXXVIII.
The Reply to the Same of Lucius and the Rest of the Martyrs.
Argument.—The Argument of the Present Letter Is, in Substance, the Same as that of the Preceding; And Therefore It is Not a Letter of Lucius the Roman Bishop, But of Lucius the African Bishop and Martyr.

1. To Cyprian our brother and colleague, Lucius,

and all the brethren who are with me in the Lord, greeting. Your letter came to us, dearest brother, while we were exulting and rejoicing in God that He had armed us for the struggle, and had made us by His condescension conquerors in the battle; the letter, namely, which you sent to us by Herennianus the sub-deacon, and Lucian, and Maximus, and Amantius the acolytes, which when we read we received a relaxation in our bonds, a solace in our affliction, and a support in our necessity; and we were aroused and more strenuously animated to bear whatever more of punishment might be awaiting us. For before our suffering we were called forth by you to glory, who first afforded us guidance to confession of the name of Christ. We indeed, who follow the footsteps of your confession, hope for an equal grace with you. For he who is first in the race is first also for the reward; and you who first occupied the course thence have communicated this to us from what you began, showing doubtless the undivided love wherewith you have always loved us, so that we who had one Spirit in the bond of peace might have the grace of your prayers, and one crown of confession.

2. But in your case, dearest brother, to the crown of confession is added the reward of your labors—an abundant measure which you shall receive from the Lord in the day of retribution, who have by your letter presented yourself to us, as you manifested to us that candid and blessed breast of yours which we have ever known, and in accordance with its largeness have uttered praises to God with us, not as much as we deserve to hear, but as much as you are able to utter. For with your words you have both adorned those things which had been less instructed in us, and have strengthened us to the sustaining of those sufferings which we bear, as being

certain of the heavenly rewards, and of the crown of martyrdom, and of the kingdom of God, from the prophecy which, being filled with the Holy Spirit, you have pledged to us in your letter. All this will happen, beloved, if you will have us in mind in your prayers, which I trust you do even as we certainly do.

3. And thus, O brother most longed-for, we have received what you sent to us from Quirinus and from yourself, a sacrifice from every clean thing. Even as Noah offered to God, and God was pleased with the sweet savor, and had respect unto his offering, so also may He have respect unto yours, and may He be pleased to return to you the reward of this so good work. But I beg that you will command the letter which we have written to Quirinus to be sent forward. I bid you, dearest brother and earnestly desired, ever heartily farewell, and remember us. Greet all who are with you. Farewell.

Epistle LXXIX.

The Answer of Felix, Jader, Polianus, and the Rest of the Martyrs, to Cyprian.

Argument.—The Martyrs Above Spoken of Acknowledge with Gratitude the Assistance Sent to Them by Cyprian. To our dearest and best beloved Cyprian, Felix, Jader, Polianus, together with the presbyters and all who are abiding with us at the mine of Sigua, eternal health in the Lord. We reply to your salutation, dearest brother, by Herennianus the sub-deacon, Lucian and Maximus our brethren, strong and safe by the aid of your prayers, from whom we have received a sum under the name of an offering, together with your letter which you wrote, and in which you have condescended to comfort us as if we were sons, out of the heavenly words. And we have given and do give thanks to God the Father Almighty through His Christ, that we have been thus comforted and strengthened by your address, asking from the candor of your mind that you would deign to have us in mind in your constant prayers, that the Lord would supply what is wanting in your confession and ours, which He has condescended to confer on us. Greet all who abide with you. We bid you, dearest brother, ever heartily farewell in God. I Felix wrote this; I Jader subscribed it; I Polianus read it. I greet my lord Eutychianus.

Epistle LXXX.
Cyprian to Sergius, Rogatianus, and the Other Confessors in Prison.
Argument.—He Consoles Rogatianus and His Colleagues, the Confessors in Prison, and Gives Them Courage by the Example of the Martyrs Rogatianus the Elder and Felicissimus. The Letter Itself Indicates that It Was Written in Exile.

1. Cyprian to Sergius and Rogatianus, and the rest of the confessors in the Lord, everlasting health. I salute you, dearest and most blessed brethren, myself also desiring to enjoy the sight of you, if the state in which I am placed would permit me to come to you. For what could happen to me more desirable and more joyful than to be now close to you, that you might embrace me with those hands, which, pure and innocent, and maintaining the faith of the Lord, have rejected the profane obedience? What more pleasant and sublime than now to kiss your lips, which with a glorious voice have confessed the Lord, to be looked upon even in presence by your eyes, which, despising the world, have become worthy of looking upon

God? But since opportunity is not afforded me to share in this joy, I send this letter in my stead to your ears and to your eyes, by which I congratulate and exhort you that you persevere strongly and steadily in the confession of the heavenly glory; and having entered on the way of the Lord's condescension, that you go on in the strength of the Spirit, to receive the crown, having the Lord as your protector and guide, who said, "Lo, I am with you always, even unto the end of the world." O blessed prison, which your presence has enlightened! O blessed prison, which sends the men of God to heaven! O darkness, more bright than the sun itself, and clearer than the light of this world, where now are placed temples of God, and your members are to be sanctified by divine confessions!

2. Nor let anything now be revolved in your hearts and minds besides the divine precepts and heavenly commands, with which the Holy Spirit has ever animated you to the endurance of suffering. Let no one think of death, but of immortality; nor of temporary punishment, but of eternal glory; since it is written, "Precious in the sight of the Lord is the death of His saints;" and again, "A broken spirit is a sacrifice to God: a contrite and humble heart God doth not despise." And again, where the sacred Scripture speaks of the tortures which consecrate God's martyrs, and sanctify them in the very trial of suffering: "And if they have suffered torments in the sight of men, yet is their hope full of immortality; and having been a little chastised, they shall be greatly rewarded: for God proved them, and found them worthy of Himself. As gold in the furnace hath He tried them, and received them as a sacrifice of a burnt-offering, and in due time regard shall be had unto them. The righteous shall shine and shall run to and fro like sparks among the stubble. They shall judge

the nations and have dominion over the people; and their Lord shall reign forever." When, therefore, you reflect that you shall judge and reign with Christ the Lord, you must needs exult and tread under foot present sufferings, in the joy of what is to come; knowing that from the beginning of the world it has been so appointed that righteousness should suffer there in the conflict of the world, since in the beginning, even at the first, the righteous Abel was slain, and thereafter all righteous men, and prophets, and apostles who were sent. To all of whom the Lord also in Himself has appointed an example, teaching that none shall attain to His kingdom but those who have followed Him in His own way, saying, "He that loves his life in this world shall lose it; and he that hates his life in this world shall keep it unto life eternal." And again: "Fear not them which kill the body but are not able to kill the soul: but rather fear Him who is able to destroy both soul and body in hell." Paul also exhorts us that we who desire to attain to the Lord's promises ought to imitate the Lord in all things. "We are," says he, "the sons of God: but if sons, then heirs; heirs of God, and joint heirs with Christ; if so be that we suffer with Him, that we may also be glorified together." Moreover, he added the comparison of the present time and of the future glory, saying, "The sufferings of this present time are not worthy to be compared with the coming glory which shall be revealed in us." Of which brightness, when we consider the glory, it behooves us to bear all afflictions and persecutions; because, although many are the afflictions of the righteous, yet those are delivered from them all who trust in God.

  3. Blessed women also, who are established with you in the same glory of confession, who, maintaining the

Lord's faith, and braver than their sex, not only themselves are near to the crown of glory, but have afforded an example to other women by their constancy! And lest anything should be wanting to the glory of your number, that each sex and every age also might be with you in honour, the divine condescension has also associated with you boys in a glorious confession; representing to us something of the same kind as once did Ananias, Azarias, and Misael, the illustrious youths to whom, when shut up in the furnace, the fires gave way, and the flames gave refreshment, the Lord being present with them, and proving that against His confessors and martyrs the heat of hell could have no power, but that they who trusted in God should always continue unhurt and safe in all dangers. And I beg you to consider more carefully, in accordance with your religion, what must have been the faith in these youths which could deserve such full acknowledgment from the Lord. For, prepared for every fate, as we ought all to be, they say to the king, "O king Nebuchadnezzar, we are not careful to answer thee in this matter; for our God whom we serve is able to deliver us from the burning fiery furnace; and He will deliver us out of thine hand, O king! But if not, be it known unto thee, O king, that we will not serve thy gods, nor worship the golden image which thou hast set up." Although they believed, and, in accordance with their faith, knew that they might even be delivered from their present punishment, they still would not boast of this, nor claim it for themselves, saying, "But if not." Lest the virtue of their confession should be less without the testimony of their suffering, they added that God could do all things; but yet they would not trust in this, so as to wish to be delivered at the moment; but they thought on that glory of eternal liberty and security.

4. And you also, retaining this faith, and meditating day and night, with your whole heart prepared for God, think of the future only, with contempt for the present, that you may be able to come to the fruit of the eternal kingdom, and to the embrace and kiss, and the sight of the Lord, that you may follow in all things Rogatianus the presbyter, the glorious old man who, to the glory of our time, makes a way for you by his religious courage and divine condescension, who, with Felicissimus our brother, ever quiet and temperate, receiving the attack of a ferocious people, first prepared for you a dwelling in the prison, and, marking out the way for you in some measure, now also goes before you. That this may be consummated in you, we beseech the Lord in constant prayers, that from beginnings going on to the highest results, He may cause those whom He has made to confess, also to be crowned. I bid you, dearest and most beloved brethren, ever heartily farewell in the Lord; and may you attain to the crown of heavenly glory. Victor the deacon, and those who are with me, greet you.

Epistle LXXXI.

To Successus on the Tidings Brought from Rome, Telling of the Persecution.

Argument.—Cyprian Tells the Bishop Successus, that in a Severe Persecution that Had Been Decreed by the Emperor Valerian Xistus the Bishop Had Suffered at Rome on the Eighth of the Ides of August; And He Begs Him to Intimate the Same to the Rest of His Colleagues, that Each One Might Animate His Own Flock to Martyrdom.

1. Cyprian to his brother Successus, greeting. The reason why I could not write to you immediately, dearest brother, was that all the clergy, being placed in the very heat of the contest, were unable in any way to depart hence, all of them being prepared in accordance with the devotion of their mind for divine and heavenly glory. But know that those have come whom I had sent to the City for this purpose, that they might find out and bring back to us the truth, in whatever manner it had been decreed respecting us. For many various and uncertain things are current in men's opinions. But the truth concerning them is as follows, that Valerian had sent a rescript to the Senate, to the effect that bishops and presbyters and deacons should immediately be punished; but that senators, and men of importance, and Roman knights, should lose their dignity, and moreover be deprived of their property; and if, when their means were taken away, they should persist in being Christians, then they should also lose their heads; but that matrons should be deprived of their property, and sent into banishment. Moreover, people of Caesar's household, whoever of them had either confessed before, or should now confess, should have their property confiscated, and should be sent in chains by assignment to Caesar's estates. The Emperor Valerian also added to this address a copy of the letters which he sent to the presidents of the provinces concerning us; which letters we are daily hoping will come, waiting according to the strength of our faith for the endurance of suffering, and expecting from the help and mercy of the Lord the crown of eternal life. But know that Xistus was martyred in the cemetery on the eighth day of the Ides of August, and with him four deacons. Moreover, the prefects in the City are daily urging on this persecution;

so that, if any are presented to them, they are martyred, and their property claimed by the treasury.

2. I beg that these things may be made known by your means to the rest of our colleagues, that everywhere, by their exhortation, the brotherhood may be strengthened and prepared for the spiritual conflict, that every one of us may think less of death than of immortality; and, dedicated to the Lord, with full faith and entire courage, may rejoice rather than fear in this confession, wherein they know that the soldiers of God and Christ are not slain, but crowned. I bid you, dearest brother, ever heartily farewell in the Lord.

Epistle LXXXII.

To the Clergy and People Concerning His Retirement, a Little Before His Martyrdom.

Argument.—When, Near the End of His Life, Cyprian, on Returning to His Gardens, Was Told that Messengers Were Sent to Take Him for Punishment to Utica, He Withdrew. And Lest It Should Be Thought that He Had Done So from Fear of Death, He Gives the Reason in This Letter, Viz., that He Might Undergo His Martyrdom Nowhere Else Than at Carthage, in the Sight of His Own People. a.d. 258.

1. Cyprian to the presbyters and deacons, and all the people, greeting. When it had been told to us, dearest brethren, that the jailers had been sent to bring me to Utica, and I had been persuaded by the counsel of those dearest to me to withdraw for a time from my gardens, as a just reason was afforded I consented. For the reason that it is fit for a bishop, in that city in which he presides over the Church of the Lord, there to confess the Lord, and that the whole people should be glorified by the confession of

their prelate in their presence. For whatever, in that moment of confession, the confessor-bishop speaks, he speaks in the mouth of all, by inspiration of God. But the honour of our Church, glorious as it is, will be mutilated if I, a bishop placed over another church, receiving my sentence or my confession at Utica, should go thence as a martyr to the Lord, when indeed, both for my own sake and yours, I pray with continual supplications, and with all my desires entreat, that I may confess among you, and there suffer, and thence depart to the Lord even as I ought. Therefore here in a hidden retreat I await the arrival of the proconsul returning to Carthage, that I may hear from him what the emperors have commanded upon the subject of Christian laymen and bishops and may say what the Lord will wish to be said at that hour.

2. But do you, dearest brethren, according to the discipline which you have ever received from me out of the Lord's commands, and according to what you have so very often learnt from my discourse, keep peace and tranquility; nor let any of you stir up any tumult for the brethren, or voluntarily offer himself to the Gentiles. For when apprehended and delivered up, he ought to speak, inasmuch as the Lord abiding in us speaks in that hour, who willed that we should rather confess than profess. But for the rest, what it is fitting that we should observe before the proconsul passes sentence on me for the confession of the name of God, we will with the instruction of the Lord arrange in common. May our Lord make you, dearest brethren, to remain safe in His Church, and condescend to keep you. So be it through His mercy.

Find this and other great works of the early Church Fathers at lighthousechristianpublishing.com.

St. Cyprian

Our Father who art in heaven, hallowed be thy name.
Thy kingdom come, Thy will be done, on earth as it is in heaven.
Give us this day our daily bread and forgive us our trespasses as we forgive those who trespass against us.
And lead us not into temptation, but deliver us from evil, for Thy is the kingdom, the power and the glory.

Amen

Hail Mary full of grace, the Lord is with thee. Blessed art thou amongst women and blessed is the fruit of thy womb Jesus. Holy Mary mother of God, pray for us sinners, now and the hour of our death.

St. Michael the archangel,
Defend us in battle,
Be our protection against the wickedness and the snares of the devil,
Rebuke him we humbly pray,
And do thou oh prince of the heavenly host,
By the power of God, case into hell Satan and all the evil spirits that prowl about the earth, seeking the ruin of souls.
Amen.